Resistible Theatres:

Enterprise and experiment
in the late nineteenth century

Resistible Theatres:

Enterprise and experiment
in the late nineteenth
century

John Stokes

BOOKS
10 East 53d St., New York 10022
(a division of Harper & Row Publishers, Inc.)

Acknowledgements

I am grateful to Elinor Finley for permission to quote from the works of William Archer and to J. C. Medley and R. G. Medley, owners of the George Moore copyright.

Jacket photograph: Scene from the Pastoral Players' version of *As You Like It*, Coombe Woods, 1884 (Godwin is seen third from the right in a friar's habit), from the Enthoven Collection, Victoria and Albert Museum.

Published in the U.S.A. 1972 by:
HARPER & ROW PUBLISHERS, INC.
BARNES & NOBLE IMPORT DIVISION

ISBN–06–4965686

Printed in Great Britain

For Faith

' . . . *the theatre is irresistible; organise the theatre.*'
MATTHEW ARNOLD

Contents

List of Illustrations

I
Introduction:
Doctrine and Repertory

It is a common tendency in theatrical histories for events and institutions to be described, if not in complete isolation, then with only a cursory acknowledgement of the social situations out of which they arose and to which they were subsequently obliged for survival. The most significant controls, the demands and habits of an audience, are too often passed by.

For no period is this factor quite so crucial as for the last decades of the nineteenth century, when theatre and theatre business began to assume a new and central position in the public consciousness—a shift that was, for obvious reasons, parallel to and even dependent upon the rise of popular journalism. The 'star system', in its modern sense, was born in the early 1880s (the adulation of the Bancrofts had been an early tremor), at the same time as members of the acting profession were once and for all admitted into respectable drawing rooms. While the popular daily papers were full of vulgar gossip about Bernhardt, journals with higher pretensions endlessly debated the 'respectability' of performers, although even they, with ill-concealed delight, could not resist indulging in the old anecdotes about unfortunate young ladies on tour.

According respectability to actors and actresses was a tacit acknowledgement not only of commerce but also of the new and powerful techniques of publicity. (An arrangement that works well, perhaps because actors are adept at submitting more refined, if not entirely fraudulent, images of their real selves.) The most important and best documented elevation of all is that of the first theatrical knight, Sir Henry Irving, whose acceptable bohemianism Max Beerbohm pertinently compared with Disraeli's. And a delightful innocence and warmth—apparently genuine—supplied the motif for a cult of Ellen Terry which lasted for more than one generation.

These are obvious and familiar milestones in the growth of our 'entertainment industry'. But the subjects of the following essays are also matters of audience and public: the birth of an opposite, a 'non-commercial' twin, whose self-consciousness resulted not from an awareness of the commercial advantages of fashionability, but from a recognition that theatres could be powerful vehicles for disseminating ideas and that the establishment of new enterprises could be a means of bringing together special and elusive social groups. The non-commercial theatres drew not only upon members of the profession but upon writers and critics, designers and painters, political revolutionaries and social reformers; men and women whose powerful engagement derived in part from the fact that in the theatre they were amateurs. There occurred then another parallel realisation—since the theatre had fallen into such a hidebound state, reform must come from the outside.

3

The call for a National Theatre, the impact of Ibsen, the 'English Renaissance' or the 'New Drama'—these are the most visible signs of revolt in the eighties and nineties, and they are inter-related: all were thought to be in direct opposition to the tyranny of the actor-manager and, in each case, were inspired by examples from the continent. Plans to subvert the established rule of commerce in the London theatre received a powerful impetus from the example of the most authoritative and institutionalised ensemble in Europe, the Comédie Française, which visited the Gaiety Theatre in 1879 for a season that attracted massive attention throughout the Press and in society. The most significant response to this visit, although it was in some ways only symptomatic, came from Matthew Arnold. The essay which he first published in August of that year marks an important moment, and for the next twenty years it was automatically referred to whenever the social role of the theatre was under discussion. 'The French Play in London' was a comparison not only between the French and English drama, but also between the status of the theatre in the two countries and the lessons to be learned from it.

'. . . the pleasure we have had in the visit of the French company is barren, unless it leaves us with the impulse to mend the conditions of our theatre, and with the lesson how alone it can be rationally attempted. "Forget,"— can we not hear those fine artists saying in an undertone to us, amidst their graceful compliments of adieu? "Forget your clap-trap and believe that the State, the nation in its collective and corporate character, does well to concern itself about an influence so important to national life and manners as the theatre. Form a company out of the materials ready to your hand in your many good actors or actors of promise. Give them Drury Lane theatre. Let them have a grant from your Science and Art Department. . . ." '[1]

Arnold's conclusion took a characteristic form: a magisterial injunction predicated on a social axiom, 'the theatre is irresistible; organise the theatre.'

A study of the Comédie Française led Arnold to rediscover the theatre as a cultural force; its conduct and traditions possessed the intellectual qualities that nurture a significant contemporary drama and that were nowhere in evidence at home.

'We in England have no modern drama at all. We have our Elizabethan drama. We have a drama of the last century and of the latter part of the century preceding, a drama which may be called our drama of *the town*, when *the town* was an entity powerful enough, because homogeneous enough to evoke a drama embodying its notions of life. But we have no modern drama. Our vast society is not homogeneous enough for this,

4

not sufficiently united, even any large portion of it, in a common view of life, a common ideal, capable of serving as basis for a modern English drama.'[2]

The English theatre had betrayed its magnificent inheritance, and resuscitation would involve two possibly incompatible changes in circumstance: the return of the middle-class audience (which had vanished, it was always agreed, with the Puritan revolution), and the introduction of state subsidy to replace the now defunct system of patent theatres.

'The system had its faults, and was abandoned; and then, instead of desiring a better plan of public organisation for the English theatre, we gladly took refuge in our favourite doctrines of the mischief of State interference, of the blessedness of leaving every man free to do as he likes, of the impertinence of presuming to check any man's natural taste for the bathos and to press him to relish the sublime.'[3]

The novelty of this essay lay in Arnold's application to the tainted world of the theatre of his own profound conviction that cultural institutions can inspire and lead improvements in the moral conduct of a nation. Not that his observations were entirely new—Henry James had chronicled past waves of French influence. In 1876 he had remarked: 'That the theatre plays in Paris a larger part in people's lives than it does anywhere else is by this time a fact too well established to need especial comment';[4] and in 1879, just before the arrival of the Comédie Française, 'The English stage has probably never been so bad as it is at present, and at the same time there probably has never been so much care about it.'[5] But Arnold was the keener propagandist, and a public figure whose ideas were familiar to a wide audience. It was Arnold who set the tone and provided the references, so that by 1883, for example, an anonymous contributor to *The Quarterly Review* could express a wish that the theatre might again become 'not only the best recreation but a moral teacher of the age, only less potent than the sacred influence of religion.'[6]

The idea of a national or subsidised theatre was not entirely original either,* and an incidental but important by-product of the French visit was the fresh attention it drew to Henry Irving's Lyceum, now unofficially recognised as England's substitute for a National Theatre. Irving's climb to a position of virtually unshakeable sovereignty over the English theatre was the dominating

* There had been fluctuating demands for a Shakespeare memorial theatre since at least 1848. In 1879 the Marquis of Townsend issued a circular with proposals for a National Theatre at Covent Garden or Drury Lane, and in the same year George Godwin, editor of *The Builder*, campaigned for a National Theatre with J. R. Planché.

phenomenon of the 1870s, to be associated with earlier achievements in actor-managership. His means—a calculated mixture of pure melodrama (in particular *The Bells* in 1871, a tremendously successful production), historical melodrama (*Charles I* in 1872 and *Richelieu* in 1873) and Shakespeare. Irving's *Hamlet*, which ran for an unprecedented two hundred performances from October 1874, was a triumph of both policy and personality, and the atmosphere of intense rivalry surrounding Salvini's London season in 1875, eagerly whipped up by the Press, served only to enhance his personal stature. When in December 1878 he took the lease of the Lyceum and refurbished the theatre, opening with a revival of *Hamlet* and following it, in April of the next year, with yet another very popular melodrama, Bulwer Lytton's *Lady of Lyons* and in November *The Merchant of Venice*, his continuing success seemed assured. The financial stability of the régime, which did allow the occasional more ambitious venture such as Tennyson's poetic dramas, was however always at risk, and crises grew more frequent as the years went by. Yet the power of Irving's charisma survived almost until the end of the century.

Attacks on the Lyceum were fairly common very early on, although not in the more established journals. Among the younger generation of critics was William Archer, whose very first book, *The Fashionable Tragedian*, written with R. W. Lowe and published in 1877, was primarily an onslaught on Irving's acting style; and while scurrilous in tone and self-consciously aware of its own daring, it did offer a radical solution to the existing undisciplined atmosphere where an actor could freely indulge and exaggerate his personal mannerisms.

'Where lies the remedy for all this?—it will be asked. Will not other actors of Mr Irving's talents meet with the same fate? All who have thought over these matters have come to the conclusion that the only remedy lies in a National Theatre, with good endowment, good traditions, good government.'[7]

Six years later Archer had been sufficiently tamed by his experience as a journalist to deliver a mild eulogy on Irving the actor,[8] but a new and serious criticism came to the fore: as a manager, he had failed to give support to new playwrights. Once again, Archer enraged the theatrical and journalistic establishment by his impertinence in attacking so fundamentally the unquestioned master of the English stage.

Moreover, many journals were controlled by Irving devotees. The most prominent was Clement Scott, for many years critic of

The Daily Telegraph, and from 1879 Editor of *The Theatre.* Scott's conservatism and moral prudery (he was later to lead the campaign against Ibsen) were notorious: with his reverence for the size and grandeur of the Lyceum, his philistinism, his simple acceptance of the need for commercial success (he even used the phrase 'the free trade of drama'), he fitted the role of cultural reactionary precisely, and was an irresistible butt for the younger generation. Still, his popularity and influence do demand full acknowledgement, and in 1896 Shaw was to write:

'The main secret of Mr Scott's popularity is that he is above all a sympathetic critic. His susceptibility to the direct expression of human feeling is so strong that he can write with positive passion about an exhibition of it which elicits from his colleagues only some stale, weary compliment in the last sentence of a conventional report, or, at best, some clever circumlocutory discussion of the philosophy of the piece.'[9]

There is a grudging truth here. In his own emotional way Scott was too generous, too involved in the real world of the theatre, and this was a firm basis for popularity: he was close to his readers. For Archer, Scott came to represent a wider target, the public itself, and Scott happily accepted the powerful role of spokesman for a mass audience. And that, by and large, is how the two critics were always to confront each other.

Whereas Scott was xenophobic, Archer's examples of ideal subsidised theatres came from abroad: from the Comédie Française and from the Meiningen Company, a court theatre from Germany which astonished London in 1881 with its massive and brilliantly organised crowd scenes. Archer was able to put these instances to good use, and his demands became more confident and more persistent, although, as this passage from 1882 indicates, the details of his solution were quite loosely formulated:

'We have got into a vicious circle, and seem likely to go on turning in it indefinitely. A frivolous public calls for frivolous plays, and frivolous plays breed a frivolous public. The public degrades the managers, the managers the authors, the authors the actors, and actors the critics, and the critics the public again. It is impossible to tell in which the impetus towards degradation originates, or where first to attempt to check it. Time, however, works miracles, and we must trust to its beneficent power. In sanguine moments I sometimes dream of "a great Perhaps" in the shape of an Endowed Theatre—not necessarily endowed by the State, but in some manner or other raised above the necessity of being always and immediately a remunerative speculation. But the words "Endowed Theatre" open a large and terribly vexed question, on whose

2

merits my own mind is as yet quite undecided, and upon which, in the present work at any rate, I cannot enter.'[10]

The issue became complicated by the fact that Archer's interest in organisation was increasingly derived from his critical judgements. Drawing on criticism of the novel, he began to develop firm criteria, rooted in the idea of 'just observation'—a reasonably flexible trust in realism that was at the same time related to moral convictions about the social function of the drama. An article he wrote in 1885 intervening in a discussion of G. R. Sims' *The Last Chance* shows these ideas in embryo.

'We are not yet within a measurable distance of an ethical drama—a drama which shall be an efficient factor in the spiritual life of the nation. But if the time for an ethical drama has not yet come, the purely fantastic drama—to use Mr Matthew Arnold's phrase—has had its day. Its exclusive reign, that is to say, is over. It will always have its place on the stage, chiefly in the form of farce, but it will no longer occupy the whole field.'[11]

In 1886 Archer published his influential book *About the Theatre*, a collection of papers more speculative in nature than his daily reviews. The first essay, 'Are We Advancing?', debated the question of whether the theatre deserved more attention from the educated. Finding some comfort in the growing popularity of the theatre and in the increasing amount of newspaper space devoted to it, he could reject the pessimistic views of those who saw nothing but decline and decadence. He recorded some slight improvement in public taste, although discriminating audiences were still only a minority. Shakespeare's public had been ideal:

'. . . an infinitely narrower, or rather more concentrated public, a public habituated to the theatre in the sense that it knew every actor in the company and every play in the repertory, yet not rendered callous and captious by the inordinate amount of theatre-going which he must endure who would keep pace with the drama of today.'[12]

He concluded with the demand, soon to become familiar, for a theatre endowed by a 'confraternity of wealthy art-lovers'.

An alternative idea was put forward in the next essay, 'The Stage of Greater Britain': a theatre whose economic problems could be eased by the production of new plays that might also be sold to America.

At this time a single event took place that both confirmed Archer's diagnosis of the situation and suggested a viable solution. In 1886 the Shelley Society, in order to bypass the censorship exercised by the Lord Chamberlain, which was causing a general discontent,[13] staged a private production of *The Cenci*. Archer, although bored by the play,[14] must have been struck by the idea of restricted performances. Why not admit the hopelessness of immediately converting the general public, and instead concentrate upon the establishment of a cadre of little theatres which would cater for the discriminating minority alone?

The Cenci was a focus of several interests, some of which will be discussed later. Certainly from this moment on, Archer's schemes recognise the impossibility of attempting a total change in public taste, and by 1889 his ideas were considerably modified, the approach more pragmatic and the aims less idealised. He now laid the blame entirely at the feet of the public: the vicious hegemony of commercial managers could never be broken while there was an economic obligation to appease public taste. What he had in mind was not an exclusively classical repertoire, 'a museum of dramatic palaeontology', but an outlet for the living playwright, and even he need not necessarily be of minimal appeal.

'Plays for which there is no effective demand, which are radically unfitted for the stage and gain nothing by representation, may be very good literature, but do not belong to the living drama. What class of modern work, then, would the non-commercial theatre welcome and foster? Why, plays that appeal to the thousands, not to the tens of thousands; plays that interest intelligent people without being sufficiently sensational, or amusing, or sentimental, or vulgar to run for 250 nights; plays in which the female interest is weak; plays that end, and must end, unhappily; plays, in fine, that do not fulfil all the thousand and one trivial conditions on which popular success is supposed to depend.'[15]

A dramatist should be free from the stifling demands of the mass public, of what was described as the 'compact majority'. He appealed to W. S. Gilbert, Sydney Grundy, Henry Arthur Jones and Arthur Wing Pinero, all playwrights that he had praised to some degree in the past,

'. . . to say whether they have not again and again found themselves consciously sacrificing artistic considerations to the necessity of conciliating the masses. Have they not altogether rejected powerful and interesting themes, which, for one reason or another, could not be treated in accordance with established formulas?'[16]

It is important to notice, and to compare with Matthew Arnold earlier, that Archer at this time still considered a state subsidy out of the question, finding it vaguely undemocratic: although even Irving had suggested the foundation of municipal theatres in the larger provincial towns, Archer was convinced that the impetus had to come from private liberality. Optimistically, he estimated that there must be 250 people in England who would be prepared to subscribe a thousand pounds each to an endowed theatre, thus providing enough capital to secure ten thousand pounds a year. A committee of trustees would be appointed, to whom only the manager would be responsible, and he suggested established figures such as Pinero, Gilbert or Squire Bancroft for this position.

Archer's schemes can only be understood in relation to what he had learnt from his day-to-day reporting of the commercial theatre. It was out of this his plans developed, a chastening experience that eventually diverted his commitment from more revolutionary projects. But he was also involved on other fronts: in particular an indefatigable championship of Ibsen, and that aligned him, if only in part, with the important group that had staged *The Cenci*.

Any account, however brief, of the impact of Ibsen on the English theatre must necessarily involve considerations of social groups, for the 'Ibsenites', as quickly picked up and caricatured by the newspapers as the Aesthetes, belonged to a particular minority, brought together as much by an interest in politics as in the theatre. Not that they had been the first to recognise the Scandinavian genius, a moment that belongs to Edmund Gosse, whose 'Ibsen, the Norwegian Satirist' appeared in 1873[17] and who placed his emphasis on the 'modernity' of the verse plays. By 1884, acquaintance with the subsequent prose dramas enabled Archer to introduce the notion of Ibsen as a more obviously social playwright, whose concerns extended beyond exclusively Norwegian issues. It was from this standpoint that he made forceful objections to Jones' emasculated version of *A Doll's House*, re-entitled *Breaking a Butterfly*.

'The adaptors, or more properly the authors, have felt it needful to eliminate all that was satirical or unpleasant, and in making their work sympathetic they at once made it trivial. I am the last to blame them for doing so. Ibsen on the English stage is impossible. He must be trivialised. . . .'[18]

In 1885, reviewing an Academy of Dramatic Art performance of the same play, and claiming that it bore no relation to what Ibsen intended, Archer's grievances were again directed against a peculiarly English weakness.

'The ultimate reasons which consign Ibsen's work to the category of the "Theatre impossible" are these: he is an idealist, and we do not understand ideals; he is a moralist, and we do not understand ethics; worse than all, his morality savours of paradox, and, except in comic opera, we abhor paradox. These objectionable things—idealism, morality and paradox—are an essential part of the fabric of his plays. Take away the warp and the woof inevitably falls to pieces.'[19]

Note here his early attention to 'idealism' and 'paradox'; Archer's preoccupation with moral form was first to restrict the force of his advocacy of Ibsen's immediate social relevance and then to dissipate in the struggle to formulate the nature of his purely dramatic achievement. His resistance to subversive ideas was latent even in a remark made soon after his first meeting with the playwright in 1881—'if Ibsen were not a great poet, he would be a rather poor philosopher.' Although his concern with Ibsen's technical innovations was occasionally perceptive, the phrases on which he allows himself to rest are lacking in vitality: 'great explorer of the human heart', 'more of a seer than a thinker', and 'there have been many better preachers, but few greater poets.'

In any case, as will be seen, Archer's enthusiasm for Ibsen was quickly contaminated by a simultaneous commitment to Pinero and Jones, a dangerous tolerance that was not, of course, always apparent either to his readers or to other commentators. His championship of Ibsen must be compared with that of a committed minority who had at first little or no access to the popular press.

Between 1880 and 1888 there were still few translations of Ibsen available, and even fewer professional productions: *Pillars of Society* (1880) and the adaptation *Breaking a Butterfly* (1884) of which Archer was so critical. The early translations, not by Archer, included Henrietta Lord's *A Doll's House* (1882) and *Ghosts* (1885). In 1888 Archer brought out *Pillars of Society* and *Ghosts* in his own version, and in the same year Eleanor Marx Aveling's translation of *An Enemy of the People* was published. The famous breakthrough came in 1889 with *A Doll's House* (Archer's translation) at the Gaiety Theatre, produced by Charles Charrington with his wife, Janet Achurch, as Nora. In 1891 the Independent Theatre staged *Ghosts*, and in the same year there were in all six productions of five of Ibsen's plays: an uncertain popularity had been achieved.

The importance of the 1889 production of *A Doll's House*, performed in front of an audience which Arthur Symons described as a 'family party', can hardly be overstated. The Charringtons' devotion to Ibsen went beyond their professional appreciation of his skill as a dramatist, for they were friends of Shaw and close to the compact world of avant-garde socialism; when Charles Charrington lectured to the Hammersmith Socialist Party in 1895, Shaw commented, 'among the Fabians, he will probably be an Impossibilist of the

Impossibilists.' Their professional behaviour was bold and pre-sumptuous and their personal commitment to Ibsen fanatical—there is the story of how Janet Achurch asked Irving for a donation towards the staging of the comedy *Clever Alice*, only to use the money for *A Doll's House*.[20] (And there are suggestions that her tragic addiction to morphine might have been a result of the strain that such lives impose.) Ill fortune dogged their career: they were obliged, under a previously arranged contract, to leave England immediately after the Ibsen performance for a two-year tour abroad. Although it made a financial loss, the event of *A Doll's House* aroused con-siderable interest even in circles that would not have dreamed of attending, and drew widespread and often scandalised attention to Ibsen as social moralist.

Engagement of this kind can be seen in the activities of another couple, the socially infamous Dr Aveling and his partner Eleanor Marx. Aveling was trained as a scientist but also translated Karl Marx, helped found the Independent Labour Party and wrote plays, mainly comedies or burlesques with the occasional more serious attempt such as an adaptation of *The Scarlet Letter* (produced by Charles Charrington in 1888) and *Dregs* (1889). He also con-tributed regularly to small socialist and theatrical magazines. Eleanor had early ambitions to become an actress, gave public recitations, and took lessons from Mrs Hermann Vezin. In 1886 she and Aveling organised an important reading of *A Doll's House* in their own home, which Shaw and May Morris attended, and they were also responsible for the School of Dramatic Art production—condemned by Archer—of the same play.

Even if they did tend to ignore Ibsen's own careful disclaimers of any didactic intent, these Ibsenites have too often been over-castigated for presenting a false image of a reformer or propagandist rather than a dramatist. The use that people like the Avelings or the Charringtons or even Shaw made of Ibsen was in fact intimately connected with their ideas of the whole programme. In precisely the same way that Shelley had been adopted by would-be revolu-tionaries, the Avelings and their associates, in seeing Ibsen as prophet of feminism or social equality, were only putting into practice an integrated concept of art and society. In October 1884 the socialist magazine *Today* contained an article on 'Women and Socialism' by Havelock Ellis, which demonstrates this process of acquisition.

'. . . Henrik Ibsen has in the compass of a short play, *Nora*, thrown into a perfectly artistic form the whole (or almost the whole) question of the independence of women as it is presented to us today. There cannot be,

Ibsen teaches us (although as a true artist, he always anxiously disclaims any attempt to teach) a truly intimate and helpful relation except between a man and a woman who are equally developed, equally independent. He has wrought out *Nora* with a keenness of insight into the most subtle recesses of the soul that is almost marvellous, and in *Ghosts*, a work of still greater genius and audacity, which there is reason to hope may soon be translated, he has again illustrated his fresh and profound way of dealing with the almost untouched ethical problems of the modern world. He has realised that the day of mere external revolutions has passed, that the only revolution now possible is the most fundamental of all, the revolution of the human spirit.'[21]

The approach here is quite different from Archer's in its appreciation of Ibsen's involvement in change: the drama, it suggests, must be able to account for a social cause and its psychological result. In 1891 Aveling, speaking at a meeting of the Playgoers' Club, denied that those who demand the truth in art 'worshipped the ugly':

'Ibsen *depicts* ugly things, but certainly does not *worship* them. Art is, or should be, the highest of all teachers. What is demanded is that plays should not simply deal with the surface, but should get at the heart of things.'[22]

A week later he lectured the same body on 'The Theatre and the Working Classes', asserting that the theatre had always ignored them, demolishing the sentimental myth that poverty and necessity could produce art, and insisting that the Club be opened to women. In the following year Eleanor Marx spoke on morality and the stage.

'She said all morality was relative, and that different ages and different people had different standards. Mrs Marx-Aveling went on to argue that all subjects were fit for the stage if artistically treated, including religion and politics. What, indeed, did we in England today mean by "morality"? Like the word "virtue" it was applied to only one special quality, and referred as to the sexual relations.'[23]

In 1894 she continued this theme with an attack on Archer and his refusal to follow through the logical implication of the domestic situations depicted by Ibsen into the whole field of social and political morality.

'Mrs Aveling split up the schools of modern theatrical principles into three: the first being that which did not desire serious emotions to be dealt with, and desired mere amusement; the second held that the stage should be a mirror of human life, and dealt with questions which affect it; the third, she said, represented by Mr William Archer, was illogical, for it allowed of the treatment of economical questions, especially in connection with the relations of the sexes, but drew the line at religion and politics.'[24]

The assumption that the theatre, and all art, is essentially relevant to the whole of life belongs to this group of opinion alone. Havelock Ellis made the same kind of point in the 1888 preface to his translations. On Ibsen's characters, for instance:

'They stand, in their stagnant conventional environment, as, either instinctively or intelligently, actually or potentially, the representations of freedom and truth, containing the promise of a new social order.'

And

'His work throughout is the expression of a great soul crushed by the weight of an antagonistic social environment into utterance that has caused him to be regarded as the most revolutionary of modern writers.'[25]

Socialists were better able to deal with a drama contained within the dialectical tensions of past and present, of social circumstance and individual ambition, than has usually been conceded. Yet it comes as a surprise to find Aveling writing burlesques and praising Irving,[26] and there is in his case a clear disjunction between theory and practice, only to be understood by an acknowledgement of the compromises necessarily involved in a search for success and of his total fascination with the theatre. It might equally be objected that his private life was very far from the free and healthy relationships that he and Eleanor publicly insisted on. But given these ironies and the occasional absurdity and piety of the demands, there must be granted to the Avelings and their associates the unquestioned virtue of championing the serious drama in a most powerful and uncompromised way. Their strength was derived from their ability to connect the work that they admired with the lives that they themselves wished to lead.

It was therefore right that much of the protest against the conduct and repertoire of the commercial theatre should come from centres of literary and political activity, and that the leading actresses—Janet Achurch, Florence Farr, Elizabeth Robins—should themselves be New Women, involved in campaigns on other fronts. As the Avelings observed, they had their predecessors in Shelley and Mary Godwin, who

'... had seen in part that women's social condition is a question of economics, not of religion or of sentiment. The woman is to the man as the producing class is to the possessing. Her "inferiority" in its actuality, and in its assumed existence is the outcome of holding economic power by man to her exclusion.'[27]

Ibsen's consistently dominating heroines offered these actresses images of themselves which intensified their sense of personal involvement, and the Ibsenite gospel was to a large extent preached by women; moreover, they were not unaware that, as Elizabeth Robins put it, 'Ibsen made reputations':

'We had come to realise how essential to success some production of judgment and action are to the actor. The strangulation of this role and that through arbitrary stage management was an experience we had shared with men. But we had further seen how freedom in the practice of our art, how the brave opportunity to practise it at all, depended, for the actress, on considerations humiliatingly different from those that confronted the actor. The stage career of an actress was inextricably involved in the fact that she was a woman and that those who were masters of the theatre were men. These considerations did not belong to art, they stultified art.'[28]

So the non-commercial theatre provided not only a platform but an environment—an extension of small and private worlds into areas of real professional equality. The theme of feminism was perpetuated in Elizabeth Robins' own *Votes for Women*, staged by Barker and Vedrenne at the Court in 1906, and even provided material for uninvolved commercial dramatists like Pinero, or Sydney Grundy and his *The New Woman* (1894). Yet there were drawbacks to the New Women's ability to identify with their parts. Shaw found Elizabeth Robins' performance as Ella Rentheim in 1897 unsatisfactory because she was 'too young and too ferociously individualistic to play her.'[29] And of course they squabbled and competed amongst themselves: there was a good deal of bickering between Janet Achurch, Elizabeth Robins and Mrs Patrick Campbell over *Little Eyolf*, and they were all considered for Paula Tanqueray in 1890—a part which, though melodramatic and bourgeois, was obviously irresistible to them all.

Shaw, more than anybody else, was aware of the potential of the actress-manageress; and Shaw it was who invariably provided the most intelligent, if sometimes unfair, critique of the functions of the entire non-commercial movement. He possessed an impetus that was crucially lacking in Archer—a coherent intellectual programme.

The Quintessence of Ibsenism (1891) had developed out of a lecture given in 1890 in the series 'Socialism in Contemporary Literature', to which Stepniak, Sidney Oliver, Hubert Bland and William Morris also contributed. It is a very Shavian mixture: propaganda and sophistry, wilful complexity and conscious simplification all combine to make a unified reading of the whole oeuvre. The key phrase, 'the will to live', belongs to Shaw rather than to Ibsen, and the plays emerge as patterns of intellectual argument, their dramatic qualities rather pushed to one side. Not surprisingly, Shaw's accounts of the plays are reminiscent of his own work. But what is of concern here is not so much the particular accuracy of his readings as the principles behind them, and the conviction that the Ibsen controversy could not be resolved 'until it is ascertained whether a society of persons holding Ibsen's opinions would be higher or lower than a society holding Mr Clement Scott's.'[30]

The first part of the book is devoted to the philosophical background. Ibsen derives from Schopenhauer: 'reason' becomes 'will', the 'objective will' becomes 'duty'. Duty becomes tyranny and is first challenged by women rather than by men as the prime victims of social obligation. Shaw, reversing the normal meanings of the terms, distinguishes between the Idealist, who sets up masks to conceal the truth and poses exterior standards as a denial of self, and the Realist, who asserts the will to live and to be himself. Women are trained to be Idealists because society always presumes that they will surrender themselves to familial duty and responsibility, and sexual desire is either concealed or sanctified in marriage. For a woman to emancipate herself she must in consequence tear down the false ideals of altruistic devotion to the family.

Three of Ibsen's early plays (*Brand, Peer Gynt, Emperor and Galilean*) are taken as philosophical investigations of idealism in heroic circumstances. From these Shaw moves to his treatment of destructive idealism in contemporary situations, social dramas where the idealisation includes public organisations and public responsibility— for example *An Enemy of the People*. In *The Wild Duck* Ibsen turns back on himself, demonstrating the dangers of destroying the essential ideals on which people depend for survival: it is Greger's truth-telling that makes Hedwig shoot herself. In *The Lady from the Sea* the call of the objective or collective ideal demands human sacrifice. What is needed is the restitution of the right to private judgement, or, to return to the terms in which Shaw began, of the demands of the rational will. Society can only be changed by strenuous individualism.

Shaw's interest in Ibsen was based on his ability to show *ideas* in action; and his fervency has an air of shared purpose that must have derived from his experience of early Socialism and the circle around William Morris. As Julian Kaye has shown,[31] Shaw's acceptance and familiarity with Marxist notions enabled him to make constructive use of Ibsen—both were seers, both concerned with society as a whole. William Morris, with his relentless insistence that social and aesthetic problems are at heart the same, offered a similar starting-point, and his inspiration, although not always acknowledged, stands behind Shaw as it does behind no other major figure in the theatre.

The gap between casual day-to-day theatrical journalism and the intense evangelising of the reformists was inevitably wide; they lived in different worlds. When a reporter from *The Dramatic Review* attended one of Morris' evenings at Hammersmith, he could only conclude lamely that 'besides all this, Socialism as here seen is a most curious type of eccentric London life, and as such alone has its dramatic interest.'[32]

Although Morris had begun his career with dramatic verse, his later opinions about the theatre have hardly survived—he probably did not have very many. According to May Morris,

'As all his intimate friends well knew, my father's antagonism to the Victorian stage was inveterate and extended especially to its representation of the chronicle plays and romantic plays of Shakespeare, where the stage convention, the modern "traditions", the tricks of diction and all the elaboration and parade of the modern setting rang falsely on an ear tuned to another key.'[33]

He certainly attended the theatre very rarely indeed, making a special exception for Shaw's *Widowers' Houses* in 1892; there was also the famous production of his own play, *The Tables Turned or Nupkins Awakened*, a Socialist morality, in which he himself played an Archbishop, and which both Shaw and Yeats attended, in 'a long narrow garret, with whitewashed roof and rafters, and red ochred walls boasting as their sole decoration a photograph of Karl Marx, an engraved portrait of Sir Thomas More . . .'.[34]

It was not to be expected that Morris would appreciate Ibsen's harsher aspects (according to his biographer, the only comment was a gruff 'very clever, I must say'[35]). But others were able to make the connections and to extend his general precepts to include the theatre. Morris wrote,

' . . . I assert first that Socialism is an all-embracing theory of life, and that it has an epic and a religion of its own, so also it has an aesthetic: so that to everyone who wishes to study Socialism duly it is necessary to look at it from the aesthetic point of view. And, secondly, I assert that inequality of condition, whatever may have been the case in former ages of the world, has now become incompatible with the existence of a healthy art.'[36]

Accept this and you realised, as Shaw put it in his moving obituary, that 'we have no theatre for men like Morris: indeed we have no theatre for quite ordinary cultivated people.'[37]

That the theatre should be for 'ordinary' people raises the most important question of all—that of audience. Minority or clique organisations might succeed in getting the right plays staged, but audiences were bound to be small; on the other hand, especially in the case of Ibsen, more regular performances and greater publicity ran the risk of the message becoming diffuse and ultimately lost.

Despite Shaw's entreaties to Irving, the only truly commercial manager who tried to stage Ibsen was Beerbohm Tree, who produced *An Enemy of the People* in 1893, and who, on moving to Her Majesty's in 1897, recommended that a portion of the gallery be set aside for the 'working man with a taste for serious drama', on the grounds that although that precise category could only be small, it was still a proportion of an immense section of the community. Though naïve and patronising, and like other of Tree's efforts, short-lived, this was at least a partial acknowledgement of the problem that Shaw had always recognised in absolute terms.

'It is clear to me that we shall never become a play-going people until we discover our fixed idea that it is the business of the people to come to the theatre, and substitute for it the idea that it is the business of the theatre to come to the people.'[38]

Or, even more challenging because of its optimistic reversal of the usual complaints:

'Dramatic Art is not going to die of commercialism in England. If it comes to that, commercialism is much more likely to die of dramatic art.'[39]

His capacity to make of Ibsen a revolutionary figure-head increased Shaw's dissatisfaction with Archer and George Moore when they defended him only in the wider context of a 'free theatre', and he was sceptical of eclectic organisations such as the Independent Theatre. In his revised *Quintessence* of 1913 he was still advocating a 'doctrinal theatre', even an evangelising 'Ibsen theatre'. The conviction that progress depended upon plays that threaten society made him doubly impatient with the English problem playwrights, and he reacted both by attacking them in his journalism and by incorporating the essence of his theories into his own plays. By taking over the form of the well-made play and the melodrama, Shaw succeeded in revealing the sentimental deficiencies within the genres themselves. The Shavian drama is essentially an argument: discussion and action are inextricably involved in each other. This is precisely the opposite procedure to that of Pinero and Jones who, although they follow Ibsen's lead in treating more controversial themes, carefully preserve not only most of the form but (covertly) almost all the moral attitudes of the conventional play.

Archer, at least, always respected the talent of Henry Arthur Jones, and had recognised it early. *English Dramatists of Today* (1882) contained an appreciation of his early work, and—like Matthew Arnold—he approved of *The Silver King* (1882). As we have seen, he objected to Jones' adaptation of *A Doll's House*, and he also disapproved of his collaboration with the actor-manager Wilson Barrett; yet after 1890 he regularly associated him with new movements, and likened his *Judah* (1890) to plays such as Pinero's *Cabinet Minister* that received his deepest admiration.

From *Saints and Sinners* (1894) onward Jones dealt with many serious contemporary matters—social reform in *The Crusaders* (1891), religious conviction in *Michael and his Lost Angel* (1896), and above all, on many occasions, the clash of hypocrisy in social and sexual morality. His main achievement was to refine the form of the well-made play so that it could deal with these subjects; a brand of ingenious but acceptable satirical comedy.[40] Yet when it came to matters of policy, the playwright who was admired by the supposedly progressive held ideas not dissimilar to those of Clement Scott: Jones was deeply and vociferously conservative, even prepared, if necessary, to defend the actor-manager.

The cornerstone of his arguments was an emphatic insistence on the difference between 'serious drama' and 'entertainment', and he was eager to exclude 'the sordid' from either category. It could be said that Jones represents a corruption of Matthew Arnold, for he upholds the centrality of the theatre only to preserve its innocence.

'1. I have fought for a recognition of the distinction between the art of the drama on the one hand and popular amusement on the other, and of the great pleasure to be derived from the art of the drama.
'2. I have fought for the entire freedom of the modern dramatist, for his right to portray all aspects of human life, all passions, all opinions; for the freedom of search, the freedom of phrase, the freedom of treatment that are allowed to the Bible and to Shakespeare, that must necessarily be allowed to every writer and to every artist that sees humanity as a whole.
'3. I have fought for sanity and wholesomeness, for largeness and breadth of view. I have fought against the cramping and deadening influences of modern pessimistic realism, its bitterness, its ugliness, its narrowness, its parochial aims.'[41]

These buoyant principles are always concerned with 'health' as well as with 'serious studies of modern social and commercial life';

and it is because they include both that they are so unconvincing. The double demand is carefully arranged to exclude a realism that is serious and modern but not necessarily 'healthy', and into that class fell Tolstoy and the Scandinavians, especially, of course, Ibsen. At the same time it elevated the kind of play Jones wrote himself.

This is part of another process of deflection. A. B. Walkley, more perceptive, had already seen through the bluff, and sharply rebuked Jones' simple-mindedness and crude Ruskinism.

'Art must be "healthy". The drama must not study vice, disease, the disagreeable, the ugly ... I venture, quite respectfully, to suggest that a course of M. Antoine and the Théâtre Libre would do Mr Jones a world of good. It would, I trust, convince him that the hope of a great future for the stage lies in perfect freedom; freedom to try every kind of experiment; freedom to be realistic or idealistic, prosaic or futuristic, "well-made" or plotless, "healthy" or pathological. ...'[42]

But by 1895, when Jones published his collection of essays and speeches *The Renascence of English Drama*, his own audience was assured; the tone was complacent and self-satisfied, and the terms and principles of reform had been skilfully modified.

Jones had certain fixed ideas about the relationship between audience and playwright. For instance the American Copyright Bill, passed in 1891, which finally made it possible for the texts of plays to be published without the risk of their being pirated, was welcomed by him, as by Archer and others, with enthusiasm.[43] To publish a play is to raise it to the status of literature, and to release it from the degrading conditions of the theatre and the egotistical demands of performers. But in his 'Relations of the Drama to Education' (1893) Jones attempted to prove that the theatre 'teaches' but is not didactic: that is, it teaches those who understand already, who have been previously educated by literature; good plays can only be written for sympathetic audiences. He very rarely considered or even referred to the alternative kinds of audience or organisation that were becoming available; instead his ideal relationship between playwright and audience suggested a deadening complicity, hardly an improvement on that fostered by the melodramas and music-halls that he so delighted in disparaging. He could even use audience demand as an excuse for bad plays, as he had done (with more justification) eleven years earlier:

'... we are concerned to break down the formation of a *ring* of dramatic authorship and to establish a *school* of dramatic authorship. And this school of dramatic authorship cannot exist until and unless there is a body of educated, cultivated opinion for it to appeal to, and to be judged by. While the English public remains capricious and fitful in its judgements, English authors will remain capricious and fitful in their work.'[44]

Jones' attitude is an example of how the basically conservative tried to appease the new threats, although the same tactics can even be found in the pronouncements of more obviously intelligent men such as Archer.

The recent interest shown in Pinero by managements and academic critics alike has provided some welcome insights into Victorian drama, but although the preference in the live theatre is now quite clearly for the farce and comedy with which he started his career and to which he periodically returned, it is still necessary to draw attention to the damage done at this time by his 'problem plays'. After some early successful farces, in particular *The Magistrate* (1885) and *Sweet Lavender* (1888), there came, in 1889, *The Profligate* and the start of a much wider and more serious reputation as a writer of plays on important contemporary subjects. No playwright attracted closer critical attention in the nineties. The sensation caused by *The Second Mrs Tanqueray* in 1893 is well known, but Pinero—like many Victorian playwrights—was prolific, writing almost a play a year throughout the nineties, and it will be more constructive to look at two later problem plays, both staged in 1895.

The Notorious Mrs Ebbsmith is set in the English colony in Venice. Its heroine, Agnes Ebbsmith, is a free-thinker who has in the past been some kind of evangelising reformist (just what this involved is never made entirely clear). She has now become mistress of a promising but egotistical politician named Lucas Cleeve. When they are visited by a messenger from Cleeve's wife, Agnes is almost persuaded to compromise her principles and conceal their liaison so that Cleeve's marriage may appear respectable and he may return to public life. She has two friends, a priest and his widowed sister, and when the priest offers her the bible as consolation Agnes, in a moment of nihilistic despair, seizes the book and hurls it in the fire. Then, suddenly overcome with remorse, she is inspired to plunge in her hand and rescue it from the flames. Resolving to withdraw from society, she deserts Cleeve, but this only makes him desire her the more.

A deputation, which includes Cleeve's wife, arrives to persuade her to take him back. But it is too late: Agnes now considers that their relationship had been 'base and gross, and wicked, almost from the very beginning,' and all she can promise Cleeve is that 'when I have learnt to pray again, I will remember you, every day of my life.'

Agnes' incredible reformation develops out of an initial distortion in her presented character. She is a neurotic (the product of a disturbed home), fearful of 'passion', and her behaviour suggests guilt from the start. Her lover's excessive vanity and caddishness is clearly intended to reinforce the moral generalisation that any relationship outside of marriage must inevitably be based on exploitation. Archer in fact started off his review of the play[45] by admitting that Agnes was a crude inaccurate type, lacking in intellectual conviction, with an improbable horror of sexual passion, who 'even in expanding her heterodoxy, unconsciously adopts the standpoint and uses the language of orthodoxy.' But he was ultimately prepared to accept this manipulation because of his commitment to the moral resolution, and halfway through the review takes on a tone of approval. The plays shows 'character working itself out entirely from within' and deals with 'the universally relevant theme of marriage in general'. It demonstrates that 'as society is at present constituted, it takes exceptional characters on both sides to make a free union any more successful than a marriage.'

But Archer overlooked that it was essential for Agnes to be inconsistent for Pinero to achieve his moral outcome. In contrast with Ibsen Pinero's women are extremely limited, and are allowed neither intellectual depth nor a full range of emotions. Archer recognised this tendency, but was either unwilling or incapable of pressing home the reasons for it, and furthermore failed to connect deficiencies in characterisation with the evasions of the play as a whole. It is true that at the end of his long two-part review he complained of 'a certain depressing negativeness—I had almost said aridity,' and noted that the play had 'no message, no stimulus, no sustenance', but these qualifications were not allowed seriously to threaten his appreciation.

Put Archer's comments beside those of Shaw and the difference in critical perception is obvious at once. Shaw, recalling Pinero's earlier plays, *The Profligate* and *The Second Mrs Tanqueray*, observed that

'. . . he conquered the public by the exquisite flattery of giving them plays that they really liked, whilst persuading them that such appreciation was only possible from persons of great culture and intellectual acuteness.'[46]

Pinero had 'invented a new sort of play by taking the ordinary article and giving it an air of novel, profound and original thought.' Shaw was absolutely right: *The Notorious Mrs Ebbsmith* is a good example of a play which is carefully designed to look and sound controversial while incorporating a conciliatory and reassuring conclusion. This was achieved by the distortion of the heroine, by suggestions that she somehow held her progressive views against her own will, by the melodramatic use of superstition and sensation to underline her essential rightmindedness. Even Mrs Patrick Campbell, who played the part first, managed to see through some of this, complaining of Agnes' unlikely inertia in the final act and wanting her to show as much headstrong enthusiasm in her revelation of the love of God as she must have had earlier when preaching revolution.[47] But Pinero, understanding only passive feminacy, let the last act stand. It is perhaps surprising, in view of its calculated appeal to the market, that the play had only a short run.

The Benefit of the Doubt was more successful, and its reception is a more subtle pointer to the ways in which Pinero's plays had become acceptable as serious drama.

Mrs Alec Fraser (née Theophila Emptage) has been sued by the jealous Olive Allingham for alleged misconduct with her husband Jack, and although the case is dismissed, the judge accords Theo only 'the benefit of the doubt'. This verdict arouses great anxiety in the Emptage household, which comprises Theo's foolish brother Claud, pompous uncle Sir Fletcher Portwood, frivolous sister Tina, and snobbish mother, all of whom are selfishly concerned with the family reputation. During their post-mortem of the case they are joined by a charitable but brisk aunt, Mrs Cloys, wife of a bishop. Both Theo and Tina have adopted the style, and style is all it is, of New Women, and much is made of this—as when Tina, frightened by her sister's predicament, promises to give it all up:

'From today I'll alter—I take my oath I will! No more slang for me, no more swears, no more smokes with the men after dinner, no more cycling at the club in knickers! I've been giving too much away—!'[48]

In fact the foundations of the Fraser marriage really are shaky, and despite the couple's good resolutions, the case does nothing to strengthen them. When Alec Fraser suggests that they go abroad to avoid any lingering scandal, Theo returns her wedding ring and disappears.

The second act is set at Jack Allingham's Surrey cottage. His uneasy celebration of the verdict with two old cronies—ageing bachelors and 'clubmen'—is disturbed by the arrival of his wife Olive. Although she is obviously wildly unstable, repentant and vindictive by turn, there are suggestions of a possible reconciliation. They in turn are interrupted by the Emptage family in pursuit of Theo. The ensuing confusion is treated as comic business, until a note arrives from Theo requesting an interview with Allingham. At Olive's suggestion, he

3

reluctantly agrees to see her, and to allow Olive to overhear the conversation, on the understanding that should nothing incriminating occur, Olive will forgive Theo and allow herself to be seen with her again in public. To complicate matters even further, Allingham also assures the forceful and upright Mrs Cloys, without letting on that his wife will be eavesdropping, that he will not permit anything to happen that might implicate or upset her niece. When it comes to it, the interview breaks down, because Theo, overwrought and tired, becomes hysterically drunk after one sip of champagne, and pleads with Jack to go away with her. Perturbed by the length of the conversation, the Emptage family burst in and Olive's plot is discovered. Theo swoons.

Both comic and sentimental possibilities are prolonged in the final act, with a quarrel between the two husbands and Olive's attempted reconciliations with Theo and her husband. Finally Mrs Cloys devises a scheme to take Theo into the bishop's London home, thus assuring her respectability until she feels able to return to Fraser.

The Benefit of the Doubt has lasted well: the comic tone almost obscures the absurdity of Theo's breakdown and the weakness of a plot that depends upon eavesdropping and 'business', and it is still enjoyable enough as a burlesque of genteel behaviour. But in its own time it was acclaimed for rather different reasons. Archer opened his review[49] with a sober attack on the Idealists (a word used, it will be remembered, very frequently by Shaw in his *Quintessence* with an opposite sense) or Ibsenites, who

'. . . professed to love the stage, and to be working both by precept and example, for a free and thoughtful and virile drama, in the near future. It has always seemed to me to show the densest ingratitude on their part that they should have nothing but sneers and disparagement for the man [Pinero] who was gallantly fighting their own battles, though perhaps with other weapons than theirs.'

He thought that the satire of the play was drawn with 'direct, sober, significant touches', and that the Fraser family was 'by no means devoid of redeeming traits'. The review is surprising because of its failure to see the comedy of the play—an omission which let Archer put forward more serious claims than it deserves. For him, the play succeeded in being both serious and wholesome:

'Thus the "comedy" is in reality a somewhat sordid character-tragedy; but it seems to me that Mr Pinero has refrained, with true artistic instinct, from making his picture intolerably grimy and repellent.'

Theo's breakdown is 'lifelike', 'inevitable' and 'daring'. The play shows the 'fluidity' of life, but—to Archer's regret—avoids a solution: it is a 'picture play' rather than a problem play. His approach is full of contradictions, and attempts to have it both ways: on one hand the play is praised for its perceptive tolerance, its technical variety and basic seriousness, on the other censured for failing to offer an 'ideal'. Archer again seems to want the acceptable tone and style of the 'well-made play' together with its conventional moral resolution, and the stirring qualities that he found in Ibsen.

It is again to Shaw's credit that he perceived the success of *The Benefit of the Doubt* to stem from the absence of such ambitions.

'Consciously or unconsciously, he has this time seen his world as it really is: that is, a world which never dreams of bothering its little head with large questions or general ideas.'[50]

When Shaw remarked that the play was an 'entirely serious work of art',[51] he meant something different from Archer. 'Serious' here did not mean sombre or even 'concerned with problems', but alludes to the play's consistency of milieu and character: it indicates an approval of technique. Only when he had made this clear could Shaw put Pinero's name alongside that of Ibsen.

'We shall presently have him sharing the fate of Ibsen, and having his plays shirked with wise shakes of the head by actor-managers who have neither the talent to act them nor the brains to understand them.'[52]

Archer's conventional vocabulary, and Shaw's playful inversions of it, have to be referred to the contemporary matrix of ideas and preconceptions that surfaced most frequently in the opposition between Realism and Idealism, a semantic area well known to historians of the theory and criticism of the novel.[53] All that need be indicated here are the associations and meanings that these words held in the often debased world of theatrical journalism: Idealism is classical, intuitive, inspirational or optimistic, and upholds some absolute ethical standard; it respects the validity of individual or isolated change. An Idealist writer may cultivate style, and aspire to the Beautiful. Realism, in contrast, admits of extreme detail, does not avoid and may even seek out the squalid, and because it rejects absolute standards of behaviour there is often an implication of a need for social or democratic reform. Confusingly, the wider and ancient term Realism was often superimposed on its more recent and confined offshoot Naturalism, but it invariably included within its range of reference Tolstoy, Zola and, notoriously, Ibsen.

Archer considered himself the champion of 'ethical realism'—a realism that discovered moral truths.[54] But then Archer seems to have held absolute standards himself, and was consistently optimistic; hence his later incapacity to persist in the exploration of Ibsen's moral relativism, his sanctification of 'serious' drama, and his continual demand for an 'ideal'. The terminology finally became quite unmanageable when the progressive Ibsenites started to be known as Idealists because of their extreme or utopian beliefs.

When Shaw attacked his Idealists he was criticising a dependence on received ideas about social morality which detracted from the freedom of the individual. When Archer wished to qualify Pinero's achievement he objected to his exclusion of the 'ideal' that gives a play seriousness, not to a failure in realism. The incompatibility of the two critics was intimately connected with their different conceptions of what the role of the theatre might be. In much of his writing Archer is torn between opposing attitudes: a tolerant eclecticism conflicts with a narrow conception of serious or moral drama. Shaw's criticism benefited from his clear and purposive aim for a doctrinal or propagandist theatre, committed to certain *ideas* and quite distinct from the commercial theatre. In his view social seriousness depended on the validity of ideas, but did not preclude an artistic seriousness that referred simply to the technical skill and generic appropriateness of the work in question. Ultimately, in its range of appreciation alone, Shaw's would have been the more tolerant approach, but it was at the same time essentially uncompromised and derived from his whole previous experience and background.

The hack journalists of the nineties too often continued to discuss Ibsen in terms of daring subject-matter and a gloomy ending. The gravest consequence of this was that it allowed English audiences to accept so-called problem plays which in fact merely upheld a conventional morality, which the sudden and incredible reformation of Pinero's heroines, the sensational gesture of an Agnes Ebbsmith, confirms.

Here was a further deflection of purpose even among reformers—the naïve welcome they accorded Pinero's new drama, and the consequent misunderstanding, certainly as far as the more general public was concerned, of Ibsen's real achievement, reveals a basic flaw of the English renaissance. Because the new dramatists arose out of the commercial system and, in their early years, had to some extent flourished in it, their later standing was essentially at odds with the pioneering performances of Ibsen—characteristically the product of small groups and private fervour. The pattern becomes familiar: the English dramatists, for flattering their audiences, were rewarded with an increased respect.

In the nineties, opposition to established management adopted various strategies: the private performance, the special season (the Charringtons at Terry's in 1893, Florence Farr at the Avenue in 1894) and the formation of societies (the New Century Theatre, the Stage Society and, first and foremost, the Independent Theatre). Few of these methods had the financial resources needed to establish an identity, none of them maintained a coherent approach. The assault persisted, the personalities survived, but their impact was dispersed.

Minority activities were in turn observed by the commercial theatre. Although Irving could never be persuaded to stage Ibsen, Beerbohm Tree, an unquestionably commercial figure, was sometimes eager to experiment with advanced tastes, though, ironically, it was Henley and Stevenson's *Beau Austin*, rightly dismissed later by George Moore as 'a sea-captain's yarn', that was the most successful of his 'Monday-Night' special performances. Tree's curiosity was ambivalent, and his late production of *An Enemy of the People* in 1893 smacks suspiciously of a commercial organisation attempting to cash in on artistic novelty.

When Tree took the Haymarket Theatre in 1887 he had opened with a series of moderately successful but quite undistinguished plays and gained proper critical attention only with Jones' *The Dancing Girl* in 1891. From the moment of his spectacular and successful *Julius Caesar* in 1898, designed by Alma-Tadema, his repertoire was dominated by notoriously vulgar Shakespearean revivals, and to those remaining outside the commercial mainstream he began to assume a tyrannical role similar to that of Irving. In contrast, some of the rewards open to the astute manager who did succeed in judging moderate public taste in new plays were reaped by George Alexander, who produced both *The Second Mrs Tanqueray* and Wilde's most popular comedies.

Professionalism could be a danger even to those dedicated to subversion, as in the case of the new actresses and the inevitable variety of parts they played. The urge to become 'men of the theatre' led others into betraying their shifting sympathies and alarmingly short memories. By 1899, less than a decade after *Ghosts*, even J. T. Grein, founder of the Independent Theatre, had been sufficiently subdued to pay conventional lip-service to the fading glories of the Lyceum, citadel of a former enemy.

'It came as a rude shock, some months ago, the message that Sir Henry Irving would no longer occupy the Lyceum. It heralded a sad ending to a vital chapter of our dramatic history. The Lyceum was, in a sense, the National theatre of the English world—the Théâtre Français of London.

The Lyceum was the embodiment of all that is refined, sumptuous and noble in English histrionic art. It was scarcely progressive, perhaps old-fashioned in its methods, but "noblesse oblige" was writ large over its porch, and inside there reigned, since Irving was its ruler, faultless decorum wedded to impressive respect of tradition.'[55]

But Grein's piece about Tree's *Julius Caesar* in 1898 should have come as an even ruder shock:

'For whoever produces *Julius Caesar* on such a scale of discreet magnificence, whoever knows how to manipulate crowds with such dexterity that Jean Jullien's words: "Realism is to transplant a slice of life to the stage in an artistic manner," become realised to the letter, is an artist of great and sensitive distinction.'[56]

The phrase 'slice of life' belongs unmistakably to the jargon and manifestoes of the advocates of naturalistic drama, Grein's old colleagues and mentors. It could hardly have been applied to anything more incongruous than the baroque extravagances at the Haymarket.

The situation can often be reduced to a formula: doctrine versus repertory. When social implication became anaesthetised by the uncritical revival of old forms it was a matter not only of resistance to new forms but of *organisation*. The 'form' of a play is never stable, especially when more than one mind has a say in the creation; it has always to be 'discovered', 'realised', or 'interpreted', which involves the demands of practical, individual and social *circumstance*. The staging of a play becomes then the making of a complex social statement, which can itself be inappropriate or out-of-turn.

A younger man who boldly embarked on a foray all his own was F. R. Benson.[57] Benson started as an amateur in the first important classical revival, the famous Balliol *Agamemnon* of 1880, but he quickly acquired considerable experience; he acted with Irving and, in 1881, was deeply impressed by the visit of the Meiningen Company. In 1883 he took over a touring company and gathered around him that collection of cricketing Shakespeareans that Beerbohm labelled 'Mr Benson's eleven'. But the pioneering tradition which instigated his extraordinary and often comic career became debased into amateurism. The Bensonians were a dilution of principle, indulging the idea of an autonomous organisation and united less by their art than by their way of life.

William Poel, on the other hand, stands out for his vigorous dedication to a single artistic cause. Determined to challenge the decadent splendours of Lyceum Shakespeare single-handed, he staged his famous 'authentic' *Hamlet* in 1881, and his irregular revivals of forgotten early plays as well as of Shakespeare continued right through the nineties. Poel's obsessive campaign, with its insistence on historical correctness and austerity, was necessarily directed against the actor-manager and his vulgarisation of the achievements of the past. Like Shaw and even Benson, Poel had found some inspiration in the teachings of William Morris for the moral import they lent to his scholarship, prophesying that 'commercialism and competition have sown the wind recklessly, and must reap the whirlwind.'[58]

The first of the essays that follow traces the theatrical career of E. W. Godwin, a crepuscular figure even to his contemporaries, as he tries to bring together a number of social and artistic enclaves with some remarkable private productions. The idea of artistic community is also relevant to the second subject, Professor Hubert von Herkomer, in his attempts to recreate Bayreuth in Hertfordshire. Finally the history of the Independent Theatre pinpoints the dichotomies inherent in the attempts made to organise a theatre by the world of literature. In each case there is a triadic relationship between text, staging and organisation, which ultimately determines the nature of the result.

But this was also a period when artistic innovation was itself becoming newsworthy, when sensation could already conceal the inertia or impotence or frustration of the truly radical, or direct attention from the steady encroachment of the commercial monolith. The serious theatre is still, necessarily, an artistic activity largely controlled by commerce and competition, and survival demands compromise; that single fact, now as then, accounts for so many contradictions and, despite Matthew Arnold's confidence, for its frequent resistibility.

II
An Aesthetic Theatre:
The Career of E. W. Godwin

Staging, like organisation, plays a vital role in shaping the theatrical experience, and its techniques and principles received an increasing amount of attention in England in the eighties and nineties. It was during these years that movements which had developed slowly earlier in the century were reinforced and redirected by new ideas from the continent, as the work of the Duke of Saxe Meiningen, of Antoine and of Lugné-Poe was displayed in a series of London visits. At the same time the heady influence of Wagner was beginning to take effect. Some innovations which now seem peculiarly twentieth-century have their origins in this period and in an international context: Stanislavsky learned from the naturalism of the Théâtre Libre, Edward Gordon Craig drew on his experience of Irving's productions and his own experiments are paralleled by those of Appia.

The drift towards domestic realism in the first three-quarters of the nineteenth century had received its final confirmation in the Bancrofts' tenancy at the Prince of Wales theatre. By abolishing the pit and carpeting the stalls the Bancrofts civilised theatre-going; and, confronted by a respectable audience in close proximity, actors were obliged to modify their performances into a more naturalistic style. The scenery for their productions offered not mere spectacle but aptness and a measure of artistic control. These tendencies were already evident in *Society* (1865), one of a series of comedies by T. W. Robertson, but it was a later production, *Caste* (1867), that caused the sensation. It was, for instance, considered remarkable that in the sets for *Caste* the rooms should have ceilings and the doors locks. The famous gusts of snow which blew into rooms when doors were opened, and the autumn park scene in *Ours* (1866), during which the trees steadily shed their leaves, showed just how literally the Bancrofts could take their realism, but it was chiefly the accuracy of their domestic interiors that was applauded. Most significantly of all, they built up a regular company, still an unusual thing to do, kept a tight control upon their actors' performances and choice of costumes, and exploited the 'long-run'—for only by doing so could the standards of the company be maintained.

But in all this the Bancrofts were working in the same directions as earlier innovators, both those concerned with what can be termed 'domestic' realism and with 'archaeological' realism, two parallel trends which had converged periodically in earlier years. Archaeology—the application of the study of architecture and costume to theatre production—had been pioneered by Macready during his seasons at Covent Garden and Drury Lane from 1837 to 1843. With the support of established literary figures (Dickens, Browning, Bulwer-Lytton, Douglas Jerrold) Macready had created unified and picturesque settings that were also, up to a point, historically accurate, and had harmonised the performances of his actors by holding proper rehearsals, a still revolutionary custom. Macready was assisted by the man who was to do most of all to improve overall standards, the first theatrical archaeologist, J. R. Planché, whose encyclopaedic *British Costume*, published in 1834, became a standard work for half a century.

Planché's researches were first seen as a dominating influence in Charles Kean's production of *King John* in 1823. Like Macready, Kean made use of scholarship in an attempt to achieve unity in his productions, although his efforts in this direction should not be wrongly emphasised: spectacle was still his final criterion and scholarship often only a means to an end. His *Midsummer Night's Dream*, for instance, involved a quite unnecessary reconstruction of classical Athens, justified in terms of archaeology.*

Despite his scholarship and the work with Kean, much of Planché's energy was expended upon burlesque. His famous collaboration with Madame Vestris at the Royal Olympic Theatre in 1831–8 resulted in a succession of farces, burlesques and light operas, albeit staged with maximum efficiency. Madame Vestris found her own brand of realism:

'Others had dealt with the dingily real; she never abandoned respectability. Even her shepherdessess carried golden crooks and her milkmaids wore silk slippers. Her realism then, although not in the least true to type and actuality, was insistent upon fidelity to normal appearances and behaviour. First of all, she banished grotesqueness in costume and acting. This in itself was no small reform.'[1]

Principles established by Planché continued through Madame Vestris' later seasons, and resulted, in 1841, in the first example of modern domestic melodrama: Boucicault's *London Assurance*, followed by his *Corsican Brothers* (1852) and *The Colleen Bawn* (1860). From Boucicault's melodrama to T. W. Robertson's comedies, with their box sets, was a short step; and thus it is more accurate to see the Bancrofts, harbingers of the long reign of the realistic domestic drama, as reformers rather than as revolutionaries.

* Allardyce Nicoll, *A History of English Drama*, Cambridge, 1962, V, 38. Fechter's stay in London diverted the trend. His *Hamlet* at the Lyceum in 1860 restaged the play as melodrama, and drew on the traditions of pantomime to introduce every possible novelty. Archaeology counted for little, the architectural style of the set was Norman, Norman costumes were worn. The purely technical reforms that he implemented were, however, valid. 'He introduced concealed footlights and semi-solid scenery, with interiors roofed with ceilings. . . .' (Laurence Irving, *Henry Irving, The Actor and his World*, London, 1951, 182.)

And it was the Bancrofts who were responsible for the renewal of 'archaeological' realism when in 1875 they varied their repertoire with a production of *The Merchant of Venice* and called upon a disciple of Planché's, E. W. Godwin, for historical guidance on its staging.

Realism, as the Bancrofts' experience showed, demanded a re-organisation of the theatre company. Because it was expensive and depended upon well-rehearsed troupes, the long-run became a condition of success, and long-runs again required regular companies. The permanent companies in Europe were held up as examples: the Comédie Française and the Duke of Saxe Meiningen's own private company, founded in 1874, which gave regular tours throughout Europe. The Meiningen in particular demonstrated the potential of a well-drilled troupe, and established once and for all the importance of designs which were more or less faithful to the text as well as the scenic effectiveness of the performers themselves when conceived as components of a stage picture. They specialised in crowd movements, each individual contributing to the symmetry of the whole, and the whole controlled by one man, the stage director (in this case the brilliant Chronegk). Their visit to London in 1881 revealed to the younger managers, and to Irving in particular, the full possibilities of 'archaeological' realism for the classic, especially the Shakespearean, repertoire.*

In England not dissimilar ideals had already been aspired to by Godwin, who was employed not by one company but as a free-lance consultant, and whose original profession had been architecture.

The architecture of the Victorian era, as all the history books record, and our cycs still tell us, was various and contradictory in its achievements. Indeed until recently the Euston arch and the St Pancras hotel, the classical and the Gothic, still stood alongside each other, also emblematising the dichotomy shown by Palmerston and Scott in the notorious Battle of the Styles, fought over designs for the Foreign Office in 1857. Living and working in what was, more than are most periods, a time of intense and conscious revival, the Victorian architect required detailed scholarly information about the styles of the past, and he was fully prepared to supply this for himself through his own researches: there was more to it than satisfying the pretensions of his patron. But the variety of styles also

---

* The influence of the Meiningen was for a long time underestimated, yet F. R. Benson's company was for many years advertised as 'conducted on the Meiningen system'. J. C. Trewin, *Benson and the Bensonians*, London, 1960, 30. See also Lee Simonson, *The Stage is Set*, New York, 1932, part 3, chapter 2, and Max Grube, *The Story of the Meininger*, trans. Anne Koller, Miami, 1965.

rested upon a further division in intention itself, for during the course of the nineteenth century the ancient and still potent architectural tradition by which a building was required to represent certain values as much as it was required to be of use, reached an apotheosis; it was eventually overcome only by the triumph of twentieth-century functionalism. A nineteenth-century public building was expected to embody social dignity, and its design, because often contradicting or concealing its real purpose, played its own part in the continuous theatre of public life.

It was logical enough then (Pugin had taken the first steps, although one could refer back as far as Inigo Jones), as the century continued, for an architect to be drawn almost irresistibly towards the exercise of his art within the theatre itself, where his skill in reconstruction was always protected by the ephemerality of the medium, and historical and aesthetic expertise could be offered as 'archaeology'. That Godwin should have already conducted an innovative career as an architect—as notable for its variety, or its versatility, as that of any of his contemporaries—was thus a highly suitable introduction for the most important stage designer and archaeologist of the late nineteenth century.

Of Dudley Habron's biography of his father, *The Conscious Stone* (1949), Edward Gordon Craig, illegitimate son of Ellen Terry and Edward William Godwin, confessed that 'most of the information that it contains was unknown to me'.

In spite of that essential source, and a few recent articles, it is undoubtedly the case that Godwin's achievements deserve fuller attention and documentation than they have so far received. This may be to do with their immense range; besides his pioneer work in the theatre he was an award-winning architect, furniture designer, scholar and historian. He was also a close and influential friend of Whistler and Wilde—he designed homes for both—and a favourite of some elements of the high society that centred on the Prince of Wales in the 1880s. He was, as Max Beerbohm vouchsafed, not only 'that superb architect', but 'the greatest aesthete of them all', a leader, an instigator and an original.

Born in Bristol in 1833, Godwin's interest in the theatre was kindled early by regular attendance at the Theatre Royal, which was then visited by the main stock companies. By 1857 he was contributing a series of theatre reviews to a Bristol newspaper, and had begun a most promising career as an architect. In 1862 he met the Terry sisters, Kate and Ellen, then appearing in Bristol, and designed a Grecian dress for Ellen to wear as Titania. Between 1862 and 1864 Godwin and Ellen Terry lost contact; she married the painter G. F. Watts, and Godwin became more and more occupied with his business in Bristol. But in 1865 when his first wife died and he opened offices in London, he began to frequent the Watts' house. A liaison sprang up, Ellen was banished from her husband's house, and after an unhappy and professionally unsuccessful period, set up home with Godwin near Wheathampstead, later moving to a house designed by him near Harpenden. This strange period of retreat was broken in 1873 when Charles Reade persuaded her to return to the stage in his new play *The Wandering Heir*. The family (two children had been born to them, Edith and Edward Gordon Craig) moved to London. While Ellen toured in Reade's play Godwin worked on his vast compilation of material on the dating, costuming and setting of Shakespeare's plays.

Between 1874 and 1875, Godwin published thirty-two articles on 'The Architecture and Costume of Shakespeare's Plays'.[2] These articles, the fruit of many years' research, together formed an immense and exhaustive work of scholarship and provided the foundation of his attack on the London theatre.*

Godwin was a fairly prolific journalist, and his writings are most remarkable for their repeated emphasis on the same demands, their extraordinary range of information and their devotion to detail. In Bristol in 1864 he was already proclaiming that

'The use of scenery, dress and other accessories directly implies an intention to reproduce the original scene, and consequently an error in either of these vitiates the whole result, nor will excellence on the part of any actor atone for the inaccuracy of his personal appearance or of the scenery by which he is surrounded. I do not need to deny that a person totally ignorant of the past may feel himself satisfied in spite of the grossest anachronisms, but his satisfaction will be that of a man who is merely anxious to be amused, entirely irrespective of any desire to be instructed, whereas I maintain that we do not go to a theatre simply to hear passionate recitations and funny speeches, but to witness such a performance as will place us nearly as possible as spectators of the original scene or of the thing represented, and so gain information of man, manners, customs, costumes, and countries—and this result is only obtainable where accuracy in every particular is secured.'[3]

The articles on the architecture and costume of Shakespeare's plays follow a set programme. First Godwin gives as precise a dating

* As Godwin pointed out in a later review (*The Academy*, 27 March 1886, 225–6) of the 3rd edition of F. W. Fairholt's *Costume in England*, first published in 1846, there had been for a quarter of a century only two cheap and accessible books on costume: Fairholt's and Planché's.

as possible to the historical period in which the play is set, second a breakdown of the complete changes of scene that it will require, third detailed suggestions for architecture and furnishings with references to actual examples or textual sources, fourth descriptions of correct costumes and their probable colour scheme, and finally some intimation of the total aesthetic style and mood that a production should aim for. Allowance is sometimes made for periods of transition in style and taste, for example that covered by the English history plays, and for the ways in which a dramatist's historical knowledge is conditioned by the other literary sources that he draws upon. The second factor was particularly relevant in the case of Shakespeare's Greek plays, where contemporary discoveries were changing ideas of the classical and pre-classical civilisations. For instance his scheme for *Troilus and Cressida* was based on Homeric sources:

' . . . assuming, that is, that Troy meant something more than the walled enclosure on the hill of Hissarlik mapped out for us in Dr Schliemann's book. For the *mise-en-scène* of the drama before us I am disposed to accept the grander view, and to take Homer's colouring of things as tolerably literal, after allowing for poetical licence.'[4]

This format is occasionally broken by side-swipes at the contemporary theatre, in particular of course at the careless habits of modern management. Such digressions could have wider implications. When attacking the way in which plays were mounted, Godwin also took advantage of the occasion to condemn, with a good deal of righteousness, all standards connected with the theatre as he viewed it, aesthetic, literary and moral.

'Modern actors and actresses have no conception of the drama directly it becomes poetry. The dignity and beauty of art are old-fashioned things, quite out of keeping with the modern spirit that delights in chaff and mockery, and fondly believes them to be the outcome of wit. To mock at love, religion, education; to jeer the unfortunate; to chaff the suicide; and ridicule the justice and majesty of the law are the things which succeed if done with a sufficient amount of absurdity, and I may add accompanied by a sufficient number of pretty girls and pretty songs. This *mockery* is unquestionably the central spirit of the age, and those who take it and mould it for the stage into an hour's amusement for us are the artists who, perhaps, best represent, and who will be most identified with, the age.'[5]

The first opportunity to put his theories and knowledge into practice came in 1875, when Mrs Bancroft asked Ellen Terry to play Portia in *The Merchant of Venice*, and Godwin to design the new production. He had already dealt with the staging of the play in extreme detail in his Shakespeare series, and now he facilitated the task by re-arranging the play into even acts or tableaux, eliminating short continuity scenes normally played in front of the curtain. On Godwin's advice the scene-painters went to Venice to make drawings from which they constructed massive panoramic settings. It is important but difficult to define Godwin's exact role in this production. He was 'historical adviser' rather than scenic designer, and forcefully denied responsibility for the costume design;[6] nevertheless tradition and Ellen Terry have it that he was responsible at least for her dress in the casket-scene. 'It was,' she recalled, 'like almond blossom.'[7] That prominent Aesthetic lady Mrs Comyns-Carr, who was later to design many of Ellen Terry's costumes, attended with her husband:

'Joe and I were present on the first night, and as the curtain rose upon Nell's tall and slender figure in a china blue and white brocaded dress, with one crimson rose at her breast, the whole house burst forth in rapturous applause. But her greatest effect was when she walked into the court in her black robes of justice, and I remember my young husband, who had rushed out between the acts to buy the last bouquet in Covent Garden, throwing his floral tribute at her feet amidst the enthusiasm of the audience.'[8]

Although not a commercial success, the Bancrofts' *Merchant of Venice* was a first vindication of Godwin's ideas. Critics heaped praise upon the artistic and historical consistency that he had imposed upon the production, even if a proportion did object that 'the play sinks beneath its load of finery and is killed by the weight of its decorations.'[9] Twenty-five years later Beerbohm Tree, speaking to the Oxford Union, claimed that

'.... it was the first production in which the modern spirit of stage-management asserted itself, transporting us, as it did, into the atmosphere of Venice, into the rarefied realms of Shakespearean comedy ... since then no doubt millions have flooded to this class of production.'[10]

1875 was also marked by the break-up of the relationship between Ellen Terry and Godwin. In January 1876 he married Beatrice Philip, a sculptress who later became the wife of Whistler. But the loss of Ellen Terry does not seem to have affected his work in the theatre. A year later he followed *The Merchant of Venice* by joining John Coleman and Samuel Phelps in a production of *Henry V*,[11] which cost some £6,000 in preparation alone. In an article published before the opening night he maintained that it was the first production on which he had been consulted *professionally*, that is, as 'archaeologist'.[12] Unfortunately this claim laid him open to attack, and a fellow architect, William Burges, pointed out a few historical inaccuracies.[13] Godwin defended himself in a spirited reply,[14] but Burges had in fact touched upon a vital weakness. Godwin himself had been dissatisfied with some of Coleman's arrangements. He complained of a cannon which looked like 'a modern pillar box on wheels', and of the use of French crossbow men at Harfleur with pikemen behind them: 'Why thus *reverse* the order and outrage not merely history but commonsense?'[15] Whether or not Burges' complaints were justified, Coleman had certainly overruled some of Godwin's suggestions—as 'archaeologist', Godwin was of course answerable to the manager, who assumed final responsibility. To resolve this situation, a recurring one in his early work, Godwin was finally obliged to invent a new role for himself, and indeed for the modern theatre: that of 'producer', a man endowed with final artistic control over a whole production, and complete power over the other participants.

As yet, however, the campaign was not firmly established, and the theatrical ventures were intermittent; it was not until 1880 that he was asked to supply costume designs for Miss Bateman's new production of *Othello*.[16] He chose for his models portraits by the Italian painters of the late sixteenth century, and Othello's first robe of deep scarlet and amber brocade was copied from a Vicelli. For the indoor scenes Othello wore a scarlet garment under a flowing blue robe, and in the last act the use of dark grey material introduced a sinister note. Desdemona's costume of dove-grey plush with undershirt of deep blue velvet, and the black and yellow outfit worn by Iago (Hermann Vezin) were taken from engravings by Jost Amman; the Doge's gown was copied from a Fialetti at Hampton Court, and so on.[17] Yet despite the attention lavished on it by Godwin, this production was not deemed an artistic success—nor did it make any money.

It is ironical that when, for the second time, Godwin was connected with a production which had a real impact on the London theatre, he received no public acknowledgement. The occasion was Irving's epic production of Tennyson's *The Cup*,[18] a classical drama requiring large crowds and panoramic vistas. The effects, obviously similar to those produced by the Meiningen Company, have best been described by Ellen Terry, who had introduced Godwin to Irving.

'There was a vastness, a spaciousness of proportion about the scene in the Temple of Artemis which I never saw again upon the stage until my own son attempted something like it in the Church Scene that he designed for my production of *Much Ado* in 1903.

'A great deal of the effect was due to the lighting. The gigantic figure of the many-breasted Artemis, placed far back in the scene-dock, loomed through a blue mist, while the foreground of the picture was in yellow light. The thrilling effect always to be gained on the stage by the simple expedient of a great number of people doing the same thing in the same way at the same moment, was seen in *The Cup*, when the stage was covered with a crowd of women who raised their arms above their heads with a large rhythmic, sweeping movement and then bowed to the goddess with the regularity of a regiment saluting. . . .

'Quite as wonderful as the Temple Scene was the setting of the first act, which represented the rocky side of a mountain with a glimpse of a fertile table-land and a pergola with vines growing over it at the top. The acting in this scene all took place at different levels. The hunt swept past on one level; the entrance to the temple was on another. A goatherd played upon a pipe. Scenically it was not Greece, but Greece in Sicily, or Capri or some such hilly region.'[19]

Though Godwin's precise function again remains obscure, there is evidence that he helped with Ellen Terry's flamboyant yellow bejewelled toga, and designed the cup itself.

In the same year Godwin collaborated with Wilson Barrett on the designs for a new play by W. G. Wills, *Juana*,[20] but despite exhaustive research into the architecture of fifteenth-century Spain and the construction of a Renaissance loggia, once again the production was not a success. Madame Modjeska, the star, refused to co-operate, and some of Godwin's work was replaced by other designs. He was justifiably irked, as he had been by Coleman's alterations to *Henry V* in 1876.

'The idea of *control* in the matter of theatrical costume has not yet got into the actor's mind, any individuality or obstinacy I have had to contend with has not been greater than experience led me to expect.'[21]

Godwin's absolute belief in the significance of what he had to offer is impressive, and was justified as his campaign gained impetus. Few reviewers now omitted a praising reference to him, and Wilson Barrett made provision for a salary of three pounds to be paid weekly during the London run of *Juana*, together with an initial payment of twenty pounds.[22] He received more commissions: less than a month after *Juana* he was designing the costumes and arranging the mise-en-scène for *Queen and Cardinal*,[23] by W. S. Raleigh, and in the following year assisted Hermann Vezin with *The Cynic*,[24] by Herman Merivale. Always concerned with artistic standards, he would attend a performance—often as the reviewer for an architectural magazine—and, during the play, cover his programme with notes and pencilled criticisms. It seems that this habit had persisted since his youth at the Theatre Royal, Bristol.* He even found fault with the archaeology of the Meiningen Company, whose 1881 tour he reviewed for *The British Architect*: he considered the Roman rabble in *Julius Caesar* to be too well-dressed, and complained that the casements built into the Elizabethan set for *Twelfth Night* (itself inappropriate) were wrongly divided into 'Queen Anne squares'. Yet the performances must have been enormously interesting to him, for the problem of manipulating crowds in harmonious patterns of colour and movement had recently been confronted in *The Cup*, and was to become increasingly important in future productions.

Although other observers had drawn the same conclusions,[25] there was no doubt a personal bitterness founded on recent experience behind Godwin's complaints that no English company could match the 'complete earnestness' of the Germans and the excellence of their stage work, which 'results emphatically in pictures, as if painted by one master hand',[26] and in his diagnosis of the causes of English shoddiness as the star system and the lack of a permanent company.

In 1882, in a further effort to establish the study of costume as a serious branch of scholarship, Godwin brought his friends together in The Costume Society, and published a rule-book and manifesto, *The Costume Society, or Society for promoting the knowledge of Costume, by copying and publishing Historical Costume from Contemporary Sources only*.[27] The objective was to produce a series of guide-books to specific periods, which when finally collated would form a kind of encyclopaedic manual of costume for the producer or scholar, a new and improved version of Planché's *British Costume*. Among those who joined were Whistler, Wilde, Wills, Vezin and Beerbohm Tree,[28] but despite the vast amount of work that Godwin put into the venture, it seems to have petered out quite rapidly. Tree was rebuked by his fiancée Maud for joining, and for associating with Godwin; she wrote to Tree that her sister Emmie 'would no more shake hands with this man than she would with a snake'.[29] Maud Beerbohm's apprehensiveness was by no means unique; he was probably still notorious for his liaison with Ellen Terry and for his reputation as a philanderer. The disapproval of his contemporaries, suggested by his nick-name 'the wicked Earl', is one reason for the occasional difficulties in locating and defining Godwin's activities.

* On the programme for *Masks and Faces* (1881), he scrawled: 'Vile combination of colours—violet and green, grey and yellow all bad singly and together.'

The following year he produced some comparatively simple designs for a drama by Robert Buchanan, *Storm-Beaten* (in which Tree had a part),[30] and supervised the costumes for the Hermann Vezin benefit matinée of *The Merchant of Venice*.[31] But for the most part the year was given over to preparations for a sensational new play, *Claudian*,[32] by W. G. Wills, presented by Wilson Barrett. Godwin and Wills, friends since their collaboration on *Juana*, retired to Broadstairs to work on the forthcoming production, and were visited by Lady Archibald Campbell, who herself had plans for Godwin.[33]

Claudian told the story of a dissolute Byzantine emperor condemned by the curse of a Christian hermit to eternal youth, the curse only to be resolved when the rock on which Byzantium was built was 'rent asunder'. It required the most detailed and strenuous research that Godwin had yet embarked upon. He plunged into the standard works on Byzantine art and architecture, read Eusebius and Appollonius Sidonius, and published his conclusions in the form of an open letter to Wilson Barrett.[34] It took another architect fully to understand the achievement:

'The foreground is a bit like Constantine's forum; to the left, solidly built, and of true dimensions, is the end of a Doric portico; to the right a portion of a circular Ionic portico; a low wall bounds the plateau, and over this we see the tops of dark cypresses among other trees and commemorative pillars, and, on a rising hill beyond, stately many-pillared structures, while, in the far distance, the blue waters of the Bosphorus and the hilly shore beyond, complete a picture of which Mr Walter Hann might well be proud. In the walls beneath the porticos we recognise the *opus sectile*, or large mosaics, of which Mr Godwin speaks in his pamphlet. The capitals and friezes reveal the coarse carving of the time, and the marble and gilding exhibit something of the costly splendour. Under one portico is a marble statue of Venus with gilded drapery and in the centre of the stage is another statue similarly treated.'[35]

The second act, in complete contrast, showed a vineyard in front of a rugged coastline and the sea. Most reviewers were more taken with the splendid earthquake in the third act, during which Claudian's magnificent palace was destroyed (a scene which Edward Gordon Craig claimed never to forget[36]).

'The moment came, and so far from being ridiculous, the effect was terrorising. With a mighty upheaval the walls, pillars, and arches shook, then split up and fell with a crash; and, in a quarter of a minute, the magnificent palace was reduced to a fearful desolation, amid which Claudian stood pale, dignified, and unharmed.'[37]

Yet Godwin, ever the perfectionist, was dissatisfied, for the costumes had involved him in a degree of compromise. As he explained in his pamphlet, information on the period was so scanty that he had been forced to collate all the available information on both the fourth and the fifth centuries, and to introduce creative variety by including as many nationalities and classes into each scene as possible. He hoped, however, that his organisation of the crowds had formed 'a succession of pictures melting into each other in imperceptible gradations.'[38]

Claudian was a scenic triumph and followed on directly from *The Cup* and the example of the Meiningen. Whether it was considered to have overcome or to have complemented the melodramatic banality of Wills' play, Godwin's 'archaeological tyranny'[39] could go no further. It was now providing a subject for cynical parodies and comments in *Punch*; and even Wilson Barrett rebelled at one stage, refusing to make an entrance in the wheel-barrow-like contraption which Godwin assured him was the historically correct means of transport.

With *The Cup* and *Claudian*, the theatre had participated in the nineteenth-century classical revival, active and growing since the first display of the Parthenon marbles at Lord Elgin's home in London in 1807. They belong with a tradition that includes, for instance, the architecture of the British Museum and the Athenaeum, the paintings of Lord Leighton and Alma-Tadema, and the novels of Bulwer Lytton. At the same time they point forward to the designs provided by Alma-Tadema for Irving's productions of *Cymbeline* (1896) and *Coriolanus* (1901) and Beerbohm Tree's *Julius Caesar* (1898). Massive and grand proportions were the means by which moods of reverence and solemnity were invoked. Godwin was also to work with Wilson Barrett on one other 'classical' project—the spectacular but unsuccessful adaptation of Lord Lytton's *Junius*.[40]

Some insight into method can be gained from an interview given in 1884,[41] when Godwin was engaged upon Wilson Barrett's successful *Hamlet*.[42] Asked if it were really possible to achieve archaeological accuracy, he replied:

'It has been determined in this case to place the date just before the reign of Cnut. Generally speaking, there are three distinct ways of putting the play on the stage, each of which has a certain amount of logic to support it. '*First*—the costumes etc., indicated by the historical date of the story. That is the period as above, which has been adopted at the Princess's. '*Second*—the costume in which it was probably originally played, viz., that in popular use in the lifetime of the author.

'*Third*—the costume of the period in which the play is acted, as adopted by Garrick.'[43]

The first method, which Godwin always attempted to use, ideally involved visits to the country in which the action of the play was set: while planning *Hamlet* he went to Denmark, and had hoped to go to Istanbul for *Claudian*. In any event he inspected every relevant museum and collection in London, researching and checking details. The designs for *Hamlet* most certainly relied upon this kind of abstruse knowledge:

'The influence of England on the Danish dress is indicated in this scene by the brilliancy of the courtiers' costumes—an influence which had almost entirely broken down the distinction between the dress of the two nations by the end of the tenth century—the date at which, as before remarked, the scene is laid.'[44]

But as critics were quick to point out when they saw the actual production, Godwin's arguments were not entirely logical. By maintaining archaeological accuracy at all costs, further and more subtle risks of anachronism were run. For some there were jars when the language, manners and customs of Shakespeare's court clashed with the rigorous authenticity of Godwin's Denmark.

The boldest move was to transfer the play scene into a garden setting, lit by torchlight and an artificial moon. Although the most obvious reasons for this were picturesque rather than practical, the added depth of stage area released by the use of an outdoor setting was potentially a significant advantage, for by breaking the tyranny of the backcloth it enabled the designer to make a real use of perspective and add a valuable third dimension to his groupings.

Hamlet completes the account of Godwin's early work in the commercial theatre, but there was one attempted reform, not confined to stage presentation and archaeology, which must be considered. In July 1881 he had called a number of the leaders of the contemporary theatre, including his particular friends Hermann Vezin and Beerbohm Tree, to the first meeting of 'The Society of English Players'. The idea behind this society was to obtain control of a London theatre and to stage there plays of its own choice, according to its own methods of presentation. Members of the company were to draw a regular salary, based on what they could expect in the commercial theatre: Godwin himself claimed an average of £20 per week, Pinero £10 and Hermann Vezin £25. Unfortunately it was this financial scheme, in itself startlingly revolutionary and clearly an ancestor of modern repertory systems, on which the plan foundered. The available records of the society, although very incomplete, tell an unhappy story.[45] The meetings cannot have been well attended, and one by one the members dropped out. None of them were prepared to rely on the company for their income, and few were happy with the salaries that Godwin suggested.

Until 1884 Godwin's idealism had only flourished, and then precariously, when subsidised by already established figures such as the Bancrofts or Irving. It was the recurrent crisis of his theatrical career that the essential autonomy of his art relied on some form of patronage, and only later did a satisfactory solution present itself. That solution, when it came, was to involve the organisation of a select group of Aesthetic colleagues in a private and uncommercial event.

Godwin's position in the Aesthetic milieu was absolutely central but hidden; he was particularly intimate with Wilde, and his undisclosed influence on the man who through his public appearances became more of a parody of the movement than its true representative was considerable. The lectures on interior decoration and dress reform that Wilde delivered on his sensational tour of America in 1881 were largely based, unacknowledged, on the teachings of Godwin, who was perhaps too scholarly and professional (or, more likely, too notorious) to receive much publicity himself. There was a curiously ironical moment in 1881 when Godwin reviewed F. C. Burnand's skit *The Colonel*, on which it is often assumed the Oscar-taunting *Patience* was based. In effect Godwin now found himself reviewing a satire of his own work and ideas; he treated it with stony-faced seriousness. First he remarked he had met the leading actress leaving the theatre in her everyday clothes and noticed that she herself wore the Aesthetic style that the audience had just been invited to ridicule on stage. He continued by praising the interior set that had been designed as a mockery of fashionable taste.

'The fact is, Mr Burnand and his co-workers in the production of this piece have given us the really artistic for the sham artistic to such an extent that it is hard to see, save for the exceptions we have made, why the very thing he has attempted to destroy should not acquire by his mode of procedure a new lease of life. There are but two scenes in the comedy, both interiors, one supposed to be founded on aestheticism, the other on common sense. Looking round the last, we find it very much upholstered with yards on yards of curtain stuff of a staring, loud pattern; an entirely vulgar, uninteresting, unpleasant apartment. But it is *this* the moral of the piece indicates as right. Turning to the other room that is presented to us as wrong, we find it furnished with artistic and simple things: a charming cabinet in walnut, designed by Mr Padgett for the

1 E. W. Godwin, *c*. 1870.
2 Ellen Terry in the costume designed
by Godwin for *The Cup*, 1881.

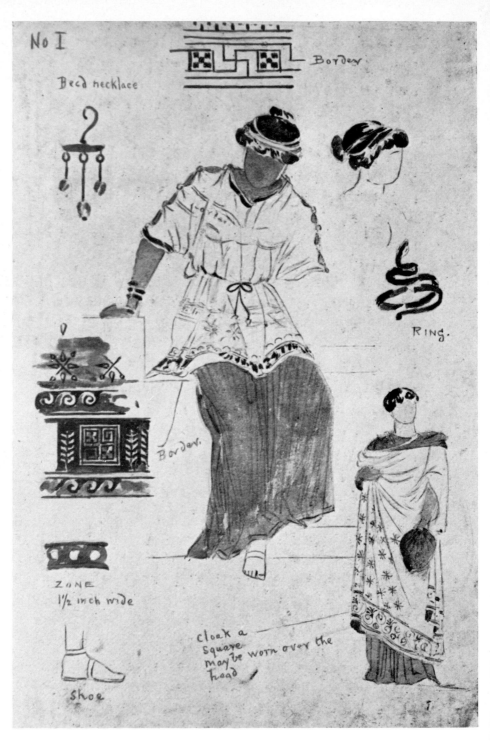

3   Page of Godwin's designs for *The Cup*.

4 and 5   *Claudian*, 1883.

PUTTING HIM RIGHT.

[Mr. Godwin, F.S.A., assisted at the arrangement of *Claudian* at the Princess's.]

SCENE—*The Rehearsal of the next Classical Drama.*

Stage Manager (to the F.S.A.).—I WOULDN'T INTERFERE, OLD CHAPPIE, WITH YOUR CLASSICAL KNOWLEDGE, BUT HANG IT, I DO KNOW MY LETTERS. S.P.Q.R. WON'T WASH. THE ALPHABET, DON'T YOU KNOW, RUNS M, N, O—P, Q, R, S!

6 and 7   The Pastoral Players' version of *As You Like It*, 1884.
top The first scene; *bottom* Lady Archibald Campbell as Orlando and Eleanor Calhoun
as Rosalind.

green room; some simple inexpensive black Sussex chairs, like those sold by Messrs Wm Morris and Co; a black coffee-table, after the well-known example originally designed in 1867 by the writer of these notes; a quite simple writing, table, matting on the floor, a green and yellow paper on the walls, a sunflower frieze, and a Japanese treatment of the ceiling (storks), and a red sun such as we see in Japanese books on hand screens, make up a scene, which, if found wanting in certain details and forced in sunflowers, is certainly an interesting room, with individuality about it, quiet in tone, and, what is most important, harmonious and pleasing.'[46]

But Godwin was happily prepared to concede the justice of deflating individual pretensions and phoniness.

'That sham art, that pretence of aesthetic culture, which holds on to the name, and practises in an absurd exaggeration a few of the outward signs of an art life it cannot understand, is a thing to ridicule, to hold in contempt, to attack and to crush. . . .'

Humourless about his own work he almost certainly was; an obituary was to comment:

'Of Godwin as a man, apart from his professional career, we can only say that his temperament was hardly calculated to attract close friendship, but he was extremely genial and pleasant company, and in all matters of art—of design, drawing, and decoration—his enthusiasm could always be drawn forth.'[47]

However, his intensity and devotion to his work could, in a certain circle, guarantee him the awe and respect due a serious artist, and also the authority to demand his own way and dispense instruction.

In the summer of 1884 Godwin collaborated with his friend Lady Archibald Campbell, queen bee of the Aesthetes, in a series of pastoral performances of the forest scenes from *As You Like It*. According to one account,[48] the idea for these originated with Lady Archibald, after she had painted the actress Eleanor Calhoun as Rosalind, using for background the woods of Coombe Warren in Surrey. This portrait inspired her, and meeting Godwin soon afterwards at an exhibition at the Grosvenor Gallery—the exhibition that contained Whistler's portrait of her—she proposed an open-air charity performance of *As You Like It*. Godwin agreed to become stage-manager, designer and general director of proceedings (i.e. 'producer'), and began to plan the production. After an initial false start—the Duke of Cambridge refused to lend his estate at Coombe— part of the adjoining grounds of Dr MacGeagh's hydropathic establishment was chosen for the setting, and a company was gathered together, mainly composed of friends but with a sprinkling of professional actors (Hermann Vezin was a special choice for Jacques).

As You Like It was staged twice, once in the summer of 1884 and again in 1885. The performances attracted a good deal of attention, coming as they did in the height of the 'season', and providing, if nothing else, an excuse for fashionable outings from the city. The élite of two worlds came to Coombe: the aristocratic, led by the Prince of Wales himself, and the artistic and theatrical, led by Whistler and Wilde; and in 1884 one man who successfully bridged the two, the Duke of Saxe Meiningen.

The setting was ideal.[49] A grove of lime trees forming a parallelogram became the 'stage', and facing it an 'auditorium', some forty feet wide and seventy feet deep, was curtained off with sage-green material and filled with three hundred chairs in tiers. This grove formed the main acting area, with natural 'wings' made out of clumps of low bushes and piles of faggots. A meadow stretched for about a quarter of a mile to the audience's left, beyond which there were more woods. In the foreground a green curtain was strung between two trees marking the extent of the 'proscenium', which was dropped by a pulley (operated by two men dressed as foresters) into a narrow trench at the start of the performance, and raised in the interval. There were, of course, no footlights, but a narrow belt of moss planted with ferns marked the foremost extent of the stage and camouflaged the trench. The action was conveniently concentrated around a large tree in the centre, near a forester's hut, with piles of oak logs beside it which could be used as seats by the actors. A wood fire gave off pale smoke which mellowed the picture, blending the colours together. ('I have never seen an illustration at once so perfect and so practical, of the aesthetic value of smoke,' remarked Wilde.[50])

As the critic from *The Era*—obviously a professional—realised, this arrangement offered radical advantages:

'A *mise en scène* of this unprecedented nature could not fail to bring into prominence in the representation itself several striking improvements on performances as constructed under the innumerable limitations and restrictions of the stage. The first of these improvements, one which, of course, everyone would naturally anticipate, was the impression of absolute reality conveyed by the acting. All the conventional symbolism, the 'make-believe' of the ordinary stage, everything which is conveniently summarised in the phrase *optique du théâtre*, the asides, 'stage-whispers', the actor taking the audience into his confidence, and so forth, became in the open-air either impossible or un-needed, and the performers were able to abstract themselves from all reference to the spectators, thus producing a sense of illusion so perfect as almost to make the audience feel like a body of eaves-droppers.'[51]

And the following year the *Era* critic developed these ideas even further, and in a wider context.

'The battle between the Idealists and Realists of the stage, between those who hold that the mounting of a play should leave much to the imagination, and those who maintain that the setting of a play should imitate reality with photographic accuracy, has long raged furiously, and is yet undecided. In Paris the opposing forces have been led respectively by the veteran critic M. Sarcey and M. Perrin, of the Comédie Française, who enjoys the reputation of being one of the cleverest *metteurs en scène* in Europe. In London we have had ranged on one side every dramatic critic of repute; on the other, the managements of the chief West End theatres and the authority, on this point by no means despicable, of Mr Oscar Wilde. Well Saturday was certainly the Realists' day out at Coombe. Not only did the mounting leave nothing to the imagination, more even than imitating reality with photographic accuracy, it was reality itself.'[52]

The reference to Wilde was perceptive, because *As You Like It* had provided him with an opportunity to pay homage to his master. No less professional than the *Era* reviewer, Wilde made very similar points:

'One distinct dramatic advantage was gained by the *mise en scène*. The abrupt exits and entrances, which are necessitated on the real stage by the inevitable limitations of space, were in many cases done away with, and we saw the characters coming gradually towards us through the bracken and underwood, or passing away down the slope 'till they were lost in some deep recess of the forest; the effect of the distance thus gained being largely increased by the faint wreaths of the mist that floated at times across the background.'[53]

Set pieces demonstrated the advantages of a 'real' perspective. The foresters entered singing, their voices gradually increasing in volume; at one stage a slain deer was seen in the distance being carried towards the fire. At the close of the performance the cast wandered away, again singing, so that they were soon lost behind the trees and only their voices could be heard, until finally even their voices were no longer audible and the curtain was slowly raised, blotting out the vista.

Realism was carried to extreme lengths with the introduction of real deer, real stag-heads and even real goats, bells tinkling in a perfect pre-determined harmony.

Godwin's famous and exhaustively contrived 'unity' attracted

49

widespread praise. Costume and setting matched exactly, each garment of a natural woodland shade yet true to both history and the play. The historical period that had been chosen was the late fifteenth century; the styles suitable for hunting and the forest. Rough materials were selected for all costumes, and the men wore 'by-cocket' caps and hunting boots. Godwin even made allowance for the varying lengths of time spent in the forest by each character and supplied some with more worn outfits than others. Working in close collaboration with the famous Art Nouveau shopkeeper Lazenby Liberty, he provided a warm-coloured russet and cinammon tunic for Rosalind as Ganymede, a very tight dress with orange-coloured bodice for Phoebe, while Celia paraded in what one spectator described as 'Liberty silks and violet silk stockings',[54] and another, Oscar Wilde, as 'a sort of panegyric on a pansy', remarking at the same time,

'I am afraid that in Shakespeare's Arden there were no Chelsea China Shepherdesses, and I am sure that the romance of Phoebe does not need to be intensified by any reminiscences of porcelain.'[55]

Touchstone was in motley of canary and red ('far too glaring', commented Wilde).

Lady Archibald herself, predictably, received most attention as Orlando. She was dressed in dark green plush relieved by a gold chain and baldrick. For the last act Rosalind appeared in a white bridal dress which Wilde found 'absolutely displeasing', but which was happily accepted by less demanding spectators.

The 1884 performances were so successful that the following year Godwin and Lady Archibald made the Pastoral Players into a formal society, repeated As You Like It, and attempted to stage a far more challenging production, Fletcher's half-forgotten pastoral drama The Faithful Shepherdesse. That a great deal of scholarly research went into this production is evident from Lady Archibald's article on the subject in The Nineteenth Century,[56] in which she traces the history of the pastoral from Hesiod through Theocritus, Spenser, and Jonson, concluding with a discussion of The Faithful Shepherdesse in the light of Jonson's and Bacon's ideas of the masque.

The setting was the same as for As You Like It with the notable addition of a large statue of Pan, carefully copied from the British Museum, to stage right. Fresh-cut grass was strewn over the ground and dotted with patches of purple clover. Beneath the statue was an incense-burning altar, also derived from examples in the British Museum. Clusters of grapes were draped upon this edifice and on a nearby sacred well, almost hidden with rushes and water-lilies. Coombe had become a sacred grove.

Around the altar, filling the grove, mingled shepherds and shepherdesses; crowned with flowers and clasping their crooks, they sang a votive hymn composed for the occasion and performed a slow dance. This was followed by the entrance of Perigot, the principal shepherd, in a chariot drawn by two dark red oxen. Beside the procession pranced horned satyrs draped with goat-skins. The costumes of Perigot and Amoret were most carefully matched: Perigot in 'diaphanous water green', buskins and a sheepskin mantle, Amoret in a 'transparent robe of the colour of a richly-tinted cocoon, edged with gold'. The shepherdesses wore clinging dresses, the fall of the drapery painstakingly copied from classical statues. Their hair-styles were taken from the same models, and like all the participants they were covered in heavy amber make-up.

The Faithful Shepherdesse was the Pastoral Players' greatest achievement, but perhaps the opportunities it offered for Godwin's ingenuity were too dangerous. At some points the performance must have seemed like a circus. One list of properties includes garlands, bay leaves, frankincense and lutes, a virtual menagerie of dogs, pigeons, sheep, goats and cows, and a hundred assorted live butterflies ordered from a Piccadilly naturalist. The outcome was predictable: Fletcher's play, which had been for both Godwin and Lady Archibald a carefully considered and very bold choice, was hardly noticed by the critics, the text being completely eclipsed by tableaux and effects. It almost became a game to spot the contemporary artists who had influenced Godwin's scenic arrangements; by popular consent the most potent influence had been Alma-Tadema, the painter most renowned for his classical reconstructions.

The classical drama, in particular the classical pastoral, had obvious attractions for the ambitious Aesthetic artist, and amongst the very many letters that Godwin received in appreciation of his efforts was one from Dr John Todhunter of Bedford Park. He had been delighted by *The Faithful Shepherdesse*:

'It was quite Arcadian, and I was much struck with the artistic ideality which reigned throughout and gave it an imaginative *naturalness* which I should have scarcely thought it possible to have given. If there was any incongruity between the classical figures and their background the fault was Nature's, who did not provide you with a more primaeval forest-glade, beautiful as the scene undoubtedly was.
'All the chances and the movements of the nymphs and swains among the trees were beautifully managed—the colour effects charming. The entrances and the exits were very well arranged and your ox-drawn chariot

a particularly happy inspiration. Altogether you have almost tempted me to write a pastoral drama since you have restored Arcadia in the midst of the nineteenth century. Are the pastoral players to be a permanent institution?'[57]

Todhunter enclosed with his letter a sonnet for Lady Archibald:

On a performance of 'The Faithful Shepherdesse' by 'The Pastoral Players' at Coombe House, 4.7.1883.

> 'If, from the Elysian haunt of Poets dead,
>   Honey-tongued Fletcher, ever thou dost look
>   On this world's change, sad for some wasted nook
>   Or sylvan glade familiar to thy tread;
> Jovially now, bending the laurelled head,
>   Smile: at thy song great Pan, who in wrath forsook
>   Our woods is come again. The pastoral crook
>   Leads in Arcadia, toil with beauty wed.
> O Shepherds blithe, fleet nymphs, whose linked glee
>   Sisters Victoria and Elizabeth,
>   Dance on, immortal is our mortal sun:
> The hymns ye move to have no note of death,
> Ye shine life's golden victories yet unwon,
>   The unfulfilled fair dreams of poesy!'

It is likely that the two men had already met—Godwin certainly knew members of the Bedford Park community—but in any case, Todhunter received a testimony to Godwin's integrity and skill from Lady Archibald: 'I can only re-iterate that there is no-one in my opinion who could ensure the success of so artistic an undertaking as this Greek play but Mr Godwin.'[58]

The outcome of Todhunter's suggested collaboration between himself and Godwin was *Helena in Troas*, performed at Hengler's Circus in May 1886. Early in the year they canvassed society for a guarantee of a thousand pounds against any losses which might result from a production of Todhunter's classical drama; rich and influential friends rallied round, the Prince of Wales himself put up a generous sum, and Vezin and Tree offered their professional services. It was decided that in the event of the production making a profit, this would be donated to the British School of Archaeology in Athens.

Not that archaeological productions of classical dramas were particularly new—they were even fashionable. In the very same week as *Helena in Troas*, a Professor Warr presented reconstructed scenes from the *Oresteia* in Princess's Hall. (These were not an outstanding success and in the inevitable critical comparisons *Helena in*

Troas came off better.) Oxford and Cambridge in particular had exploited the idea: there had been Balliol's celebrated production of *The Agamemnon* in 1880, in which the scenery was constructed from drawings by Burne-Jones and which, on its brief transference to London later in the same year, was attended by Robert Browning and George Eliot as well as Irving and Ellen Terry; and there had been the performance of *The Eumenides* at Cambridge in 1885. In 1882 *Alcestis* had inaugurated the famous series of open-air productions at Bradfield. All these had been able to draw upon both recent and established research; for instance J. W. Donaldson's standard *Theatre of the Greeks* reprinted regularly since its publication in 1836.

Godwin now set about finding a locale, and after rejecting both a lecture theatre in a Kensington museum and Princess's Hall, which Tree judged 'unsuitable for scenic effects', he finally hit upon Hengler's Circus in Great Pulteney Street, a large indoor amphitheatre some forty-two feet in diameter, normally used for equestrian displays and circuses. He had the arena boarded over and converted to the traditional classical arrangement of orchestra, proscenium and 'thymele' (altar).[59] A new artificial floor was painted with geometrical designs in a reddish shade which gave the effect of tesselated marble and which the chorus found useful as guides when taking up their positions.

From the centre of the semi-circular stage rose the thymele, bearing in gold Greek characters the name of Dionysus. Behind it stood a reconstruction of Priam's palace, with a portal in the centre whose entrance was concealed by a large crimson curtain painted with a lion motif. On either side open arches revealed distant ramparts, painted vistas of the Aegean and far-away purple hills. The raising of the curtain disclosed two massive bronze gates, with to stage right a golden image of Aphrodite.

However unified and impressive it might have appeared, this setting had a mixed ancestry, for while the basic architecture of the palace was derived from the Temple of Empedocles at Selinunte, the murals, painted as if in relief, represented scenes from the wars of the Centaurs and Amazons, and were after the frieze at Phigaleia. The proportions were almost exactly those of the theatre of Bacchus on the Acropolis. Godwin had corresponded with A. S. Murray at the British Museum, who had supplied him with examples of classical altars, censers, decorations and so on. In any case, besides being an enthusiastic advocate of Greek costume, Godwin himself had considerable knowledge of the art and architecture of the classical world. In his article 'The Greek Home according to Homer'[60] he discussed Mycenae at great length, making use of

Schliemann's *Tiryns, The Prehistoric Palace of the Kings of Troy;*
although it was later objected to *Helena in Troas* by other informed
persons who had followed Schliemann's excavation that Godwin's
designs were not of the epic age itself, but rather those of Periclean
Athens. Nonetheless, the overall effect was for most people once
again 'like one of Mr Alma-Tadema's pictures magnified and
turned into stone'.[61]

The basic costumes of Priam and Paris were of contrasting shades
of red: Priam (Hermann Vezin) wore the white Phrygian cap, a
white 'chiton' and crimson 'peplum', while Paris (Beerbohm Tree)
was bare-armed, the thongs of his sandals crossed to the knee, a
short scarlet chiton reaching to his waist. He carried a small sword.
Helen (Alice Murray), her hair bound by a chaplet of golden leaves,
had the most conspicuous costume, of white silken gauze with a gold
border over a chiton of golden yellow—pale shades that contrasted
with Hecuba's deep turquoise and Oenone's greyish blue. All the
coloured costumes were set off by the constant background of the
chorus, who were dressed in chitons of unbleached calico. These
fifteen girls were bare-armed, peplums double-folded, hair bound
by a single gold fillet. Helen was attended by two hand-maidens:
Miss Hare in plain white, and Mrs Oscar Wilde (who reviewed the
production in *The Lady*) in a sea-green woollen chiton edged with
gold, her hair gathered in a knot and filleted with sea-green ribbon.

The costumes brought together two contemporary interests, for
the suitability of the chiton for English everyday wear had been a
major debating point in those circles concerned with dress reform,
which at various times had included G. F. Watts, Oscar Wilde and
Godwin himself. In fact Wilde's well-known championship of the
garment in lectures and writings was not only fanciful and impractical, but also somewhat behind the times. In the late seventies
severe arbiters of taste such as Mrs Oliphant and Mrs Haweis had
wisely rejected the chiton on grounds of climate alone. But of course
Helena in Troas permitted a demonstration of the elegance of the
costume, as had *The Cup*, without submitting it to any practical test.

To tell the truth—and some did so at the time—Todhunter's
laborious verse play about the death of Paris did not deserve the
attention lavished on it by its producer; it was to be appreciated,
if at all, for the particular kind of spectacle it presented. It opened
with the long crimson curtains slowly parting. At that same moment
the chorus entered from lower doors on either side of the stage,
chanting the opening lines rhythmically and slowly. At the climax
of their chant the leader, throwing her peplum down in front of the
altar, instigated a rhythmic processional dance. For the remainder

8 and 9   *The Faithful Shepherdesse*, Coombe Woods, 1885.

top The setting, with the statue of Pan in the centre; *bottom* Perigot and Amoret in their oxen-drawn chariot.

10 and 11   *Helena in Troas*, Hengler's Circus, 1886.
top Group photograph of the ladies of the chorus; *bottom* Watercolour impression of the production by H. M. Paget.

of the play they arranged themselves in small statuesque groups on the altar steps or below the line of the stage.

Unfortunately the chorus was not a success. Although they formed their groupings with commendable grace, during the more active moments their lack of rehearsal was all too apparent, and the need for more time with their 'aesthetic drill-master' was remarked upon by all critics.

Yet the weakest part of the production was undoubtedly Luard Selby's music and his chorus and orchestra of amateur musicians.

'Singing, chiefly in unison, a kind of accompanied recitative, they contrive to keep in tune with each other, but neither in tune nor time with a band which is some distance away and whose conductor is evidently supposed to follow, not guide, the chorus.'[62]

Perhaps this was not the point, for as Oscar Wilde pointed out, one of Godwin's advances on earlier classical productions had been to let music and choreography play their part without resorting to the large-scale extravagance of *The Cup*.

The actors fared rather better in critical estimation, although the poor acoustics at Hengler's deprived the audience of many of Todhunter's lines. It was agreed that one moment in particular struck a highly discordant note: this was when, during the last scene, Oenone, pursued by Paris, flung herself from the battlements with a ghoulish shriek. Wilde considered it to be destructive of the impersonality so carefully built up until that point:

'. . . the harsh realistic shriek with which the nymph flung herself from the battlements, however effective it might have been in a comedy of Sardou or in one of Mr Burnand's farces, was quite out of place in the representation of a Greek tragedy. The classical drama is an imaginative, poetic, art, which requires the grand style for its interpretation and produces its effects by the most ideal means. It is in the operas of Wagner, not a popular melodrama, that any approximation to the Greek method can be found. Better to wear mask and buskin, than to mar by any modernity of expression the calm majesty of Melpomene.'[63]

Wilde's response was important and right; seeing beyond the merely picturesque appeal of *Helena in Troas*, he recognised that the sudden focusing of attention on the personality of one actress intruded violently upon the mood which Godwin, with all the disadvantages of an amateur company, had managed to evoke. Wilde understood that his great achievement had been 'mood' rather than 'action' or 'plot'.

'The performance was not intended to be an absolute reproduction of the Greek stage in the fifth century before Christ: it was simply the presenta-

55

tion in Greek form of a poem conceived in the Greek spirit; and the secret of its beauty was the perfect correspondence of form and matter, the delicate equilibrium of spirit and sense.'

The summer of 1886 was remarkably active. In July, Godwin organised open-air performances of *Fair Rosamund*, an adaptation of Tennyson's *Beckett*, at Conizaro Woods, Wimbledon Common, for which he studied Tasso's *Aminta* and Ramsay's *Gentle Shepherd*. Genevieve Ward appeared as Queen Eleanor and the production was a moderate success, for by now performances by the Pastoral Players had almost become a traditional event. However the play offered Godwin no new challenge: he had, perhaps, exhausted a medium. In May he superintended rehearsals for the famous private production of *The Cenci* by the Shelley Society, for which Todhunter wrote the prologue, but Godwin's name appeared neither on the bills nor in the programme.

Then he made a surprising, though ambitious, blunder. He hired the Opera Comique throughout July and, once again in collaboration with Hermann Vezin, prepared a production of *The Fool's Revenge*, Tom Taylor's old adaptation of *Le Roi S'Amuse*. Despite the most lavish Renaissance costumes and setting and an Aesthetic programme which reproduced the autograph of each member of the company, the result was disastrous, and the production ran for only four days. It would appear that the motive behind this scheme was to transfer the principles of group initiative and the power and influence of fashionable society explored in earlier experiments to the commercial theatre, and so perhaps to break the traditional dictatorship of the London managers and their relentless round of farce and melodrama. The strategy was certainly intelligent —an unacknowledged forerunner of the subsidised theatres suggested by Archer a little later—but the execution was clumsy. Not only did he choose the height of the season, when many London theatres were closed, for the inauguration of his venture, but that his aristocratic amateurs were incapable of sustaining their parts was a weakness pounced upon by the press:

'The chief object of this production was to afford an opportunity for the *débuts* of Mrs Mackintosh and Miss Steer, ladies of fashion with some pretensions to personal beauty, but neither of these débutantes were possessed of any unusual histrionic ability.'[64]

Godwin was in a vulnerable position, because for this production he had at last publicly styled himself 'producer'. Having assumed all responsibility he now received all blame, and the reactionary manager John Coleman, with whom he had quarrelled over the

1876 *Henry V,* took advantage of the opportunity to scorn his ingenuity.

'Let us . . . render unto Caesar the things which are Caesar's!; let us take off our hats to Godwin, the renowned; Godwin, the architect and archaeologist, Godwin, the manager and stage manager; Godwin, the scene painter and inventor of the Pastoral Player; Godwin, the Great Man Milliner.'[65]

Coleman's heavy sarcasm was wasted, for two months later Godwin was dead.

His example was to survive him in a number of ways. Most importantly, he was the first producer in the modern sense, one man endowed with complete control over a production. In fact, the arrival of the 'producer' was not to be officially announced in *The Theatre* until 1889; under the title 'A Few Words for the Unseen', an anonymous contributor then paid tribute to a new profession, taking as text the increasingly common phrase, 'produced under the direction of . . .':

'These few words, which have appeared lately on the bills of many a London theatre, are generally passed over unobserved by the playgoing public, and often by the critics. It is a great mistake to think that the man who looks after the production of a new play is merely a stage manager. Stage managing is a business; producing a new play is a gift which can neither be taught nor acquired . . . the play-producer, or *metteur en scène,* must be proficient in every branch of the dramatic art. Not only must he be capable of arranging for the production of a new play with the scenic artist, costumier, master carpenter, property master, gas man, limelight man, musical director, the manager or manageress (as the case may be)—and now of late one more trouble is added to his work, viz., the electrician—but he has also to study the actors, and actresses engaged for the play, to harmonise the colour of the scene and furniture with that of the dresses worn; he must know the rudiments of music, dancing, and elocution, for it may fall to his lot to have to produce a farce, a comic opera, burlesque, domestic drama, comedy or farcial comedy, a melodrama, tragedy or whatnot . . . he is, as it were, the master hand which pulls the strings. In conclusion let me point out that it is time that the fact should be recorded of his existence.'[66]

Even though written three years after his death, it is hard to resist thinking back to Godwin's achievements on reading this belated plea for recognition of the comprehensive responsibilities of the producer. Versatility is a talent in its own right, and the demands made upon it are always greater than the mere sum of a man's abilities.

When the rules of the Pastoral Players were drawn up in 1885 his position had been ratified, and he had officially assumed responsibility for all aspects of the society's undertakings. These responsibilities were jealously guarded and he expected acknowledgement of his work. A year earlier he had written to a newspaper demanding this recognition, whilst at the same time attempting to disguise personal motives.

'. . . A propos of the open-air performance of *As You Like It*, which I am glad to say was acknowledged to be a decided success, can you tell me what has happened to the dignity and impartiality of the press?
'The writer of the long article in the *Daily News* of Thursday was not ignorant that the whole affair was planned and superintended by me; but he carefully avoids all mention of my name, and even gives another man who had nothing whatever to do with it the credit. Other papers have more or less adopted a similar line. This can hardly be accident, as my name was printed on the programmes, and I received as manager a most cordial acknowledgement from the audience of Wednesday.
'To me, as you know, these things are not of much moment; but to Lady Archibald Campbell they are vexations, as indicating a spirit antagonistic to hers, for her appreciation of my gratuitous art-work has been thorough and uninterrupted.'[67]

The issue was probably not so simple. There is little doubt that Godwin courted publicity as far as his work in the theatre was concerned (this was not the first letter that he had written to the press by any means), principally because without it his long campaign could not succeed. Moreover, amateur performances were a convenient vehicle to further highly professional ambitions that were never fully realised. Yet he left few statements of general aesthetic principle. Most of his published articles were detailed and scholarly, and it was left to two of his friends, Lady Archibald Campbell and Oscar Wilde, to transform and transmit his ideas. And it says something about the unsystematised nature of his ideals that living in the same context they reached rather different conclusions about the final character of his achievement.

A year after Godwin's sudden death Lady Archibald wrote an article on the pastoral plays. In part an obituary of Godwin, it also contained an exposition of a theory of Art that was both tortuous and tautological.

'It has been said that the artist is the man who recognises art in Nature, the man who knows what is the natural material capable of being aesthetically treated, and where it is to be found; for art can only be exercised under conditions, and to such conditions it is not always in Nature's power to conform. The conditions, for example, of dramatic art are imitative, as are those of all other arts, yet the drama can never be strictly said to be imitative of Nature, but only representative. To transfer life to the boards of the theatre demands a just appreciation of the difference between real and dramatic conditions; so that the spectator who goes to the play and (as many spectators do) institutes a *direct* comparison between the actor and the man, criticises on a false basis, and does not appreciate the artistic conditions.'[68]

But, she continued, commercial realism failed because it was 'the realism of the common-place', as opposed to representation of the Natural, which necessarily embraced the Beautiful. She rejected not only the pseudo-realism of the modern, which only intensified the pull between Nature and Art, but also the simple artificiality, the masks and stilts, of the Attic stage. 'We demand complexity, we demand sympathy, we demand character, we demand Nature.' Her realism depended upon a concept of Nature as norm, and the pastoral plays were perhaps its only possible realisation,* for the simple equation of Nature and Beauty failed to account for *Helena in Troas*, a production that was 'artificial' in its dependence on the reconstruction of the archaic convention. She avoided this difficulty by making reference to the 'ideal':

'The pure keynote of beauty was again struck, and, line and colour taking the place of language, the play ultimately reverted to that plastic ideal which lies at the basis of all Greek art.'

And so the aim that she attributed to Godwin became modified into representation of the principles of harmony within Nature, to which even the actor must be subordinated.

'The composition of stage effect and the art of acting generally, whether indoors or outdoors, meant for his wonderful genius what the art of musical composition meant for the wonderful genius of Wagner—it meant growth, originality, freedom from tradition. As art-director of our natural stage, he urged more than ever on the actor (whether that actor occupied the principle *role*, or that of the silent super) the necessity that the ordinary *technique* of the stage must be held by him subordinate, and sacrificed to pictorial and realistic effect.'

But the contradictions could be reconciled—'he assimilated art to Nature, and Nature to art.'

* Not all were as confident that the pastoral plays had resolved the problems. The subject was controversial. See for instance Freeman Wills, 'Open-Air Theatre', *The Dramatic Review*, 18 July 1885, 394, and the reviews of *The Faithful Shepherdesse* in *The Era*, 6 June 1885, and *The Dramatic Review*, 1 August 1885, 4.

A year earlier Lady Archibald had published her strange testament *Rainbow-Musick, or the Philosophy of Harmony in Colour-Grouping*, in which a theory of harmony had been proposed. Behind it lay the theories of both Godwin and—as she acknowledged later—his close friend Whistler.

'The fundamental principles of decorative art with which Whistler impressed me, related to the necessity of applying scientific methods to the treatment of all decorative work; that to produce harmonious effects in line and "colour-grouping", the whole plan or scheme should have to be thoroughly thought out so as to be *finished* before it was practically begun. I think he proved his saying to be true, that the fundamental principles of decorative art, as in all art, are based on laws as exact as those of the known sciences. He concluded that what the knowledge of a fundamental base has done for music, a similarly demonstrative method might do for painting. The musical vocabulary which he used to distinguish his creations always struck me as singularly appropriate, though he had no knowledge of music.'[69]

Rainbow-Musick was based on the assertion that certain laws, 'as true, though not so self-evident, as those of mathematics',[70] operate in any work of art. For examples of the successful manifestation of these laws she chose, predictably, the colour schemes of the pastoral performances and Whistler's 'Peacock Room', which achieved harmony through the counterpoint of blue on gold, gold on blue. The musical analogy was certainly familiar and *Rainbow-Musick* concluded with a treatise on the chromatics of colour, by which the seven primary colours were said to harmonise with the seven gaps in an octave. Wagner was another acknowledged mentor, and although the performances with which Lady Archibald had been associated were of a quite different kind, her ideas bear a distinct resemblance to those which inspired Herkomer's 'Pictorial-Musical plays', the subject of the next chapter. A further process of assimilation had taken place, and Godwin's practical exercises in archaeology had become part of a total theory of art.

In 1885, Godwin had written seven articles on archaeology for *The Dramatic Review*, a journal with which Wilde was also connected. In these he reiterated what had become the familiar principles of his method: above all the idea that although practising a 'modern science' the archaeologist must needs 'be an *artist*, endowed with the sense of form and colour, having constructiveness well developed and in sympathy with the dramatic purpose.'[71] The modern stage-manager's commitment to technical realism failed because the plays that he presented were themselves startlingly *un*real, the characters unconvincingly and poorly acted. On the other hand the better the play the more essential the need for correct and careful staging. Thus '. . . the higher poetical drama represented by Shakespeare demands, first of all for its costume, scenery, and property, artistic treatment,' and the 'unity of design' guaranteed only by a single designer having complete freedom to control all aspects of production, including the costumes worn by star performers. Archaeology is not so much a desirable addition, a mere extra touch, as a fundamental principle of dramatic art in which the demands of the historical and the aesthetic imagination are satisfied and united.

'The very phrase *Archaeologically correct*, like the loose expressions used in, so-called, art criticism is stupid. You cannot have "bad Archaeology" any more than you can have "bad art", but you can try the sham in both.'[72]

These articles, although not presented as such, were particularly topical, and belonged to a nexus of discussion to which Wilde also contributed.

If his public enthusiasm for the Pastoral performances and *Helena in Troas* had been a welcome advertisement, Wilde, that great synthetiser of ideas, was able to make use of Godwin's precepts on other occasions to serve his own ends. Godwin's influence on him outside the theatre has already been mentioned; less familiar is the background of archaeology to 'Shakespeare and Stage Costume',[73] the first version of the essay that appeared in *Intentions* (1891) as 'The Truth of Masks'. Wilde was replying to a remark by Lord Lytton:

'The attempt to archaeologise the Shakespearean drama is one of the stupidest pedantries of this age of prigs. Archaeology would not be more out of place in a fairy tale that it is in a play of Shakespeare.'[74]

With a long and thorough catalogue of references, Wilde sought to establish Shakespeare's awareness of the scenic value of costume. Since he was obliged to indicate the historical respectability of archaeology, he suggested that it had inspired and sustained medieval masques and pageants:

'Archaeology to them was not merely a science for the antiquarian; it was a means by which they could touch the dry dust of antiquity into the breath and beauty of life, and fill with the new wind of romanticism form that else had been old and out-worn.'[75]

From past uses of archaeology, he turned to its foremost contemporary exponent and to *Claudian*.

'From such materials, for instance, as the cloak of Theodosius, materials with which the majority of people are probably not very familiar, Mr Godwin created the marvellous loveliness of his first act of *Claudian*, and showed us the life of Byzantium in the fourth century, not by a dreary lecture and a set of grimy casts, not by a novel which requires a glossary to explain it, but by the visible presentation before us of all the glory of that great town. And while the costumes were true to the smallest points of colour and design, yet the details were not assigned that abnormal importance which they must necessarily be given in a piecemeal lecture, but were subordinated to the rules of lofty composition and the unity of artistic effect.'

His idea of the nature of archaeology was a significant one:

'For archaeology, being a science, is neither good nor bad, but a fact simply. Its value depends entirely on how it is used, and only an artist can use it. We look to the archaeologist for the materials, to the artist for the method.'

From this it followed that the stage-manager had to be both archaeologist and artist, and once again Godwin served as example. The open-air *As You Like It* fulfilled both requirements: worn and faded costumes, for instance, were both accurate and aesthetically pleasing. Unity in the theatre, unity of the kind characteristic of the work of the Pastoral Players, could be achieved only when the theatre was 'under the power of a cultured despot'. The implication was clear: the ideal 'cultured despot' was Godwin, and 'Shakespeare and Stage Costume' a tribute from pupil to master.*

A full understanding of the assumptions behind Godwin's work required a knowledge of the social milieu in which he operated, and sympathy with the ideas circulating within it. When William Archer replied to Wilde with a commonsense refutation of extremism, his argument, although powerful enough, missed the presence of an essential Aesthetic conviction that a perfect work of art is answerable to no-one or nothing outside itself, a conviction that Godwin had recently alluded to in his *Dramatic Review* articles and that had been re-asserted by Wilde. Archer commented:

'To attack archaeology is foolish, says Mr Wilde; "one might just as well talk disrespectfully of the equator. For archaeology, being a science, is neither good nor bad, but a fact simply." But archaeology, as applied to stage decoration, is not science but art, and as such may be good, bad, or indifferent.'[76]

* However it should be pointed out that Godwin knew of the essay and, I would say typically, insisted that Wilde make full acknowledgement of his debt to him. Letter from Wilde to Godwin, 20 June 1885, in *The Letters of Oscar Wilde*, ed. Rupert-Davis, 1962, 176–7.

His obviously sensible point that there was little evidence to suggest that Shakespeare's awareness of costume and architecture would be any more accurate than his notions of real history or his knowledge of the geography and customs of civilisations outside of Elizabethan England, was therefore little more than a surface objection, although a rebuttal that Wilde's pseudo-scholarship deserved. Moreover Archer failed to admit that Godwin's archaeological productions had been generally acknowledged, in terms of scenic design alone, to be superior to most of the other work current in the theatre at that time.

Other critics of Godwin and archaeology understandably concentrated upon particular examples rather than upon general principles. A writer in *Macmillan's Magazine* a little later said of Greek tragedy that:

'The hero of one of those old tragedies must have looked very like the hero of another; and in the trailing robes, the masks modelled on strictly preserved types, and the measured declamation of the actors, deviations from the normal arrangement were rarely allowed to distract attention from the central action of the story.'[77]

He made a distinction between this classical tradition and the plays of Shakespeare, where external characteristics of individual appearance and behaviour were obviously important (ignoring the possibility that an exact reproduction of the classical method might also benefit from archaeology). And he warned against allowing the archaeologist so much control that an appetite for the authenticity of non-essentials destroyed the impact of the drama itself and changed an audience's traditional understanding of a play and its characters. Historical accuracy, picturesque staging, and effective drama do not—as they do for Godwin and Wilde—necessarily coincide. Another writer, this time in *The Dramatic Review*, normally a stronghold of the archaeological camp, found proof of archaeology's failure to sustain a whole production in Godwin's unsuccessful *Fool's Revenge*:

'Archaeology, which is, after all, an essential but subordinate art, has had to do duty for the whole of Art, and has proved unequal to the task—hence the failure.'[78]

But for Wilde, whose solidarity with Godwin was social, aesthetic and programmatic, these objections were swept aside, and Godwin became his model of the true artist. The visual harmony of his productions had an aesthetic impact devoid of sensation; 'impersonality' was reached through scholarship. Wilde's claims advanced archaeology beyond the picturesque towards a coherent and sophisticated theory of theatre. He had admired the classical form of *Helena in Troas* in particular, which had carried its own innate 'impersonality', transcending the historical and offering a real purity of ideas and sensations born of 'the plastic clearness of outline that the Greeks so desired.'[79]

When 'Shakespeare and Stage Costume' was re-published as 'The Truth of Masks', a further concluding paragraph had been added.

'The essay simply represents an artistic standpoint, and in aesthetic criticism attitude is everything. For in art there is no such thing as a universal truth. A truth in art is that whose contradiction is also true. And just as it is only in art-criticism, and through it, that we can apprehend the Platonic theory of ideas, so it is only in art-criticism, and through it, that we can realise Hegel's system of contraries. The truths of metaphysics are the truths of masks.'

This appendage, and the new title, made more explicit hints from the original essay, and introduced a favourite paradox—that of the mask as real opinion, real personality. Archaeology became a similar 'mask'. Godwin's realism became Wilde's reality, his scientific technique a conscious attempt to achieve aesthetic 'impersonality' through artistic unity. The use of Godwin was not just parasitic; Wilde absorbed the older man's work into his own theoretic construction.*

Godwin's career had a strange coda. Augustus Moore, infamous editor of *The Hawk*, attempted in 1890 to expose a society swindle by which prominent people had been persuaded to donate money to a bogus charity, and in the course of this exposure implied that Godwin's Greek theatre had been a similar charity swindle. Whistler, who had married Godwin's second wife after his death, infuriated by this slur on his character, followed Moore to a first night at Drury Lane and, during the interval, attacked him with a cane, crying out 'Hawk! Hawk!'. There was a scrimmage from which Moore emerged the victor. Naturally such a scandalous incident made front-page news, but in almost every case the newspapers had to explain who Godwin had been and few got further than 'a deceased friend of Whistler'. Godwin's fame had been short-lived.

His work was continued by two totally opposed factions: by the great actor-managers, Irving and Tree, who corrupted 'archaeology'

---

* He may also have made practical use of Godwin's example, as his later scheme for Charles Ricketts' planned production of *Salome* suggests. 'Did Wilde actually suggest the division of the actors into separate masses of colour, today the idea seems mine!', Ricketts was to write in 1913. (*Pages in Art*, 1913, 243.)

into 'spectacle', and by a small minority of theatrical reformers, antagonistic to realism, who absorbed the example of the small amateur production and the principles of harmonious décor.

One of this minority was John Todhunter, the author of *Helena in Troas*. He was born in Ireland in 1839 and attended the Medical School of Trinity College, where he formed literary friendships with Edward Dowden, Standish O'Grady, Alfred Perceval Graves, John Butler Yeats and others; and, despite the medical training, he became Professor of English Literature at Alexandra College, Dublin, in 1870. He travelled widely in Europe, wrote essays and in 1876 published his first volume of poems, *From the Land of Dreams*. In 1881, Todhunter settled in a house he had built for himself in Bedford Park, and began to devote his life to the writing of poetry and plays.

Alcestis (1879), a dramatic poem, made use of classical devices. As Todhunter explained in the preface, 'to the sympathetic reader's imagination I trust the frank anachronism between modern sentiments and their legendary settings.' With *Helena in Troas* the question of anachronism did not arise; it was not so much an attempt to create a contemporary poetic drama from a classical model as conscious imitation, in which Godwin's methods of production ensured archaeological authenticity.

However, although Todhunter had no real talent as a playwright —a fact that was recognised by all but a very few of his contemporaries—*Helena in Troas* was by no means the end point of his ambitions, and he continued to have ideas of his own. A dedicated Shelleyite, his prologue to *The Cenci*[80] offered that play as a prototype for the dramatic poet, and contrasted two kinds of theatre:

> 'Can your eyes
> Delight their sense with tawdry properties,
> The pomp of theatres, the glittering shows
> Of the mummers' art; with tinsel, joys and woes
> Posturing before a painted scene. . . .'

and,

> 'This curtain green
> Of common baize, the stage's homely screen,
> Turns to the pall that hides the inmost cell
> Of Tragedy.'

Classical methods were one alternative to 'the pomp of theatres', and although *Helena in Troas* had required rather more than the

'curtain green of common baize', he pursued his search for simplicity and classical grace with his next play, *A Sicilian Idyll* (1890),
a studied imitation of the Theocritan pastoral.

The first and most important of the play's four productions[81] was
at the Clubhouse at Bedford Park, a large bare room, wood-panelled,
with a large tile and wood fireplace beneath a classical relief, and
a very small proscenium stage and conventional heavy velvet
curtains at one end of the room. In the published text of his play,
Todhunter described a very ambitious classical setting: it is difficult
to believe that the Clubhouse could have managed anything so
exotic, and a review in *The Stage* confirms these suspicions.

'It was careful and fluent—careful as one might have been sure seeing
the intelligence bestowed upon it, and fluent, as one might have been in
doubt seeing the table-top stage for the common movement. The cramped
space, indeed, was a serious difficulty throughout. The figures of the
dramatis personae, disproportionate in so small an area, made sadly asym-
metrical scenes—with more than a Tademaesque suggestion in design.'[82]

The shortage of space and consequently of potential perspective
was crucial. Godwin's work obviously stands behind *A Sicilian Idyll;*
but his professional experience and financial backing had enabled
him to choose more suitable settings (Hengler's Circus and Coombe
Woods, both large areas).

Photographs and drawings show a backcloth that is reminiscent
of the seascape visible through the columns of Priam's palace in
Helena in Troas; the pastoral trappings obviously derive from *The
Faithful Shepherdesse*; and a statue of Dionysus was similar to the
Pan which graced Coombe Woods. The stage was lined with falling
draperies, and the cloth-covered floor (probably an arrangement of
rostra) was strewn with garlands. The draperies served a very
different purpose from the green curtain used in the Pastoral performances, which had formed a harmonious background and had
blended with the foliage in a 'natural' way. Todhunter's curtains
also supplied a harmonious background, but they were recognisably
artificial, reduced the need for perspective scene-painting, and
concealed the identity of the Clubhouse. Greek dresses were worn,
whose sinuous qualities Godwin had already exploited in *Helena in
Troas*, and their loose folds were intended to form changing patterns
in the chorus.

Yet in every respect the standards of production were amateurish,
and to the professional critics it seemed that archaeology had, in
the hands of Bedford Park, become merely an excuse for Aesthetic
nostalgia. For the most part the performers were sadly below par,

and except for Florence Farr, who survived by virtue of her voice, none emerged unscathed.

The most spectacular moment of *A Sicilian Idyll* was a Bacchic dance by Lily Linfield. What Godwin had hardly managed at Hengler's Circus failed dismally in Bedford Park. As one cynical onlooker put it, 'her sprightly daring suggested that the can-can was thoroughly understood and appreciated in Arcadia,'[83] and another critic was reminded of a Salvation Army rally.[84]

Fortunately the production was somewhat stronger by the time it moved to St George's Hall, and although it had little chance of commercial success, it benefited from a larger stage, and the occasion was said to be 'full of solemnity and fashionableness.'[85] But when it was put on together with Todhunter's *The Poison Flower* at the Vaudeville in 1891 the West End critics knew precisely on what grounds it was to be dismissed.

'Well, that may be all very interesting in art-loving Bedford Park, but it is death to the unenlightened Strand. What the object of the entertainment may be we have not the slightest means of knowing. Why these authors should descend upon the stronghold of light, amusing and farcial comedy, and storm its fortress with blank verse we cannot say.'[86]

A Sicilian Idyll was passed over as the product of an esoteric cult; it was the highly professional Clement Scott who, although harsh in his judgements, saw through to the real flaw in the enterprise.

'Very little was in the dramatist's favour at the Vaudeville matinées arranged to exploit the classical works of this earnest dramatist. He wanted scenery; he did not get it. He wanted *style* and *décor* on the stage: he found tawdriness. He wanted music: it was execrable. He needed dancing: it was amateurish to the last degree. Last, and most important of all he wanted what all classical playwrights want—elocution. He met with incoherency and the worst form of mumbling.'[87]

Todhunter's efforts towards the creation of a new poetic drama seem to have stopped with *A Sicilian Idyll*, and his later work developed at a tangent to the early plays. *The Poison Flower*, a dismal failure, was a closet drama adapted from Hawthorne's story, and *The Black Cat*, produced by the Independent Theatre in 1893, was an acknowledged 'realistic drama', an experiment in 'Ibsenism' and 'character'. Finally there was *A Comedy of Sighs*, a drama of the New Woman, which was staged by Florence Farr's pioneering but brief management at the Vaudeville in 1894, together with W. B.

Yeats' *The Land of Heart's Desire*. Todhunter himself described how the play,

'. . . . with its somewhat "impressionistic" sketches of character, and observations from the ordinary type of a "well-made" play, proved to be "too lightly tempered for so loud a wind" as blows upon British bugbears —"modern women" and the like.'[88]

For whatever reason, the production was disastrous.

There never was an Aesthetic theatre, there never has been, there probably never can be; for the rights of playwright and audience will always take precedence over those of designer and producer. But Godwin's example, transformed and hardened into doctrine, survived to the twentieth century in the dreams, in both cases so rarely realised, of at least two men: Edward Gordon Craig and W. B. Yeats.

To the young Yeats in Bedford Park, fascinated by the legend of *Helena in Troas* (which he probably did not see) and the experience of *A Sicilian Idyll*, it seemed that Godwin had found ways of achieving a theatrical mood, essentially religious in nature, that could sustain a poetic drama; and he wrote of *Helena in Troas* that it was a new attempt 'to redeem the drama by mingling music and poetry, to add a new convention to the stage.'[89] Godwin's principles of simplicity and harmony, reinforced by later findings and experiences, were to guide him through the years of struggle in Ireland and towards the discovery of the Noh.

In the case of Craig the legacy from father to son was largely indirect, passed on through the spectacular example of Irving and what he, in turn, had taken from Godwin. We do know that *Claudian* made an indelible impression, and the classical ideal of space and clarity of outline, the use of a restricted colour range, and above all the authoritative placing of the performers within a scenic whole— all must have been important influences. There are also seeming contradictions. Godwin had always insisted that perspective depended upon stage buildings constructed in their actual size and proportion; these his son wilfully distorted in order to create his startling abstracted effects. It had been Godwin's belief that authenticity and precise detail could by themselves reveal the essential nature of a play; Craig went in what looks like an opposite direction by condensing the stage picture into a single, concise but suggestive statement. But 'unity' and 'control' had always been Godwin's watchwords and there is consistency in the fidelity to principles strong enough to outlive 'archaeology' and to inspire another single vision and single-minded devotion to the art.

III

A Wagner Theatre:
Professor Herkomer's
Pictorial-Musical Plays

Photograph of Miss Margaret Griffiths as *The Sorceress*, 1887.
iss Griffiths was Herkomer's second wife and sister of his first wife Lulu.

Painting by Herkomer of a scene from *The Sorceress*.

(facing page 81)   Scenes from *An Idyl*, 1889.

⬥ SCENES ⬥

From Professor Herkomer's Pictorial Music-Play. "An Idyl."
At the School of Art, Dyrcham, Bushey.

JACK AND MEG PREPARING SUPPER.

THE SMITH'S BALLAD.

"There lived a maid in Avondale,
A winsome lass was she . . . ."

THE FORGE.

"Work, my lads, till set of sun.
Work, for duty must be done."

In 1882, the year of the first production of *Parsifal*, Londoners had the chance to see and hear most of Wagner's major works within the period of two months. In May and June Hans Richter conducted *The Flying Dutchman, Tannhäuser, Lohengrin, Tristan und Isolde* and *Der Meistersinger* at Drury Lane with a full company and elaborate scenery from Germany; and in May the first performances in England of *The Ring* cycle were staged at Her Majesty's by Angelo Neumann's touring company. That they had been rehearsed under the supervision of the composer himself and were performed with scenery and properties from the original Bayreuth production of 1876 was no guarantee of approval:

'So far as concerns the scenery, dresses, decorations, armour and c., lent by the King of Bavaria, we must say that the scenery was of the poorest kind—such as would probably be jeered at if exhibited at one of our minor theatres. The dresses were appropriate, but the steam apparatus was not well arranged, and the clouds of steam which should have hidden personages and scenery during changes of scene, frequently failed to realise this design.'[1]

These seasons offered a further chance to confirm rumours and resolve controversies, for when Bayreuth had opened with *The Ring* in 1876 most English reports had had some difficulty in maintaining an adulatory tone. At that time expectations had been uniformly high, encouraged by regular accounts of Wagner's schemes since the first announcement of plans for the Festspielhaus. Details of the design for the auditorium had been studied even during its construction, and in 1874 *The Practical Magazine*, for example, had provided diagrams and a ground plan together with a lengthy quotation from the master himself explaining the theoretical justification for the most important innovation—a sunken area between proscenium and audience to house an invisible orchestra.

'On this point Wagner remarks: "I have named this great space, extending from below the level of the stage, and the width of the *parterre*, up to the roof, the "Mystic Abyss"; because, as I tell my friends, it separates the reality from the ideal. My idea in rendering the orchestra invisible is to prevent the technical apparatus of musical production attracting attention from the stage. Between the audience and the perception of a picture presented there should be no interruption, there should be no intervening reality between the audience and the ideality if we would produce perfect illusion. But as you see, the innovation made a change in the structure of the theatre necessary; we had to exclude the system of tiers of boxes and confine ourselves to the amphitheatrical formation, by which we afford accommodation for fifteen hundred persons. I banish footlights and prompter's box, and leave only a framework, as it were, for the stage pictures. In front of the orchestral space the architect devised a second proscenium, the effect of which will be, in its relation to the proscenium proper, to produce the illusion of an apparent further removal from the scene. The effect will be that the audience, though fancying the scene to be far removed, will nevertheless perceive it with the clearness of immediate vicinity; and then a further illusion will be produced that the persons on the scene will appear in increased size, in superhuman form. But of all this I have written much. I think, however that most persons fail to comprehend the distinct character I give to the orchestra, as an illustrative organism, to occupy the place of an ancient Greek chorus—a high, invisible language appealing constantly to the audience, revealing, recalling, expounding." '[2]

Nor was the success of this device questioned when put into practice:

'. . . the absence from view of all such executive machinery as orchestra, prompter and footlights made the drama intensely real to the audience, who seemed to be "assisting" at it in a very forcible sense of the term.'[3]

What did provoke disagreement in 1876, even amongst convinced disciples, was the appropriateness and efficiency of actual scenic effect. Here again it was not a question of misunderstanding the master's intentions. Franz Hueffer, to whom above all must be credited the dissemination of Wagnerian ideas and information in England, wrote before the opening:

'A drama so full of strange and new situations as the *Ring of the Niblung* requires for its adequate performance a more than usual amount of taste and mechanical resource. Wagner has theoretically and practically advocated the legitimacy of scenic effects as long as they are organically connected with the action of the drama. It is indeed difficult to perceive on what grounds purists object to a group of human figures, or a beautiful landscape being made use of to create that perfect illusion of which the realistic spirit of modern art stands in need. Only where these accidentals are treated as the main object they become detrimental to the economy of the drama; a perversion of aesthetical principles of which the contemporary stage offers but too many instances.'[4]

In 1876 the reservations were about the success of the new machinery at Bayreuth in creating the required effect, and the appropriateness of the high romantic fantasy of the sets, constructed by the Bruckner brothers from Hoffmann's designs. For some English members of the audience the use of steam to create sky and cloud phenomena, or as in *Das Rheingold*, submarine effects, was impressively lavish but hardly novel. And 'regarding the scenery itself, I cannot say that anything astonishing was presented to an English eye' was a typical comment about the sumptuous painted sets. For others paraphernalia, reminiscent of pantomime, reduced the grandeur of conception; yet two effects were picked out for approval—the moments of daybreak in both *Siegfried* and *Götterdämmerung*, and the leaping red flames of Siegfried's funeral pyre:

'Nothing more terribly real was ever put upon the stage. . . .'[5]

'At Bayreuth, by ingenious combinations of colours projected on steam, the gentlest gradations of light and shade were obtained, exquisite combinations through all the varied light-tones from morning to night; clouds, lightning, moonlight, really illusive instead of ludicrous—details absolutely necessary indeed to the due setting forth of an heroic picture, but none the less difficult of attainment.'[6]

The idea of an annual pilgrimage to Bayreuth was rapidly to become established, and with it the notion, promulgated by Wagner himself, that *only* at Bayreuth could the operas be seen as their composer intended them, for only at the Festspielhaus were there facilities for their complete representation and hence the unique Wagnerian experience. The legendary associations of the locality and the special significance of seeing Wagner performed in his native land were combined with the atmosphere of a ritual occasion depending on a spectacle that simply could not be reproduced elsewhere.

When Bayreuth reopened in 1882 with *Parsifal*, the controversy about staging became more intense. It centred upon the lurid garden scene, crammed with giant plants, which was based on the paintings of Paul Joukowsky. This spectacle so horrified the young Adolphe Appia that he went away immediately to start work on his own revolutionary alternative, and also provoked Wagner's own famous remark that 'having invented the invisible orchestra, he now wished that he could invent the invisible stage'.[7] But the real *tours de force* of the production were its transformation scenes: solemn, slow-moving shifts of vast flats to suggest the heroic journey to the castle of the Grail. These were admiringly described in *The Theatre*.

'Technically this is what happens: the whole of the elaborate "set" forest moves across the stage, forming a quadruple panorama, the realistic effect being much heightened by the front portions moving much quicker than the back. The tree "cuts" are succeeded by rocks, in which are seen, first natural caves, and then artificial passages partly lined with masonry. The front panorama then shuts in the stage with a front cloth representing a stone wall, close to the proscenium. After remaining stationary for *thirty seconds* only, instead of being drawn off, it sinks, and reveals the magnificent set scene of the cathedral hall—a built dome with built cloisters all round. . . . The whole of this elaborate change is accomplished with perfect smoothness, not a creak or sound of any sort betraying the means.'[8]

Here, if anywhere, was tested the ability of what was currently available in stage machinery to convey the progress of the music-drama, and its success was again disputed by the discriminating. A report in *The Theatre* might legitimately emphasise the purely technical achievement, but there were, and had been for some time,* others who were sufficiently informed to probe more deeply into aesthetics. Bayreuth gave them the opportunity of seeing put into practice ideas and theories long understood and assimilated.

It was, to put it briefly, Wagner's belief that the combination of music, the medium most capable of evoking intense emotion, with poetry, or more correctly with drama, in which emotion is also placed and defined, might result in an artistic experience of a more sublime and revelatory nature than either is capable of realising alone. With the Greek theatre as ideal and inspiration, the opera was to become then not a composite of duets, arias and choruses, but a dramatic unity, its music rooted in and inextricable from its story or myth. George Eliot, probably without even having consulted Wagner's own writings, understood as much in 1855:

'Wagner would make the opera perfect musical drama, in which feelings and situations spring out of *character*, as in the highest order of tragedy, and in which no dramatic probability or poetic beauty is sacrificed to musical effect. The drama must not be a mere pretext for the music; but music, drama and spectacle must be blended, like the coloured rays in a sunbeam, so as to produce one undivided impression.'[9]

Many, like the prominent musicologist the Reverend H. A. Haweis in 1877, were content for the most part to expound the doctrine and leave its practical implications alone:

'Wagner had the unconscious but inflexible hardihood to take up each art in turn, weigh it, and find it wanting. Each fell short of the whole reality in some respect. Painting leaves out motion and solidarity, sculpture possesses solidarity without motion, and usually without colour. Poetry without drama appeals to the senses chiefly through the imagination; in itself it has neither sound, colour nor solidarity. The spoken drama lacks the intensity which it is the unique function of musical sound to give; whilst mere pantomime, whether of dance or drama, lacks the indefinite suggestion of sound as well as the definite suggestion of words; and, lastly, musical sound alone provokes the eternal "why?" which can only be answered by associating the emotion raised with thought, for music

* *The Musical World* in 1871 contained translations of 'A Communication to my Friends'. The first volume of Ashton Ellis' mammoth edition of the prose works, which contained 'Art and Revolution' and 'The Art Work of the Future' was not to appear until 1892.

alone is without solidarity, colour or thought, whilst possessing motion and soul in the highest perfection.'[10]

More searching critics were disturbed by the incompatibility of music to the other arts. Edward Gurney in 1883 distinguished between music, a *presentative* art, and poetry, painting and sculpture, *representative* arts. Music creates 'absolute' experiences from elements which do not exist outside of it. However,

'Some natural tolerance of ungrasped or ungraspable sound may be admitted: there are doubtless persons who easily resign themselves to regard its presence as a vaguely emotional background to the passing scene, getting subdued or emphatic, bright or gloomy, at appropriate places, like the gestures of the actors or the clouds that figure so largely in the Wagnerian stage-effects.''[11]

Gurney was here questioning the need or appropriateness for music to receive support from any other media at all, and this at a time when similar questions were beginning to be asked about the non-musical drama. For Henry James, disguised as Dorriforth in his seminal dialogue of 1889 'After the Play', there was the possibility of a basic incompatibility between the essential requirements of a drama made up of expressive gesture and language and current demands for the fullest possible means of representation.

'*Dorriforth:* ... The face and the voice are more to the purpose than acres of painted canvas, and a touching intonation, a vivid gesture or two, than an army of supernumaries.
'*Auberon:* Why not have everything—the face, the voice, the touching intonations, the vivid gestures, the acres of painted canvas, *and* the army of supernumaries? Why not use bravely and intelligently every resource of which the stage disposes? What else was Richard Wagner's great theory, in producing the opera at Bayreuth?
'*Dorriforth:* Why not, indeed? That would be the ideal. To have the picture complete at the same time the figures do their part in producing the particular illusion required—what a perfection and what a joy! I know no answer to that save the aggressive, objectionable fact. Simply look at the stage of today and observe that these two branches of the matter never do happen to go together.'[12]

That was in June, a few months before G. B. Shaw, himself no admirer of spectacle for its own sake, was prompted by a visit to Bayreuth to corroborate the inadequacy of what was being done there, and to enter the controversy about *Parsifal*. 'Wagnerism', Shaw was to end, 'like charity, begins at home'; there was no need for performances of the operas to be confined to Bayreuth.

'. . . *Parsifal* can be done not merely as well in London as in Bayreuth, but better. A picked London orchestra could, after half a dozen rehearsals under a competent conductor, put Herr Levi and the Bayreuth band in second place. Our superiority in the art of stage presentation is not disputed, even by those who omit Mr Herkomer and the Bushey theatre from the account.'[13]

In 1889, that reference to Herkomer and the Bushey theatre was topical enough. A year later even the young W. B. Yeats, overwhelmed by amateur performances in Bedford Park, themselves inspired by the example of E. W. Godwin, could allude to Herkomer's activities in Bushey as a model for an annual dramatic event:

'If successful and there is every likelihood of its rousing even more interest than Professor Herkomer's yearly play at Bushey, there is some talk of getting up an annual venture of this same kind, a sort of May Day festival of dramatic poetry.'[14]

Another member of the Bedford Park audience made a different kind of comparison, coining a new adjective in the process:

'But what I do give unqualified praise is the pretty scene . . . full of warmth and colour and brightness, and abounding in Herkomesque effects.'[15]

The second comparison may have been naïve and misleading, for Herkomer's theories and productions represent a very different approach to stage décor from that of Godwin, and one that incidentally Yeats was to bypass completely, but readers of *The London Figaro* would have understood the allusion.

William Archer's articles over the same two years, 1889–90, contain many references to Herkomer, as for example in his reply to 'After the Play':

'True, there is an element of puerility in our present craving for scenic display. We are like children with a new toy; and we can think of and play with nothing else. But presently (in a generation or two) the novelty will wear off. We shall no longer be content with mere decoration; and in the meantime we shall have mastered the decorative arts, which at present time have mastered us. Have you seen Professor Herkomer's ingenious experiments at Bushey? The Professor is doing excellent work in carrying scenic illusion to the highest power, developing its utmost possibilities . . . It is conceivable that Richard Wagner's forecast may be right, and that the drama, instead of developing along realistic lines, may blend into the "great art work of the future", reuniting with dance and song, with painting, sculpture and architecture in a vast symbolico-poetic whole. In that case our present enthusiasm for scenery is part of the main current of tendency and not a mere eddy in the tide.'[16]

76

The fascinated but confused response in England to the problems of staging Wagner is one way of approaching the subject of this essay, the 'ingenious experiments' of an understandably forgotten Victorian whose contemporary eminence depended not upon his work in the theatre but upon a highly respectable and much publicised career as a painter.

As one of the most highly rewarded artists of his time, Hubert von Herkomer is above all a figure of success; his story has to do with public taste and, like other members of the Victorian Parnassus, a skilful combination of eccentricity and conventionality. The man who became Slade Professor of Fine Art, who ended his career painting national heroes (both Baden Powell and Cecil Rhodes sat for him) and a large portion of established society, indeed who finally painted royalty, was born in Bavaria in 1849 to a family of peasant craftsmen. His father, also called Hubert, was the second of the four sons of a mason and became a skilled woodcarver, later building his own house in Waal. Two of the elder Hubert's brothers were also craftsmen, John a carver and Anton a weaver, and as boys all three were encouraged to develop traditional skills, one of which was the modelling of the familiar Bavarian Nativity reliefs out of painted wood and cloth, first stiffened with glue and then decorated with gilt. The three brothers went on through the normal stages of apprenticeship to become professionals, and a family community was established. This was disrupted when John decided to emigrate to America, and was soon followed by Hubert, taking with him his three-year old son and his other brother Anton. They stayed for a year in New York, then moving to Rochester and later to Cleveland, Ohio, living as far as possible on what work their specialised skills could obtain. In 1857 Hubert's family moved to England and settled where they got off the boat, in Southampton. His wife took up work as a music teacher, while the woodcarver began work on a large and ornate cabinet, which he subsequently found himself unable to sell. The early years were arduous and poverty-stricken. But the son inherited talents from both parents, quickly developed some musical ability, helped his father at his workbench, and began a long series of watercolour drawings copied from *The Illustrated London News* and other magazines. During these hard times his father renounced smoking, drinking and meat-eating, setting an example of abstinence which his son was always to profess and probably, in such minor matters, to maintain.

Prosperity came very slowly—first a commission obtained by Uncle John, still in America, for four life-size carvings of Evangelists after models in Nuremberg, which allowed father and son to cross to Germany to work, study carvings and visit the opera. On his return Hubert became a student at the South Kensington Art School, whose teaching methods by the 1860s were well established as the orthodox training for most young artists and were to remain so at least until the end of the century. He immediately found them frustrating and unacceptable, recalling later:

'The teaching at the Kensington Schools led me nowhere in my art. There is something wrong in a system for the training of art-students that does not awaken the power of "seeing" the artistic aspects of nature, or help the student to grasp the meaning of "quality" in painting. Not a criticism was given me that would have led me to either. I did endless studies, all of uniform merit, or de-merit, and all were quickly and easily done. Judging them now—impersonally—and with the experience of years in teaching, I can clearly see how a *word*—the right one at the right moment—would have put my young mind on the right track; I should have recognised the identity upon which my future depended.'[17]

At South Kensington he came under the influence of Frederick Walker, whose famous and influential painting 'The Bathers', showing a group of nude figures upon the banks of an English river, was hung at the Royal Academy in 1876 to immense critical acclaim and to controversy among artists.

'There were hot discussions in the life-room at Kensington about Walker's work. It was flat, chalky and ill-drawn to some; to others it had the light of nature, and was above all things unconventional.'[18]

Herkomer left the Art School and returned to Southampton, where he sketched and did watercolours. He then moved back to London, attempted to join some Christie Minstrels as a zither player, and took the first important step of his career by contributing black and white work to *The Graphic*, a paper which in the early years of its existence exercised a powerful influence upon young artists and brought them into close contact with everyday subjects. Herkomer submitted sketches of gypsies and men at work, sketches that we might now count amongst his very few durable achievements; and it is not entirely surprising that they should have later appealed to the young Van Gogh, who in the early 1880s devotedly collected copies of *The Graphic* and held Herkomer's work in particular esteem.[19]

It was now that Herkomer began to experiment with oils, and he saved some two hundred pounds for a holiday in Bavaria, where he began work on his first important and commercially successful painting.

' "After the Toil of the Day", it was called, and represented a street with old sunburnt wooden houses on the one side, and a river bordered with apple trees on the other. The old people and the children were sitting on the benches, with more able-bodied peasants returning from the fields. It was the spirit of Walker that entirely guided my feelings in this picture. Although thoroughly Bavarian, and although painted on the spot direct from Nature, I had in it two strong points that indicated Walker, viz., the apple trees and a herd of geese.'[20]

Apart from the justly acknowledged debt to Walker there were other reasons for the painting's impact. Herkomer had hit upon two powerful ingredients of success: first, like Millais, the popular genre of the elegaic peopled scene, second, the unfailing appeal of narrative detail. But his account of the methods and intentions behind this work is also significant.

'The effect was evening, thus enabling me to get Walker's warmth of colour. I painted it on an absorbent ground, made by my father which gave it that *dry*, fresco-like appearance that I thought so essential, in those days, to oil-painting. And although it was *flat*, and wanting in what we now talk so much about—"planes" and "values"—it certainly had a charm in its quality not to be replaced by mere photographic realism. Faces were carefully stippled up as in water-colour, and there was in the workmanship that odd admixture of excessive finish with undue sketchiness.'[21]

The confident distinction between carefully achieved effect and 'mere photographic realism' is deceptive. In fact Herkomer was to become fascinated very early on by the 'camera obscura'. He wrote ominously to his uncle Hans in 1876:

'I have at last found my art master in the shape of a large Camera Obscura, which I have had made. Nature is reflected and translated as it ought to be painted.'[22]

In the winter of 1873 financial stability permitted Herkomer to marry, and to rent a cottage with his parents in the then comparatively isolated village of Bushey, near Watford. This he furnished in the Aesthetic manner, with Morris wallpaper, oak cabinets and blue and white tiles; one room was blue, the walls of Japanese leather-paper, its ceiling toned to match, another room was all yellow.[23] The marriage was to be a disaster, but the career flourished. Herkomer's next painting, the immensely popular 'Chelsea Pensioners', was sold for £1,200, and was praised by established painters such as Lord Leighton and George Richmond. In 1878, two years after the first performance of *The Ring*, Wagner visited London to conduct concerts of his own music at the Albert Hall, and Herkomer, unable to persuade the great man to sit for him formally, based a portrait on sketches made during rehearsal; this was eventually presented to Cosima. His desire to paint the composer at this particular time is interesting and unexplained.

From then on the portraits came thick and fast—Tennyson in 1878, Ruskin the following year—and with them further economic security. On the death of his mother, Herkomer was able to build in Bavaria a monument to her memory in the shape of a romantic tower over a hundred feet high, named 'The Mutterhorn'. He did continue with the narrative pictures, for example a painting with life-size figures entitled 'Life, Light and Melody', completed in 1882, and later experimented with etching, mezzotint and even enamels, but from now on it was the portraits that dominated his output, and in 1882 he made the first of many highly profitable visits to paint fashionable society along the Eastern sea-board of the United States. In this way the foundations were laid for an immense commercial success, guaranteed by wealthy patrons and a regular production. In two and a half months of 1882, thirteen portraits were completed which brought him £6,614; over nine months of the same year, his earnings came to over £11,000. His frenetic energy became legendary:

'His theory of life is the very antipodes of that contained in the French aphorism which insists upon it that "le mieux est l'ennemi du bien". He is never content to let well alone, but is always seeking for the better. He changes, he shifts, he revises and redecorates and rearranges; so that his environment has the attribute of an endless variety of aspect, and its circumstances seem gifted with an innate and peculiar capacity for metamorphosis.'[24]

Style and market established, Herkomer exploited both to the full, and perfected a mode of portraiture dependent upon likeness and effect alone, whose main criteria were those of photographic realism.

Yet in a lecture published in 1904, he was to discount the relevance of photography for the painter, except as a guide to lighting effects, for it imposed—upon the portraitist in particular—an obligation to produce accurate likeness above all else.

'... photography has not only *not* assisted art, but has been a direct cause of much degeneration in modern art. It has altered "seeing" in the young artist, and has lured him into "bit painting", and thus caused the beginning of a decay in real design which is to be deplored. It has engendered a literalism devoid of sentiment and nobility. It has caused laziness and a disposition to avoid trouble.'[25]

By this date the objection was old-fashioned indeed, and it is an indication of Herkomer's insularity that it should have been made at all, especially without reference. More to the point and part of an established procedure would have been to observe the effects of photography upon Impressionist painters, in terms either of what they had appropriated or, more likely in the case of a realist of Herkomer's school, of what they had discarded. Particularly imprecise is his endorsement of the idea that the subject of a work of art should be treated according to the temperament of the artist, because at no time does he reveal just how much freedom of interpretation he is prepared to allow.

Herkomer's fear of photography is directly related to his un-avowed belief in realism, and a glance at his own portraits, or at the comments of his more discriminating contemporaries, makes this absolutely clear—for the work produced by this advocate of 'artistic interpretation' was, of course, particularly in its lighting effects, crudely photographic. In fact Herkomer had little more control of the possibilities of his medium than he did of its theory, and realism remained, as it always had been, ideal end enough. Certainly critics in the vanguard of the nineties, George Moore and D. S. MacColl, involved as they were in the prolonged struggle to estab-lish Impressionist ideas in England, referred to him with nothing less than contempt, Moore being characteristically violent:

'In the north room I was particularly distressed by two life-size portraits by Professor Herkomer—Sir George Gabriel Stokes, Bart., and the Rev. John E. B. Mayor. I am uncertain which of these portraits it would be most unpleasant to live with. The portrait of Sir George would drive me into a lunatic asylum, the portrait of the Rev. John E. B. Mayor would drive me to suicide. Suicide is better than lunacy, so on that ground, and on that ground alone, I should cast my lot with Sir George if necessity compelled me. Truly, it is impossible to imagine anything more vulgar than these portraits, and I do not readily distinguish how and where they differ from richly-coloured photographs. Tempted by an odious curiosity I examined them more closely, and I seemed to discover strange analogies between them and the well-known light and shade of photo-graphy. I do not mean that Mr Herkomer is or should be made professor of the gentle art of the camera, but he seems to be more than a platonic admirer of the machine.'[26]

Although Herkomer made continuous disparaging reference to the camera, he admitted to using it as an aid when planning a painting. This in itself is telling, for the camera records only the relations of light and shade, and often the success or failure of a photograph depends entirely upon the effectiveness of that relationship, although we may feel that it also tells us something about the nature of its subject. The colour photograph (unless the print has been deliberately retouched or tinted) in the same way shows us only a colour relationship controlled by the distribution of light. As with many of his contemporaries, Herkomer's vocabulary of 'tones' and 'values' should be connected with the photographic, for these words tend to refer to relationships of light and are founded in objective realism; they should be distinguished from the ideas of tone or value relations operating *within the picture itself* that were to overcome them. Confusingly, this distinction was not maintained at all consistently in the art writings of the time.

Quite as interesting as the conventional acumen and financial astuteness that earned those vast sums is the eccentricity with which they were spent.

Plans for his home Lululaund, to be 'the most beautiful house in England', originated during the first tour of America, and the American architect H. H. Richardson was commissioned to undertake the design. Nothing was to be bought, but everything to be individually manufactured on the site, from the woodcarvings to the stonework. Large-scale research was undertaken:

'It will be an addition to England, unique as it is noble. He has kept the masses, giving the greatest dignity of style and using 13th century Gothic with a Romanesque feeling. This is as it ought to be, because we enter the house and immediately feel the development of style, having advanced from the 13th century to the 15th century in the decoration and inner structures.'[27]

The exterior of Lululaund was built from grey 'tufa' limestone specially imported from Bavaria, chosen for its weatherworn appearance and varied with broaded courses of red sandstone. Attention was lavished in particular upon the front elevation, where the dominant feature was a huge Romanesque arch joining two round turrets and supporting an ornamental gable. Long stone balconies extended from this on either side. To the left rose up a solid square tower, intended to support a never completed *campanello* spire. The effect was described as representing the artistic character and development of Herkomer's national heritage: there was considered to be no incoherence between the Romantic arch and the almost entirely Gothic interior.

An enormous drawing-room contained a panelled ceiling, carved cross beams, a large stone fireplace and a music gallery above, with windows that resembled stained-glass but were in fact made from a combination of painting and draped gauze. The master's studio, the least decorated room, had walls that were covered with a greenish gold metal leaf, and silver pewter electric light brackets. Each bedroom followed its own colour scheme—as for example the all-yellow 'Midas room', with its gold leaf walls. But the greatest showpiece of all was the dining-room, crammed with carvings of interlaced branches, with at one end a vast relief entitled 'Human Sympathy', showing half-nude female figures, delicately tinted and voluptuously posed. These figures, it was said, had originally been entirely nude, but were later, in the interests of propriety, partially draped in muslin stiffened with plaster of paris.

Lululaund, which Herkomer moved into in 1894, cost a reputed £80,000, and it was here that the 'lion of Bushey' entertained his students and admirers with musical soirées, Sunday afternoon receptions and private lectures, occasions that were evidently uncomfortable and claustrophobic.

'One peculiarity of the house was that after entering it one felt imprisoned. However beautiful the outside world might be, nothing could be seen of it, for there were only slots of windows, so high that none could look through them.'[28]

Lululaund was in the tradition of the great mansions of the late Victorian Academicians: Frederick Goodall's 'Graeme's Dyke', built by Norman Shaw in 1870, Alma-Tadema's villa in St John's Wood, and Leighton House, the grandest of them all. Herkomer's home was more than just a folly: it was both one man's monument to his own endeavour and, like the castle it resembled, a stronghold in which to protect his legend.

'We listened, the crowd stood spell-bound on the stairs. Presently I whispered, "What wonderful time he keeps; I had no idea the Professor was a musician as well as a painter." "He can do anything he wishes", was the response. Then his cousin, Mrs Herkomer, interposed, "It is the pianola he is playing." The pianola! And here were we all holding our breath, listening in awe and reverence. Strange that no one seemed to see the comic side of it; perhaps some did, but it was not apparent on the faces of any amongst whom I was standing.'[29]

In October 1883 the Herkomer School, an institution that was to last for twenty-one years, was founded at Bushey with twenty-five students. Based on a dual concept of a residential community and an autocratic teaching system designed to counteract the 'tradition' of South Kensington, the school offered a strict and austere timetable.

'. . . painting from the nude living model from nine until three, five days in the week; drawing in charcoal and pencil from the nude model from seven until nine; on the Saturday morning, a village model was requisitioned for head painting only.'[30]

Locally their surely very innocent moeurs aroused curiosity.

'They live in the small houses of the village, and impart quite a Bohemian touch to the rustic surroundings. These students enjoy a thoroughly unconventional existence. They call on and pass pleasant afternoons with one another; chaperones are not in evidence and are not wanted. To have the privilege of passing an afternoon with some of these knights and dames of the brush affords a charming contrast to the ordinary "at home" where the stilted methods of society are *de rigueur*.'[31]

And although fees were nominal and the Professor claimed to receive no remuneration whatsoever, he was conveniently provided with a permanent free labour force for whatever experiments he might choose to embark upon and, it cannot be doubted, for completing paintings and thereby maintaining his output. Many students lingered on in Bushey and settled there, forming a permanent colony that lasted long after the school closed in 1904.

There was of course a remarkable irony in the establishment of an Arts and Crafts community by this highly commercial painter, but the great man remained oblivious to it, continually evoking a spirit that he had done as much as anyone to destroy. 'The old spirit of reverent craftsmanship has gone, and the new spirit "Business" is without reverence for anything.'[32]

Late Victorian artists were, notoriously, of many kinds: they included both William Morris and Lord Leighton. It might be said that Herkomer attempted to embrace two attitudes, two ways of life, and that the lesson to be drawn from his activities was that professional success could exist quite comfortably alongside professed amateurism. When he took up work in the theatre, it was as an 'experiment' or 'hobby' and not to be confused, either in theory or in practice, with the serious business of painting. Nevertheless amateurism became at least an excuse or disguise for the inadequacies of his theories.

In 1887 Herkomer began to satisfy his interest in the theatre with a performance of *The Sorceress*, a play without words contrived by the painter with himself in the leading role. Distinguished guests, including Ellen Terry, Edward Gordon Craig, F. C. Burnand and Augustus Harris, were invited to a charity matinée; they travelled from London in a special train, were met by carriages and driven through the decorated High Street to the Herkomer estate.[33]

The Sorceress was a great success, and was repeated the following year in a disused chapel which Herkomer and his pupils had converted into a remarkable auditorium modelled on Wagner's Festspielhaus at Bayreuth. Although his declared intention had been simplicity, the artist as always could not resist an opportunity for ornamental woodcarving and decoration: a frieze adorned its pitch-pine walls, stencilled patterns covered the panels of the ceiling, and a finely carved design of oak leaves ran along the front of the gallery. Despite these excrescences, the theatre did contain important innovations. Footlights, usually a border of gas jets around the proscenium, had been abolished, and replaced by an irregular pattern of *electric* lights carefully positioned to bring out muted effects of light and shade on the stage itself. Within the auditorium electric lights were suspended from elegantly wrought ironwork holders. There were no wings; the sides of the stage receded and tapered off, an arrangement that both sharpened perspectives and improved acoustics. A Wagnerian touch was also noticeable in the use of a screen to hide the orchestra from view, and slightly later, in the attempt to bring stage and auditorium together by painting the interior an undistracting sober dark blue.[34]

The sensation of the production was Herkomer's new stage moon.

'Nothing in these days has been seen more beautiful in scene painting than this, in which a pale and full moon, seen through a foreground of trees and wild rocks, gradually yet imperceptibly sinks in the sky, wherein a line of grey night-clouds are visible just above the horizon, while the intervening sky-spaces become first faintly yellow and then rosy with the light of the approaching dawn.'[35]

Not surprisingly, the moon attracted far more attention than the entertainment itself, which William Archer described as

'. . . neither drama nor opera, nor ballet; it was simply, as the programme puts it, a "romantic musical fragment". A series of *tableaux vivants*—studies in plastic chiar'oscuro—accompanied by music and interspersed, that, I take it, is a fair description of *The Sorceress*.'[36]

An Idyl, Herkomer's next work, was a major advance, although again the plot was little more than banal. He described it as a 'Pictorial-Musical' play:

'It was based upon the fantasy of a painter who used as pigment living colours and a magic canvas, his mind all aflame with the excitement inseparable from a new experiment.'[37]

Music played a key part, and was written by Herkomer and conducted by the eminent Wagner conductor, Hans Richter. This link probably went further, for there were clear suggestions of a more than permissible similarity between Herkomer's themes and those of the German master.

'Nobody ... could hear the children's chorus in "An Idyl" without thinking of the dance of the apprentice in "Die Meistersinger"; the smith's first song, without recollection of Hans Sachs; the opening of the third act of "An Idyl", without a thought of 'Das Rheingold"; or the theme which accompanies the entrance of the knight in the last act, without a sneaking kindness for the "Siegfried Idyll".'[38]

Herkomer's latest stage-effects astonished his audiences. Archer compared them to 'a page of William Morris materialised',[39] and another critic commented upon

'... the still evening with its purple haze, sunsmitten mist, moonlight, and the broad plain and streets flooded with sunlight. And then the joyous wedding party, with the children scattering flowers, and the rejoicing of the villagers as the procession enters the smith's house, all show admirable taste and management, with an eye and feeling for picturesque effect it has rarely, if ever, been our privilege to see elsewhere.'[40]

This was all quite easily managed, of course. The properties were very conventional: grass was simulated by dyed matting, the sky was of canvas, and the mist composed of wisps of muslin. Nevertheless, as Herkomer explained, *An Idyl* was '. . . vital in its lesson to my students, demonstrating to them, as it did, the art of "picture-making" with living models, in a real setting.'[41] 'Picture-making' explains his intentions precisely. 'It was to be a reproduction of nature, as the painter sees it, and not to be the semblance of nature usually seen and accepted on the stage.'[42]

The scenario of *An Idyl* was simple enough, and only the first sequence need be described in detail. It opens with a picture; based on one of Herkomer's early oil-paintings (probably 'After the Toil of the Day'): a narrow street in a quiet fourteenth-century village, the gables of medieval houses on each side. It is an autumn evening, and shadows lengthen over the open landscape visible at the end of the street. In the foreground there is a blacksmith's forge, while on benches before the houses the old people of the village sit and sing their evening song, children playing around them. This scene is interrupted by a passing hunting party, one member of which, FitzHugh, remains behind briefly to ascertain the home of the beautiful Edith, the blacksmith's daughter. As the hunting party moves on, so the tones of the Angelus are heard, and an old woman begins to entertain the children with a story, until again disturbed, this time by the return of the reapers with Edith at their head. She is approached by her lover, Dick o' the Dale, and her rebuttal causes him to refuse to accompany the dancing; however, FitzHugh re-enters and breaks into a brisk dance tune. Only Edith fails to participate in the ensuing dance, standing self-consciously apart until the villagers leave and she is left alone. FitzHugh steals up behind her, takes her hand and kisses it, and sings her a love-song. As this ends, Edith is summoned indoors by her father and FitzHugh exits singing a gay song, watched by the troubled blacksmith, who sinks upon a bench and starts up an old ballad whose unhappy story is being re-enacted by his daughter.

It is clear from this résumé that action is determined by opportunity for stage effect. Formal entrances and exits and the display of isolated figures permit the use of perspective and provide settings for song, while gesture and expression are limited to those required for the simplest, most recognisable emotion. The first act exploits the scenic possibilities of work at the smithy, the lengthening shadows of evening and nightfall announced by a rising moon. The second act, less varied, features a static domestic scene as the setting for a recapitulation of the blacksmith's ballad, and the third act, bathed in bright daylight, includes a chorus of children who scatter flowers before the arrival of a lavish wedding party. 'Pantomimic action' and 'pictorial situations' were Herkomer's unashamed intention, based on 'a simple story with a touch of nature'.[43]

'I wish only to make the effects as true to Nature as I possibly can; and only artistic natures, and lovers of Nature who have looked enough at Nature to remember her effects, can be my judge.'[44]

The professed aim of *An Idyl* was to bring together, in an experimental way, the two arts of painting and music.

'There was just story enough to give reason for the changes of pictorial effects, and music enough to attune the mind of the spectator to the pictures.'[45]

It was, he reiterated, an experiment in scenic art carried out by a painter, and his private theatre was a place in which

'. . . he could experiment in scenic art, in grouping figures, and in story-making, only changing his canvas for the stage in order to express with real objects and real people the thoughts he placed ordinarily upon canvas with brush and colour.'[46]

The deliberately vague definition 'Pictorial-Musical play' (which replaced the evasive 'fragment' or 'pageant') is, as he acknowledged,

7

a way of avoiding the word 'opera', which in turn carried its own overtones of 'drama'.

'The first word denotes the plastic picture; the second, the musical sounds that attune one to the picture; and finally, the word play, to give sufficient motive for the display of the two arts—painting and music.'[47]

The picture comes first, the music 'annotates' the picture, and the story is the excuse or justification for the whole thing. These are of course simple divisions, *un*Wagnerian and naïve, yet Herkomer, although he often seems to be talking merely of tableaux, makes frequent comparison between the arts. 'To put it concisely, the basis of the graphic arts is nature; of music, it is thought, emotion.'[48] And,

'Music is the most natural expression of human emotions. Man, when jubilant, or overcome by thankfulness, must sing. In itself, music is the purest of all the arts. A tune cannot be immoral; it is made to appear so by its being attached to immoral words. Alone, a tune can be vulgar, common or banal, but never immoral, or, I may add, blasphemous.'[49]

Herkomer always started with his picture: music and story came later, and the actors, or mimes as he called them, were merely components. Hence the very limited settings—predominantly sunsets, sunrises, and weather effects—because the number of naturally changing vistas is few, and hence too the emphasis on the creation of 'mood'. When mood replaces theme, and harmony becomes the only possible ideal, the unification of the arts has become a very reduced ambition indeed.

The next in the series was *Filippo*, an adaptation of Coppée's popular *Le Luthier de Crémone*, performed in June 1890 and repeated in June 1892. Herkomer played the title part of a hunchback. The stage showed cornfields full of seemingly real stooks of corn, and there was a magnificent storm scene, with a novel and splendidly contrived rainbow effect.

The final production, which was performed for six afternoons in January 1893, was *Time's Revenge*, by W. L. Courtney. Herkomer was a great success in the part of Gaston Boissier.

Herkomer's enterprises attracted the attention of the professional theatrical establishment, and in 1892 he was invited by H. A. Jones to lecture to a special audience which included Edward Gordon Craig, Beerbohm Tree, Mary Moore, Hermann Vezin, Lily Langtry, Alma Murray, Charles Wyndham. The subject, 'Scenic Art', was introduced by Squire Bancroft as one 'never before touched upon by a lecturer'. Be that as it may, in fact Herkomer's suggestions were either impractical or already well known.

He began by emphasising that his attitude to the problems of staging was a practical one. Since the dramatic and pictorial qualities of a play were inseparable, responsibility rested upon the designer to provide the best possible facilities for the staging of a drama. 'Shakespeare in a barn' simply would not do. What Herkomer demanded was *illusion*, an acceptance of the artificiality of the scenic art. Maintaining that the creation of illusion depended, first and foremost, upon lighting rather than upon the painted set, he rejected open-air performances on the grounds that 'the actuality of nature and the artificiality of the actor's situation can never blend.' Herkomer fails to distinguish between the artifice of the drama itself and scenic artifice, which may be intrusive and destroy involvement; he thinks all can be resolved by upholding a *perfection of illusion*:

'I hold the stage to be the medium through which the greatest truths in nature can be brought home most directly to the minds and hearts of the people, and all the arts can, to their fullest capacity, be united in the most complete form of human expression. But we should not be satisfied until all the arts are placed on equal footing, *not necessarily of importance, but perfection.*'[50]

'Artistic whole' depended on the presence of one mastermind and a full use of all available technical machinery. The objective was the creation of a mood that harmonised with the dramatic situation:

'It is this mood or aspect of a scene that should, to my thinking, reflect that of the actor, or else strengthen it by the force of contrast.
'Just as an atmospheric effect, or a scene in nature, produces that indefinable condition of the mind that one calls a "mood", so ought a scenic effect on the stage to impression itself on the mind of the spectator by its poetic and picturesque fitness.'

Herkomer's equation of 'stage scene' and 'picture' was used to justify three innovations. Comparing the position of spectators at a Royal Academy Exhibition with that of the audience in a theatre, he called for the abolition of footlights, survivors of the days before electricity was available.

'We all know that the light from within the proscenium alone cause heavy shadows on the face of the actors as they approach the front of the stage, and that these shadows *must* be relieved by some lights *in front* of the proscenium. But where to place them? Nobody will be rash enough to say that light can ever come from the ground in nature. Therefore, to place lights on the ground, under the noses of the actors, cannot but destroy all chances of obtaining truthfully the aspect of nature on the stage. If footlights were only becoming to the actors, one might put up with the unnatural effect they produce. But here again the verdict must be against them.'

The parallel here was with the art of the portrait painter, who must select a perfectly congruous background and a natural light that reveals the essentials of his subject's features. He gave two examples: the work of Frederick Walker, and the results achieved by a camera obscura, which shows exactly the amount of actual or diffused light within a framed area. His own solution had been to soften the faces of the actors by placing a group of lights at eye-level on each side of the auditorium, about ten feet from the proscenium.

As with the sunken area at Bayreuth, containing orchestra and conductor, a plain darkened auditorium contributed to the sense of involvement. By abolishing all distractions and barriers audience and spectacle are in direct confrontation; the illusion stands or falls on its own terms.

The one barrier that remains is the proscenium arch, whose presence Herkomer not only accepted but went some way to utilise, on grounds fundamental to his whole theory:

'I take it that the proscenium should be to the stage picture what the frame is to the easel-picture. It should separate the picture from the surroundings.'

But if frame is to picture as proscenium is to scene, whereas the painter can suit the size of his frame to his picture, the size of the proscenium remains the same whatever it contains. To surmount this problem Herkomer suggested a more complicated reform: the telescopic proscenium, a device that could be made to contract or expand according to the requirements of each scene.

'The scenic-artist, by the aid of this contracting proscenium could, with the collaboration of the stage- and acting-manager, carry out all the laws that govern pictorial composition in art.'

This would mean that, for instance, a small cottage need no longer be presented as being of the same dimensions as a castle banqueting hall: the 'telescopic proscenium' was demonstrated on an ingenious model theatre.

Another piece of machinery suggested was a gigantic gauze screen, arranged on a principle of adjustment '. . . similar to that of breakfast dishes whose covers turn back on a hinge and finally settle underneath,' which would eventually open up the possibility of creating many effects by the use of reflected light, like a magic lantern. With his final suggestion Herkomer unwittingly gave the lie to an aim of simple pictorial realism. The evening scene, *pièce de résistance* of *An Idyl*, had been achieved by the placing of a sheet of gauze in front of the painted backcloth but at some distance from it. The surface of the backcloth was built up and modelled with plaster of Paris, paper and glue, in much the same way that Nativity scenes had been constructed by his Bavarian ancestors. By playing lime-lights first through coloured glass and then onto this raised surface, it had been possible to reproduce the shapes of moving clouds and even to cast lengthening shadows—in short, to achieve a changing stereoscopic effect, enhanced and softened by the gauze. Such effects might well be described as an illusion of nature, but the Professor did not leave it there, and added a further and significant prophecy.

'. . . . I see a possibility of bringing living people within the focus of a lantern so constructed that they shall be reflected back onto the gauze surface, and again be repeated innumerable times until the heavens would live with spiritual figures. If life were only not so short; if money were only more plentiful for such experiments; if somebody else could do my painting work, I would produce a fairy-phantasy such as man has only seen in his dreams.'

A 'fairy-phantasy' is a very different matter from the pictorial representation of nature.

The theatrical journals were, in general, scornful of Herkomer's theories. (*The Theatre* did not even review the lecture.) *The Dramatic Review* pointed out that the method of lighting was thoroughly well known, and was used particularly for pantomimes, when additional brightness was required. As for the use of gauze to soften distances, this had been common practice with scenic artists for the last twenty years. *The Stage* agreed that Herkomer had little new to offer, and like *Dramatic Opinions* was most concerned with the new and expensive theatre that would have to be built to house a telescopic proscenium, and to accommodate 'the minimum number of persons in the maximum amount of space'.

The closest that Herkomer ever had to a champion was Archer, and even he viewed the experiments rather cynically at first. Archer did, however, fully recognise the points of similarity between Wagner's vast undertakings at Bayreuth and Herkomer's domestic charades at Bushey. Both were committed, he said vaguely, to 'unification of the arts', and the final development of a 'total art', and Archer referred to Herkomer's theatre, actors, painters and musicians as one vast 'art city', or 'art machine',[51] 'Pantechnicon' and 'Künstlerstadt'.[52]

In fact Herkomer was not completely in sympathy with what was being done in Bayreuth. Although his own reforms were still based upon the *principles* of painting, he could see quite clearly where Wagner had gone wrong. 'Richard Wagner still held the erroneous idea that scenic success lay in the painting, and always endeavoured to employ the best artists';[53] '. . . the scenery at Bayreuth is vulgar and tawdry to a degree.'[54]

Archer's early misgivings about the Bushey experiments are expressed in his review of *The Sorceress*:

'It meant no more than the scales of chords whereby a musician essays a new piano. Mr Herkomer wanted to test both the human and mechanical portions of the instrument he has devised for himself, and chose this means of doing so. So far as it went, the experiment was successful; but it did not go very far.'[55]

He realised that music, scenic effect, and even elaborate lighting technique reduced rather than extended an actor's potential; dramatic action would inevitably become subservient to the hopeless pursuit of realism.

'All that is truly dramatic—facial expression, definiteness of form, precision of gesture—is sacrificed to a tantalising approximation to the impossible.'

Herkomer reached the limits of his own inventions with the series of scenes known as Pictorial-Musical plays, for without specially contrived tableaux, the lighting devices lost their point.

When in later years Archer came to view Herkomer more favourably, it was as part of a general movement towards improved standards. Puzzled by Irving's *Macbeth*, which attempted a realistic set while still relying on limelight to pick out the actors' faces, he turned to Herkomer for advice, who predictably recommended that Irving use electric light.[56] Disturbed by the difficulties involved in joining sky-borders, painted flats and bare boards into a realistic total perspective, he was told by Herkomer that the solution lay in the imitation of the great painters, old masters who had perfected 'circular panoramas'.

To the extent then of a move towards realism in scenic art, Archer sympathised more with Herkomer than with those 'two-board-and-a-passion' men (by which he may have meant William Poel) who resented all aids to their 'heroic imagination'.[57] But although Edward Gordon Craig paid belated tributes—'I think our stage owes something to Herkomer . . .'[58]—it is hard to believe that his realism amounted to very much. Herkomer's main contribution was probably to introduce more sophisticated ways of using electric light. And there was also that miraculous stage moon.

One of the most prominent elements in nineteenth-century aesthetics is a preoccupation with the idea of synaesthesia, and although its past history is an awesomely complex one to trace, a start can be made by referring to the classical precedents that were often invoked. In the *Cratylus* Plato considers names to be imitations compounded of elements that bear an onomatopoeic resemblance to the objects they refer to: 'Do you agree with me that the letter ρ is expressive of motion and hardness?', asks Socrates.[59] But because this level of imitation is only partial, it is decided that names are also governed, imperfectly, by convention, or *language*. A comparison of the skill of the name-giver in imitating the essence of the object with the arts of the painter and musician, who imitate colour, or figure, or sound, produces the conclusion that names have a double nature. Nevertheless Plato's comparison of the arts does presume in part an isomorphic relation between art and object; both possess a similar essence.

Aristotle, on an occasion often referred to by aestheticians, speaks of colour harmony as operating like that of sound, within a system of *ratios*.

'It is likewise possible that these may subsist after the same manner with symphonies, for the colours which are in the most proportional numbers, on these symphonies are these which appear to be the most delightful colours, such as the purple and the light red, and a few others of the same kind; and for the same reason as there are but few delightful symphonies, there are but few delightful colours; but the other colours have not a ratio.'[60]

Goethe's *Farbenlehre*, known in England through Eastlake's translation of 1840, bears in its conviction that colours must be studied as physical appearances an acknowledged similarity to the treatise *De Coloribus*, also often attributed to Aristotle. Goethe expounds the anti-Newtonian idea that colours are produced by colourless means according to the *density* of the medium interposed between pure light and the beholder. A theory of relative colour value could be used to support principles of contrast and gradation in painting; for instance, Eastlake's notion that warm colours are produced by the 'interposition of dark transparent medium before a light ground'.[61] For exponents of synaesthesia Goethe's treatise gave some confirmation to two hopes: first that it might be established that colour shades suggest certain emotions or poetic values, for example 'as pure yellow passes very easily to red-yellow, so the deepening of this last to yellow-red is not to be arrested. The agreeable, cheerful sensation which red-yellow excites, increases to an intolerably powerful impression in bright yellow-red';[62] and secondly that further investigation might be repaid into the idea that both colour and sound 'are referable to higher formulae', an idea that Goethe himself expressed with some caution—'both are general, elementary effects, acting according to the general law of separation and tendency, of undulation and oscillation, yet acting thus in wholly different provinces, in different modes, on different elementary mediums, for different senses.'[63]

In the course of the nineteenth century, several different versions of synaesthesia were developed: an aesthetic that evoked equivalences between one area of sensation and another—for Baudelaire music and poetry, for Rimbaud words and colour; Wagner's belief that total expression could only be achieved by a bringing together of media, each of which would be but a component; and finally a search for natural laws that link the perception of various stimuli. In this story, the central and most fertile paths, the notion of *correspondances* ('the contingency of the arts'[64]) and, to some extent, the unification of the arts, will be pursued less closely than the practical experiments of scientists and pseudo-scientists. Inevitably there was overlapping and interchange, but here the problems of verbal language will be passed over and attention directed mainly at those who emphasised the visual arts.

The most bizarre experiments attempted to find some basis for synaesthetic experience in physics (or pseudo-physics) and to invent methods and machines for its practical demonstration;* and it is with these that the phenomenon known as 'Colour-Music', in which Herkomer was to take a belated but significant interest, belongs. In June 1895 A. Wallace Rimington read at the St James's Hall a paper entitled 'A New Art. Colour-Music', announcing his fervent desire to demonstrate the ability 'to deal with colour in a new way, and to place its production under as easy and complete control as the production of sound in music.'[65] This manifesto offers one of the simplest versions of the idea that colour, once released from static form and placed under *mobile* control, will not only exercise an emotional power comparable to that of sound, but will operate according to natural laws of harmony:

---

* Recent discoveries in the theory and physiology of perception are also relevant. See for example 'On the Physiological Causes of Harmony in Music', a lecture delivered in 1857 and published in 1873, in *Helmholtz on Perception*, ed. R. and R. Warren, 1968.

'After the Toil of Day', painting by Herkomer, 1872.

'Towards the Close of Day', drawing by Herkomer of Act I of *An Idyl*.

A MOONLIGHTER AT BUSHEY.

Professor H⸺rk⸺m⸺r, A.R.A., instructing Master Henry Irving and Master Gussie Harris how to illuminate "The Inconstant Moon." ("*The Moon was not like the Moon ordinarily seen on the stage.*—*Vide general journalistic opinion on the* "*Herkomer Opera.*")

18   Cartoon in *Punch*, 1889.

Herkomer's house and practice in Bushey

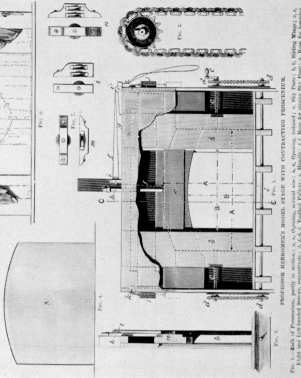

PROFESSOR HERKOMER'S MODEL STAGE WITH CONTRACTING PROSCENIUM.

Fig. 1.—Back of Proscenium, partly in section; A, a, Opening, normal size; b, b, Opening, reduced; c, Sky Piece; b, b, Sliding Wings; c, c, Right and Left-handed Screws, respectively; d, d, d, d, Toothed Pulleys; e, Handle; f, f, Rope for raising Sky Piece; g, Rope for lowering same; h, Guide; i, i, Pulleys; j, j, Counterbalance Weights, working over Pulleys k, k; l, Shaft connecting Pulleys d, d. Fig. 2.—Section on Line A B. Fig. 3.—Sliding Sky Piece; b, Sliding Wing; a, Guide; i, Pulley. Fig. 4.—Front View of Toothed Pulley d, and Connecting Chain. Fig. 5.—Greatest Size of Opening. Fig. 6.—Least Size of Opening. Fig. 7.—Method of Raising and Lowering the Curtain; the dotted lines represent the Curtain lowered; n, n, Pulleys. Fig. 7.—Elevation and Side View of Pulleys m, n, and i respectively.

20   Diagrams of Herkomer's model stage in *Magazine of Art*, 1892.

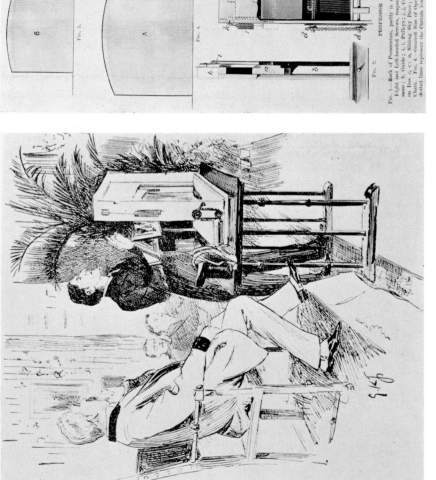

19   Drawing of Herkomer demonstrating his theories on a model stage at the Avenue Theatre. From *The Daily Graphic*, 29 January 1892.

21   Photograph of the Colour-Organ designed by A. Wallace Rimington. Above the keyboard are apertures in which colours appeared when the appropriate note was struck.

22   Herkomer in a still from *The Old Wood Carver*.

'In painting, colour has been used only as one of the elements in a picture, although perhaps the greatest source of beauty. We have not yet had pictures in which there is neither form nor subject, but only pure colour. Even the most advanced Impressionism has not carried us that far.'

All that is required to implement this release is the mobilising factor, the means of instigating change:

'. . . and with this changefulness, the three great influences of *Time*, *Rhythm*, and *Combination* slow or rapid and varied. Colour thus is freed from the trammels of form, and dealt with for the sake of its own loveliness.'

Since time, rhythm and combination exist in music, Rimington proposed that colour sequence could be correlated to a musical score; and for this purpose he had invented a machine called the Colour-Organ. And although it could be objected that the determining of colour sequence by written music was still a form of control, that could be countered by the suggestion that sound and colour were in some way subject to the same higher natural laws. Certainly Rimington was able to find one time-honoured instance in natural phenomena of colour harmonies that changed without an encompassing form.

'I have said that to a large extent in nature colour is presented to us without mobility. Exceptions to this proposition will easily occur to us. Who has not experienced a profound emotion, partly joyous, partly melancholy, produced by the grand procession of glorious schemes presented by many a sunset? Here the changes are for the most part slow and solemn; red becomes orange, orange gold, gold again melts to delicate green and blue by almost imperceptible transitions. Numberless combinations and proportions of every colour, in ever-varying and progressing harmony, march with slow and stately measure into the night.'

It was not until 1912, with the publication of *Colour-Music* (for which Herkomer wrote the introduction), that Rimington supplied a full description of his invention. Here he claims that colour can have an almost religious emotional effect, potentially as powerful as that produced by music. Although he repeats the similarities in the physical nature of light and sound waves, the real need is to establish some kind of emotional analogy between the two, and not necessarily any scientific equation.

The Colour-Organ makes possible an entirely new art, neither wholly music nor wholly colour, but taking contributions from both. It consists of an ordinary piano keyboard connected either to a series of small apertures on a large board or to an arrangement whereby coloured patches can be projected onto a screen. The playing of a note on the keyboard automatically produces a particular colour or shade (for instance, middle C corresponds to deep red), whose intensity varies according to pressure. The playing of a chord produces a sequence or 'harmony' of colours.

What the Colour-Organ did achieve, it would seem, is a means of regulating the duration and intensity of a colour sequence, but it by no means solved all the problems. As Rimington was obliged to concede, only a very few of the resulting colour sequences might be unquestionably attractive, and this made the choice of suitable music extremely limited; moreover, any projection of colour must have contours, that is, have a formal value, however diffuse or erratic. These problems Rimington did not claim to have solved, instead he again indicated the kind of natural model he was aiming at: the changing patterns of a sunset and the beauty of natural iridescence. And to support his own sense of the as yet undiscovered and unrealised power of pure colour, he turned to Wagner, whose personal delight in rich colour was well-known, to the paintings of Turner and, from the world of science, the discoveries of Helmholtz and those who, like Gruber, had suggested that principles of colour association exist within the human mind.* These references are significant, for Rimington's own conclusions are modest: the new art's most important function will be to stimulate those who work in the old arts—painting and decoration—and to awaken the numbed responses of the inartistic to the emotional power of colour.

Many experimenters admitted to finding themselves on very sticky ground when it came to attempting to relate their theories to the work of more conventional artists. One of the strangest rationalisations was provided in William Schooling's article 'Colour-Music', written in 1893 with apparently only a slight knowledge of Rimington's work and published two years later.[66] Schooling saw recent Impressionist painting as an instance of devotion to colour overriding matters of accuracy and detail. Liberate colour entirely, offer a new art method utilising colour alone, he suggested, and artists would turn to work in monochrome, directing all their attention to subject and black and white 'tones'. The warrant for this prophecy lay in Schooling's own brand of aesthetic Darwinism. If the evolutionary process were one from the simple to the complex, of differentiation, and if with this movement came a breaking down into separated organisms, then in aesthetic terms art would also sub-divide into separate components. Thus primitive utterance had

* Professor Gruber of Romania reported to The International Congress of Experimental Psychology held in London in 1892 of experiments in the association of certain vowels and diphthongs with colour. (*Nature*, 11 August 1892, 363.)

divided into song and speech, primitive ritual had bifurcated into dance and drama, and music had finally separated itself from dance. In each case the new offspring is discovered to be able to convey ideas as a self-sufficient medium. Music, as far as Schooling is concerned, conveys emotional ideas through phrase and harmony. The arrival of electricity, making new inventions possible, may finally release colour from representative painting, which will be split irrevocably into the *monochromatic* (where form and subject are preserved) and the *polychromatic* (based on colour ideas alone, probably organised in a non-formal way). Schooling's argument is an idiosyncratic reversal of the tendency to elevate the power of colour through comparison or unification with the other arts. Clearly Wagner did not automatically fit in with his conclusions.

Both Rimington's and Schooling's ideas had long been anticipated. In a short treatise published in 1844, D. D. Jameson had proposed another version:

'. . . a new music called *colour-music*, a practical system of which is now constructed for the first time; and to apply some of its principles to render the study and practice of *sound-music* easier and more popular than they are at present; by substituting distinct and definite sensations, which, being the language of nature, are at once understood, for the arbitrary mnemonics now in use.'[67]

Jameson referred back to a machine constructed by the seventeenth-century Jesuit scientist Castel, author of *Optique des Couleurs*. Castel's machine failed through its incapacity to correlate a note's duration and volume to the intensity of a colour or to the area it occupied. Jameson constructed an apparatus based on the use of *transient, reflected* colours. It consisted of a dark chamber lined with bright tin plates, pierced by twelve round apertures containing glass globes, each filled with translucent coloured liquids. To the outside of each globe was fixed a lamp, and within it a movable opaque cover connected to the keys of a piano. This made it theoretically possible to relate the percussion of the keys to the reflected light according to the length and vibrative intensity of each note.

In fact, the colour sequences produced by Jameson's construction were still completely controlled by the music, and, as he admitted, it offered no guarantee of colour *harmony*. He claimed that a study of the most successful combinations should provide the basis from which an understanding of the natural laws linking the two modes might be deduced; yet while constantly affirming his faith in the existence of such laws, he made no attempt to articulate them. His treatise concludes with demonstration only, specimen harmonies, patterns made up of blocks of colour.

The search for a relationship was continued by J. W. Macdonald in his *Analogy of Sound and Colour* (1869), where the end point was the discovery of a reliable theory that would allow a painter to exercise scientific method in his selection of colour; Macdonald worked out a 'colorific scale' through an equation of colour and note, and went on to analyse famous paintings in these terms. Yet clearly all he succeeded in doing was to substitute as far as he could musical terms for those of painting.

'The musical analogy extends to every branch of the pictorial art. In Canaletto's "View of the Grand Canal" ... the common chord of the tonic, and of the sub-dominant, alternate and inverted, show the skill of the contrapuntist. In this picture there is a multiplicity of according tones of colour, tinting the varied architectural masses. The sky supplies a dominant, to compensate for the want of it in the buildings, and is sufficiently near to complete the perfect chord; it contrasts also with the greenness of the water in the canal, which forms the sub-dominant, or 4th interval, according with the qualities of the 6th and 8th, in the architectural part of the picture. The latter chord never fails to produce an agreeable effect, when it can be introduced with propriety.'[68]

Although Macdonald poses an exact physical resemblance between colour and sound, others speak only in terms of parallelism or analogy. Thus W. F. Barrett in 1870:

'At the outset let us remark that no attempt will be made to show the identity of light and sound: it is their resemblance, their parallelism, and not, of course, their oneness we wish to establish. A parallelism that probably is metaphysical as well as physical; so that the estimation of beauty of colouring and harmony of sound may, hereafter, be found to resolve themselves into mental actions essentially the same.'[69]

And F. J. Hughes (a relative of Darwin's) in 1883, despite complex musical theory and diagram, could only offer in the end a concept of divine harmony.

'The complex work of harmony is governed by the laws which are originated by the Creator; every note performs what He has willed, and in tracing these laws let us not be indifferent about their Author, but ever bear in mind that the *source* or fountain of the life and activity of harmonies arises from the Power who created the machine, and who knows how it will act.
'The fountain or life of musical harmonies and colours is E, or yellow; the root B, or ultraviolet: these being, in fact, tints and shades of white and black.'[70]

The mystic note is characteristic and was to become increasingly dominant.[71]

Theories linking sound and music operated most happily when colour was taken as a self-sufficient medium, separated from the traditional methods and function of the painter committed to the representation of objects and scenes. It was generally agreed that music, as the most abstract of arts, represents, if it can be said to do so at all, emotion only. Haweis made the distinction between the two arts very clearly:

'Music is the creation of man. He does not reproduce in music any combination of sounds he has ever heard or could possibly hear in the natural world, as the painter transfers to his canvas the forms and tints he sees around him. No, the musician seizes the rough element of sound and compels it to work to his will, and having with infinite pains sub-jugated it and tamed it, he is rewarded by discovering in it the most direct and perfect medium in all Nature for the expression of his emotions.

'The Painter's art lies upon the surface of his world; its secrets are whispered by the yellow cornfields spotted with crimson fire, and the dappled purple upon the hills; but the Musician's art lies beneath the surface.'[72]

But even Haweis had gone on to ask for a system for the notation of colour as precise as that applied to music, and a mechanism that would control what he called the 'velocity', that is the duration and rhythm of a colour sequence. He suggested that the use of fireworks might solve the problem.

Comparisons with other arts depended upon the assumption that colour possessed an inherent ability to evoke certain ideas or emotions, which could either be combined with other media or isolated as expressive values in themselves. Allowing colour an independent meaning or making it a component or reinforcement of an inclusive *total* idea, in the Wagnerian sense, was sometimes only a matter of emphasis. But Schooling for one had noticed an apparent contradiction in the two approaches:

'It would seem that the added definiteness thus given to music by the constant association of ideas with sound or musical phrases is eminently in accord with the general principles of evolution, and I may be permitted to add in parenthesis that this innovation by Weber, developed by Wagner, is the most likely reason for such music as they have given us being "the music of the future", and that by a curious contrast the effort to combine many arts in one production so characteristic of much of Wagner's most elaborate work is from the abstract point of view a retro-gression.'[73]

Yet because the use of the leitmotif presumes that a musical phrase can repeatedly evoke the same response, Schooling was finally able partly to resolve the problem by extending the notion to include the medium of colour.

So much for science. An exact physical equivalence between colour and sound expected the existence of a common principle or set of natural laws; but the longed-for advance from analogy to exact connection remained elusive.

In the programmatic aesthetics of visual artists, these scientific experiments, which held their own fascination, could at least be alluded to; though here the need was more often only to suggest similarities between the arts rather than to discover their common principle. Vocabulary alone could easily be used to establish analogy, and the titles of Whistler's paintings—'Harmonies' and 'Symphonies'—are an obvious example. Lady Archibald Campbell, disciple of E. W. Godwin and Aesthetic synthetiser, whose activities have been described in the previous chapter, wrote in *Rainbow-Musick*:

'That there is one vocabulary in use expressive of all the fine Arts is significant of their Oneness; and if we study, separate, and compare the fine Art sisterhood individually, we see that the exactitude of treatment demanded from the one fits as directly the requirements of the other, the science of harmony being pre-eminent over all.'[74]

But Lady Archibald's 'science of harmony' can be verified only in terms of a similarity of method and description among the arts, and, like some heavenly Platonic idea, is darkly apprehended only in its phenomenal instances.

In his very qualified introduction to Rimington's book, Herkomer cast some doubt upon a theory that claimed to have found a precise connection, and suggested for the Colour-Organ a less ambitious role. The contemplation of pure colour sequences 'without form' would stimulate a painter's colour sense, by acting as a 'tonic' for his sensibility:

'To sit at this instrument and improvise for half an hour whilst watching the ever varying combinations of colour on the screen produced by the playing, is not only an unspeakable delight, but of real health-giving effect on the sense of colour. How much more valuable as a stimulant is mobile colour than the fixed colours of a rug, which the eye gets accustomed to, and which thereby act no longer *as a tonic*.'[75]

Herkomer will allow only the psychological affinity between the effects of colour and music *felt* by artists and musicians, that accounts for common terms of expression such as 'note' and 'tone'. Nevertheless there was a significance in his contributing this preface, and a discussion of the context of experiment and belief out of which Rimington's strange invention arose provides a further frame of reference to account for Herkomer's own experiments in the Pictorial-Musical plays.

If Herkomer's comments on Rimington's ideas were very sketchy and relied on received formulas—'Mr Rimington's mobile colour system seems to me a method to enable one to *see sound* and *hear colour*', Rimington himself betrayed a strong antipathy to what had previously been advanced aesthetics, in particular, even now, to the theories of Impressionism. His ideas were still rooted in a conviction of nature as norm and absolute, and showed a more than eighteenth-century confidence in the monistic simplicity of representation.

'Within the last twenty or thirty years, however, a desire to study and enjoy colour for its own sake has sprung up, and the art of painting has tended somewhat to devote itself to the production of pictures in which colour is the chief factor, and Whistler and others, with some appreciation of musical analysis, have gone so far as to call their pictorial works "harmonies" and "symphonies". But in most pictures colour has necessarily remained subservient, to some extent, to their subjects, and in any case a picture cannot give more than one colour scheme, or the solution of a very few problems in colour within the boundaries of its frame. Once painted, moreover, that scheme, harmony or symphony, or whatever the artist may call it, remains fixed and unaltered. At most it is a chord or two of colour, or a single colour phrase, even though much may be sacrificed in expression of the subject of the picture, or even in truth to nature, to make that chord or phrase harmonious and interesting.'[76]

But the question of linear colour change within a single pictorial scene Herkomer had already encountered in the problems of theatrical representation.

By the turn of the century mystical beliefs such as theosophy were playing a major part in the search by suggesting that the simultaneous stimulation of more than one sense could produce a manifestation of an ultimate creative force, the hidden spirituality within the material representations of art. Revelation would come through participation in the artistic event. Rimington's bizarre machine was used to attempt at least one such moment: the catastrophic performance of *Prometheus*, the *magnum opus* of the Russian composer and mystic Scriabin, at Carnegie Hall in 1914. This work, which in its entirety was to require some two thousand performers, was Scriabin's first step towards the realisation of a colossal 'Mystery', which by synthetising every sense in a ritual experience involving performers and audience together (even perfume was to be used), might initiate a spiritual transformation of the world. Scriabin's 'Mystery' extended the Wagnerian concept of revelation through participation, while placing less emphasis on the mythic or allegorical elements of pattern and drama, and shifting the attention to abstract spirituality.

Nor is it surprising to find the pioneer of non-objective painting, Wassily Kandinsky, writing in 1909 a play called *Yellow Sand* or *The Giants*, which with its directions for music, staging and the use of coloured lights was yet another attempt to synthetise the arts in terms of a semi-abstract, semi-symbolic theatrical representation. Kandinsky, like Mondriaan, reinforced his belief in abstraction with mystic doctrine from theosophy and the teachings of Rudolf Steiner; but for him the connection between media could only be established in terms of emotion or spirituality, and not through scientific principle. Even a 'construction' depends not on distribution of mass or geometry but on things inexpressible and innate.

Kandinsky's theatre made use of three elements: musical movement, pictorial movement and artistic dance movement (he admired Isadora Duncan). As pictorial composition is made up of form and design, so his stage composition uses those three elements to create a 'counterpoint of movement', working within the dimension of time. As Kandinsky himself put it, movement and design had been added to Scriabin's Colour-Music:[77] contributions towards a spiritual transformation, formal dictates that relate to the justifications for abstraction. 'The question is not whether the coincidental outer form is violated, but only, if its quality depends on the artist's need of certain forms irrespective of reality pattern.'[78]

An artist like Kandinsky is concerned to express *universals*—this becomes the main reason for abstraction and, although he perpetuates the notion that music is the most spiritual of the arts, there is as basis for his theory the idea that the bringing together of different art forms reveals a universal closer to the ultimate, each medium still retaining its own unique characteristics. And if each colour does make its own impression, or give out its own vibration, then the human faculty must be spiritually tuned to receive that message. Thus

'Even the simplest effect varies in quality. The eye is attracted by light colours and still more by the lightest, warmest ones. Vermilion attracts and stimulates like the flame eternally craved for by all men. The bright yellow of a lemon hurts the eye after a while, as a shrill trumpet may disturb the ear. The eye becomes restless, is unable to fix its gaze for any length of time, and seeks distraction and rest in blue and green.'[79]

Form, although 'nothing but the separating lines between surfaces', also contains its own 'inner' meaning, known as 'necessity' or 'the eternally objective'.

Any discussion of the several versions of synaesthesia, the experience defined by Gombrich as 'the splashing over of impressions from one sense modality to another',[80] must have to do with relationships; for each version searches for a basis on which they may be founded, whether in mysticism, physics or aesthetics. It can be called a search for language. When serious artists or critics investigate these questions, they face one immediate problem: how to estimate the value or effect of a sense impression. There are two solutions to their dilemma. One is through an expressionist theory, which presumes an innate value within the medium; most often this is colour, sometimes it is form. This value will still operate, or operate even better, when freed from its established context or language. The other solution presumes that language is always present. Although subverted or parodied, the effect of the work of art still depends upon the remembered language or habit, which is only temporarily threatened or suspended—some accounts of cubism depend upon this. It is a system of alternatives.[81]

An objection to expressionist theory must be that if each element possesses its separate innate value, then the *language* of art must be very limited: a supposition that can be discounted by a simple comparison between disparate kinds of art; for it is one of the interests of the study of art that there should be differences to discover. An even stronger objection, which results from this, is that expressionist theory ignores structure as a component or control of the whole. *All* expressionist theory breaks down when it has to presume a connection, both innate and formal, between not only kinds of sensation but also between sensation and its apprehension, and yet cannot admit some idea of language or conventional matrix.

In the notion of a new art of Colour-Music, there lies a telling aesthetic cul-de-sac, both avant-garde and anachronistic at the same time. The Wagnerian example, on the other hand, was readily assimilated by revolutionary artists in the furthering of new directions. Kandinsky seized on the 'spirituality' of a pure medium.

'His famous "leitmotif" is an attempt to emphasise heroic personalities beyond theatrical expedience, as make-up and light effects. He employs a definite "leit" motive, which is a pure musical medium. This motive is, so to speak, a musically expressed spiritual atmosphere which precedes the hero, to effect a spiritual radiation felt from afar.'[82]

The film director Eisenstein, who produced *The Valkyrie* at the Bolshoi, wrote:

'Wagner proved to be a quite natural step in my creative path.
'In Wagnerian opera I particularly appreciate the epic quality of the theme, the romanticism of the subject and the surprising pictorial nature of the music, which calls for poetic and visual embodiment. But what most attracted me in Wagner were his opinions on synthetic spectacle

8

which are to be found scattered throughout the great composer's theoretical works. And the very nature of Wagner's music drama confronts producers with the task of creating internal unity of sound and sight to the production. 'The problem of the synthesis of the arts is of vital concern to cinematography, the field in which I am principally engaged. Men, music, light, landscape, colour and motion brought into one integrated whole by a single piercing emotion, by a single theme and idea—this is the aim of modern cinematography.'[83]

Eisenstein, polymath that he was, knew the *Farbenlehre* too, but when investigating the possibilities of 'chromophonic' montage, asserted the ultimate control of the artist over his material, denied the existence of higher laws that govern relationships, and finally decided against a mystic explanation of colour value.

'This means that *we do not obey some "all pervading law" of absolute "meanings" and correspondences between colours and sounds—and absolute relations between these and specific emotions*, but it does mean that *we decide which colours and sounds will best serve the given assignment or emotion as we need them.*
'Of course, the "generally accepted" interpretation may serve as an impetus, and an effective one at that, in the construction of the colour-imagery of the drama.
'But the law laid down here will not legalise any absolute correspondence "in general", but will demand that consistency in a definite tone-colour key running through the whole work must be given by an imagery structure in strict harmony with the work's theme and idea.'[84]

It is hardly surprising then that he should have devoted so much of his energy searching for a grammar for the language of film.

And there is another way in which the cinema fulfilled an earlier quest. It had been a common belief (one that even Kandinsky inherited) that the essential difference between music and painting was that painting could only represent one instant at a time, whereas music could only be durational. In the art of the cinema these opposites are finally reconciled.

Although there is, to be honest, little in his previous career to suggest the real inevitability of the progression, it is at least fitting that Herkomer should end by experimenting with film.[85] In October 1913 he read to the Playgoers' Club a short paper entitled 'About Cinemas', announcing at the same time that he had founded with his son Siegfried the Herkomer Film Company. Between then and his death in the spring of 1914, the company was to make at least nine films at new studios constructed out of the remains of the old theatre, which were later sold to the actor A. E. Matthews. Unfortunately it is almost certain that no copies of these have survived, and all we have to suggest the kind of work that Herkomer produced are a few stills, some uninformative public statements and interviews, and their titles (in themselves sufficient indication of subject-matter): *A Highwayman's Honour*, which took ten months to make and involved the burning down of a cottage, *The Old Woodcarver* (a prose synopsis of which was published), *The Grit of a Dandy*, *Love in a Teashop*, and *The White Witch*. The films were obviously for the most part melodramas, adventure stories, or costume dramas reminiscent in period and setting of the Pictorial-Musical plays, and probably often featuring the already established open-air pursuit. Herkomer played the leading parts himself, and would accompany their showing with his own organ music.

The company was inaugurated as a campaign for both moral and technical improvement.* For instance,

'An entertainment need not necessarily consist only of constant thrills, and excitements and sensations, and the feeling that is growing against these forms is one of the best signs of our times.'[86]

The suggestion that the manager of a picture theatre should suit his programmes to each class of audience—one for the rich, one for the poor, one for the old, one for the young—is confirmation of Herkomer's extreme and ineradicable understanding of social convention. The proposed technical improvements were slight enough too.

'I should think the black and white artist never had such a chance as now, with the cinema at his side. . . .'[87]
'But my great ideal is to present films from the artist's point of view. At present almost all suffer from the somewhat crude realism of the camera. What I want is less realism and more art. Some of the films one sees are enough to make an artist weep. Those awful continuous greys—those foreground figures, sometimes dazzling white, other times a dense black! It needs an artist to superintend the lighting of a film. It is just the same with the setting of the scenes. Too frequently it dominates the picture when it should be nothing more than an accessory, just as the artist uses a landscape background for figures.'[88]

Just as he had approached scenic design from the point of view of the artist (for all he minimised the importance of painting), and had produced on stage what were essentially a series of panoramas,

* For a more generous assessment, see Rachael Low, *The History of the British Film, 1906–14*, I, 1949, 105–06: 'The historical significance of his film activities lies not in artistic or commercial achievement, but rather in his position as a link between socially accepted culture and the still vulgar "art of the people".'

Herkomer considered the potential of the cinema in terms of *composition* and *arrangement* alone; apparently unaware of sequence or even perspective, as before he could only offer vague affirmations of the 'natural' and the 'real'.

'Do I think the moving picture tends to develop and improve a love of art in the people? I do—most decidedly do because as an artist I look at the film from the point of view of the artist and what, as a rule, do I find? A perfect study in black and white, of all that is beautiful in nature. Why, there are thousands of people who never look at nature, who never realise its marvels, who never see its beauties—and who will never see them unless they are brought right under their noses. And that, to my mind is where the Kinematograph is paramount, for it is gradually educating the people to love "the thing beautiful" and revealing to them a storehouse of knowledge that is interesting as well as lovely. Therefore it must tend to develop and improve a love of art even in the uncultured. How does the artist regard the Kinematograph? I speak as an artist when I say that kinematography *is* an art, and I am absolutely lost in admiration of the beautiful settings, the perfect acting, the wonderful light and shade, and above all the splendid stage management one sees in so many moving pictures. It almost goes without saying, therefore, that the kinematograph is and must be regarded by every artist as a great and real help in his work. The moving picture is action emphasised in pictorial form. It is nature revivified. And, as such, it should prove of the utmost service to the art student.'[89]

Although Herkomer did in fact prophesy something like television and stressed the education potential of film (his dislike of literature comes out very strongly here), as before, new media and new methods fail to provoke in him thoughts of new messages, new subjects. Energy, ingenuity, versatility cannot be ends in themselves, and Herkomer's myopia and conventionality once again prove disastrous.* If the plays had simplified the example of Wagner to the point of banality, if the theories of Colour-Music had merely been intriguing, so the discovery of the cinema, late as it was, was used only to confirm principles held for a lifetime.

Yet he had come so close to real connections. What was the variable proscenium after all but a way of suiting perspective to subject, that is, of making proportion relevant as in a painting but

* But not, it should be stressed, his remarkable curiosity. For instance, 'It is now some twenty years since Mr Muybridge came down to me to lecture to my students on animal locomotion, bringing his camera with him; and a most interesting demonstration it was. Those photographs were a great revelation, and were probably the beginning of the picture-film of today, hidden though it was from the mind of man at that moment.' (Letter to *The Daily Telegraph*, 12 December 1912.)

also allowing that relevance to change and develop?* And that is just what the cinema can do so concisely, indeed what it must do through the simple operation of the panorama, the close-up and the tracking shot. In England G. A. Smith was using close-up as early as 1900,[90] and the refinement of the technique until it became part of the acknowledged elemental grammar of film is, in all histories and legends, credited to D. W. Griffith.

Wagnerism attempted to bridge the gap between audience and spectacle not by involving audience within it but by eliminating the most obvious barriers within the auditorium and uniting all elements towards a single response. The search for a correlation of sound and colour also suggested a total coherence in the work, and in responses to it. The cinema, as Eisenstein above all realised, immediately provides an answer—it is simply unable to operate in any other way. It is well known that early film-makers and theoreticians anticipated the incorporation of music and colour before either was really technically feasible, and experiments in pre-recorded music (a different matter from the semi-improvised accompaniment of a piano player) and the tinting of black and white film began very early on. It is just possible that Herkomer, who did after all dislike sub-titles ('. . . often a subterfuge to escape representing action'),[91] who realised that the cinema would require a new kind of acting ('No eye-rolling!'), and who always maintained his faith in the visual image, was groping towards such perceptions; but it seems unlikely.

'The moving picture is *the* thing of the future. . . . A well projected image on the screen requires so little elucidation and conveys so much more in a clearer way than the written or spoken word. And we all love pictures don't we?'[92]

Significantly, when Eisenstein attacked the suggestion, put forward with statistical backing, that the natural proportion for a painting was the rectangle, he did so by expressing contempt for the habits of a school perfectly exemplified by Herkomer's early narrative paintings:

'The statistical paradox of Mr Jones derives probably from an undue weight placed upon compositional proportions of the nineteenth-century pre-impressionistic period—the worst period of painting—the "narrative" type of painting. Those second- and third-rate paintings, right off a

---

* Herkomer was not alone in thinking of this device. Steele Mackaye patented his 'Proscenium-Adjuster' in the US in 1893. See P. W. Mackaye, *Epoch. The Life of Steele Mackaye*, 2 vols, 1927 and A. N. Vardac, *Stage to Screen*, 1949.

progressive highroad of painting development, and even today far surpassing in volume the new schools of painting, abundant even in the neighbourhood of Picasso and Léger as petty-bourgeois oleographs in most concierge offices of the world!

'In this "narrative" group of painting the 1:1.5 proportion is certainly predominant, but this fact is absolutely unreliable if considered from the point of view of pictorial composition. These proportions in themselves are "borrowed goods"—entirely unconnected with pictorial space organisation, which is a painting problem. These proportions are bare-facedly borrowed—not to say stolen!—from—the stage.

'The *stage composition* each of these pictures intentionally or unintentionally reproduces, a process in itself quite logical, since the pictures of this school are occupied not with pictorial problems, but with "representing scenes" —a painting purpose even formulated in *stage* terms!'[93]

More even than this, Eisenstein indicates the place of photography in this complex story with a breadth of reference unknown (or perhaps inaccessible) to Herkomer:

'And from the moment in which painting liberates itself by an impressionistic movement, turning to purely pictorial problems, it abolishes every form of aperture and establishes, as an example and an ideal, the framelessness of a Japanese impressionistic drawing. And, symbolic as it may be, it is the moment for the dawn of—photography. Which, extraordinary to remark, conserves in its later metempsychosis, the moving picture, certain (*vital* this time) traditions of this period of the maturity of one art (painting) and the infantilism of its successor (photography).'[94]

Unable to move beyond nineteenth-century principles of realistic and narrative painting, Herkomer fell back, as always, on the morality of subject matter and the idea of harmonious composition.

Peter Wollen has written of the cinema:

'It poses in the most acute form the problem of the relationship between the different arts, their similarities and differences, the possibilities of translation and transcription; all the questions asked of aesthetics by the Wagnerian notion of the *gesamtkunstwerk* and the Brechtian critique of Wagner, questions which send us back to the theory of synaesthesia, to Lessing's *Laocoön* and Baudelaire's *correspondances*.[95]

It is only very recently indeed that critics have begun first to unravel these strands and then to attempt an aesthetic able to confront the advent of film. Among the practitioners of the new art there have been only a very few, possibly only the genius Eisenstein, who have been sufficiently intellectually engaged to investigate and fully comprehend what they were creating.

Put alongside those of the cinema, the conventional resources of the theatre may seem feeble. (Fortunately there were other means of survival; Max Reinhardt, most Wagnerian of all the early modern directors, showed the way in which the picture stage might be destroyed by bringing the drama out into the auditorium where actors and audience intermingle, perhaps even interchange.) If we appropriate Eisenstein's terms again and compare the 'spatial/pictorial' with the 'temporal/pictorial', it is clear that only within the cinematic medium can the second easily be realised. In other words the proscenium theatre cannot make any complex or changing comment on figure (action) and background (situation). To this extent only was Herkomer right to see 'harmony' as the theatre's final achievement, and harmony the early film directors soon discarded as any simple intent. But Herkomer's crude aesthetics never got beyond a sense of the absolute and static criterion of the 'pictorial'. It is salutary to notice how innovations and new ideas in scenic art ran almost exactly parallel to the birth of the cinema, and yet how few of the new theatre designers acknowledged that volcanic event. If it is true that *how* we see affects or even *is* what we see, then here is a reminder that it takes some time for us to realise, if we ever fully do, the extent or nature of the change. For the theatre designer there could be only one way out—the creation of a décor of suggestion rather than of representation, which remained essentially the same in its material construction, but which could change its significance or the 'extent' of its presence; and this is what was achieved in the work of Edward Gordon Craig and Adolphe Appia through the use of fundamental shapes which could change their significance simply by changing their position or through a rearrangement of light. The move, inevitably, was to be towards the abstract and the symbolic, for if photography had altered the purpose of painting, then the cinema would alter not only the purpose of décor but of the whole drama.

The story of Herkomer is perhaps interesting for its oddity more than anything else, but it does, in some ways, provide a tragi-comic allegory of English culture in the visual arts over four decades. The establishment of a patriarchal community essentially immune to outside influences and yet almost totally dependent upon the world for its survival, without even a special doctrine but only an uncritical reverence for craftsmanship, could so easily become a protection for the amateur. Above all, the refusal or inability to theorise is all too often a particularly English characteristic. It is as a part of this long history of obliviousness and delay that Herkomer belongs—an example of curiosity without understanding and competence without originality. It is, as always, only much later that we can trace the true directions and see what was once considered an 'experiment' revealed as a retreat. It is a very English story, for like other immigrants, Herkomer finally emerges as more English than the natives.

IV

A Literary Theatre:
The Lessons of the
Independent Theatre

The inauguration of the Independent Theatre is one of the an-
nunciatory events in the history of naturalism, and as such pre-
figures many of the requirements and methods of our contemporary
theatre. As Eric Bentley long ago remarked, 'to search out all the
naturalism in modern drama we would have to look almost every-
where,'[1] an assumption which has now become the received starting-
point for other studies. Even in the latest revised edition of what was
Drama from Ibsen to Eliot and is now *Drama from Ibsen to Brecht*,
Raymond Williams preserves the closing remark, 'It must be obvious that what is meant by the "rejection of naturalism" is ordinarily a rejection of its earliest particular conventions';[2] but by
making a distinction between the naturalist 'assumption', which
survives, and the naturalist 'conventions', which change, he is only
furthering what was, in its origins, a similar awareness of the
pervasive power of this nineteenth-century idea of what the drama
can do. In which connection Williams also makes overt acknowledgement of the social determinants that are always, if sometimes
invisibly, a presence in his book.

'There have been hardly any difficulties with naturalism in the majority
middle-class theatre and its derivations; it is a self-evident, though to
others mainly boring, tradition. But important naturalist drama developed,
historically, in just that period of liberal revolt against orthodox liberation,
of individual revolt against the form of bourgeois life. Its means were the
"free theatres" which sprang up across Europe (often interwoven with
nationalism but still connecting with each other) between 1860 and 1900.
What was becoming available as a style was used to push an action
beyond the ordinary terms of the beliefs on which it depended. The self-
evident reproductive element in naturalism was joined by the alternate
emphasis of direct exposure. The passion for evident truth burst beyond
the forms of self-evident truths.'[3]

Although Bentley's treatment of a changing form is more abstract
than that of Williams, who frequently alludes to the tensions within
a changing European society, both would undoubtedly agree about
the lasting significance of naturalist expectations. But in England
there is more that remains to be explored—in particular the ways
these were nurtured in an atmosphere of revolt. Less reassuring
circumstances of contemporary tactic and reaction have been passed
by in the interests of historical continuity.

In this account then one preoccupation will be with supplying
further historical evidence in support of an already established
conviction about the resilience of the naturalist drama, with the
repertoire of the Independent Theatre as instance. The organisation
of such a theatre is product and part of a social context (obviously

including both audience—what they expected and what was expected of them—and the mechanics of staging) which can either open up possibilities or shut them off.

The simple justification for the whole is that theatre is by definition an un-private art. Not only is it a corporate creation, involving writers, directors, actors and whatever other artists are needed to put something upon a stage; without an audience it cannot, in any normal sense, be said to exist at all.

These inescapable conditions provide the historian of the nineteenth-century theatre, who is in any case restricted to contemporary verbal descriptions for the most part, with a particularly demanding task. Although the method used here might appear simple—direct reportage of what was said, and presumably felt, at the time, a list of reviews—what was discussed is not necessarily what was suspected, known, or pursued, and there is an inevitable (and easily justifiable) temptation: to under-estimate the contemporary impact of what may now seem to be myopic or wrong-headed responses, or alternatively to find in them too many indications for the future. The desire to find a tradition is always there. Allowance too has to be made for those journalists who were expected to provide regular excitement in their weekly column. For such reasons a study of this kind must on occasion make a rigorous attempt to maintain the synchronic view, and produce only the closest possible documentation of critical moments.

The twentieth-century need for an art that above all confronts or even anticipates social crisis is shared by both artist and critic, but it can become a paradoxical drive in the theatre. Often reformers urge that the art can only *resume* its centrality by *developing* its forms. It is said that the survival of the theatre depends upon its social position (at its crudest, the 'habit' of theatre-going, at its more ambitious, the communal event), yet its performances must be startling, awakening, even shocking. It must belong to the society that it is attempting to change; that is, it would sometimes seem that the theatre must move in two directions at once. Probably the most interesting and important aspect of the Independent Theatre is that it was the first major, and reasonably permanent, organisation to emerge in England as an answer to this partly economic dilemma.

Whereas the previous essays have been concerned with the activities of individuals and the special social resources available to them in carrying out their schemes, an account of the Independent Theatre must take a different approach from the start, because it was a formally created institution, a Society, finally a Limited Company, organised by a group of people who shared only *similar* concerns and alignments. Supporters of the Independent Theatre were not united by background or nationality or even by interests outside the theatre, although, it must be said, to wage war against Farce and Melodrama was very much to attack the spirit of the age, and advocates of new means and new forms (or of the revival of ancient forms) were united if only in their self-conscious alienation from the popular mainstream.

The Independent Theatre lasted from 1891 to 1898—an important period of time, its importance only partly due to the influence of the Independent Theatre itself. It was not always at the very centre of things, although its repertoire and the disagreements among its members do reflect changing tastes in a fluctuating situation. It is as the most prominent *case-history* that it is to be considered, as model or as mirror; and although some twenty-eight plays (some of them one-acters) were produced in the seven years, it will be necessary to examine closely only those whose selection stands out as symptomatic.

Before considering repertoire, there is a need to determine how the Independent Theatre conceived of itself at the outset. One immediate problem here is in identifying a single controlling personality. Although he must take most of the credit for its foundation and its subsequent organisation, J. T. Grein never operated without a supporting committee made up largely of people with ideas of their own. There are now two lives of Grein—his wife's memoirs (written with considerable outside assistance),[4] and a long biography by Father N. H. G. Schoonderwoerd,[5] which pays much attention to Grein's relations with the continent, and in particular with his native Holland; yet the overriding impression conveyed by both books is that Grein's energy was primarily directed toward matters of execution and was not backed up by a consistent critical taste. In this he differed from his colleagues—from George Moore and Shaw, for example. Nor was Grein a significant or even particularly competent professional writer: his own plays are weak, conventional affairs, his journalism lacks edge.

The most useful approach may be to examine the slogans and catch-phrases associated with the Independent Theatre and their particular fields of reference. While staging a play cannot really be divorced from 'interpreting' it, having ideas about it—a major difference from Herkomer and Godwin, who had been chiefly involved in new methods of presentation—the staging of Independent Theatre productions attracted almost no attention at all: the play and, to a much lesser extent, the acting was the thing. So the subject of this chapter will initially require a switch of attention from designers to writers; from the theatre as 'mood' or as 'picture' towards the theatre as 'literature'.

The Independent Theatre laid claim first and foremost to being a 'literary' theatre; and the nature of that claim will have to be investigated, for the 'literary drama' as a phrase in polemic was sometimes used to elevate the status of the text, and sometimes, in a wider context, merely as a term of approbation. Then again to the general public (who didn't have much to do with it) the Independent Theatre was regarded as a 'naturalist' theatre (and therefore, such being the semantic overlay involved, as belonging within the wider traditions of realism). The starting-point must be a look at the current meanings and applications of that difficult term.

In his preface to *Thérèse Raquin* (1873) and later in *Le Naturalisme au Théâtre* (1881) Zola had laid down powerful prescriptions for the naturalist drama; empirical observation rather than constructed plot, psychological study founded on scientific method. All aspects of theatre—text, acting, décor in particular—would need to undergo revolutionary change. Whereas in the classic drama, because mankind is presented in abstraction, and situation is of metaphysical not historical relevance, the conventions of an idealised acting area and non-representative backcloths are appropriate, the new drama, in keeping with the preoccupations of the age, would require realistic sets; which, to Zola, meant the exact reproduction of an actual or typical locale. Characters and their actions could only be explored and understood when examined within the context which conditioned their behaviour. Décor would no longer 'represent', it would 'be'; it would strive to reproduce as exact an illusion of environment as possible, to its precise dimensions; it would be photographic.

'Le décor exact s'est imposé de lui-même, peu à peu, comme le costume exact. Ce n'est pas une affaire de mode, c'est une affaire d'évolution humaine et sociale.'[6]

'Tel est le rôle de décors. Ils élargissent le domaine dramatique en mettant la nature elle-même au théâtre, dans son action sur l'homme.'[7]

The logic of the argument derived from Zola's implicit and explicit comparisons with the novel: as location is to the novel, so décor is to the theatre. It had two main concomitants: first, settings would tend to be confined to single rooms, and domestic rooms at that, consolidating the idea of auditorium as the 'fourth wall', and secondly, character and action would derive from the setting, with behaviour motivated by what was possible, credible and normal within it; the actors would no longer be required to further the illusion attempted by the setting, but would instead be conditioned by it.

Zola's ideas were not accurately carried out until 1887, when a gas-works clerk called André Antoine founded the Théâtre Libre, an amateur company that presented the plays of young French writers as well as Ibsen, Strindberg and Tolstoy. Zola's patronage helped the Théâtre Libre to become an immediate sensation, and it soon became the archetype of the anti-establishment theatre in France.

Antoine fervently believed in Zola's prescriptions. For example an early production, Tolstoy's *La Puissance des Ténèbres* (10 February 1888) was a revelation for one contemporary critic because:

' On voyait pour la première fois, sur une scène française, un décor et des costumes empruntés aux habitudes quotidiennes de la vie russe, sans enjolivements d'opéra-comique, sans ce goût du clignant et du faux qui semble inhérent à l'atmosphère du théâtre.'[8]

Antoine's loathing of the lavish formality of the Comédie Française was epitomised in a lambast against their production of *La Parisienne*, which complained that its set was, simply, uninhabitable.[9] His own productions relied on real furniture and properties (even real sides of beef in *Les Bouchers*) and created sound and lighting effects that were as natural as possible.

That he should have been impressed at the same time with the Meiningen Company, most admired for its spectacle, its size, and not by any means for its domestic interiors, may seem contradictory. But as he expressed in an enthusiastic public letter to Sarcey, what Antoine found to admire in the Meiningen was 'ensemble-acting', not just the harmonious manipulation of large numbers, but that each member of the ensemble was an actor in the fullest sense, however minor his role, creating a visible character on stage.[10] Antoine's formula for naturalist acting amounted to a simple but absolute mimesis, but when put into practice by his predominantly amateur company, it led to misunderstanding, first in France and then, more severely, in England.

Before the visit of the Théâtre Libre to London in 1889, English theatre-goers' knowledge of Zola had been confined to popular and highly melodramatic adaptations, in particular Charles Reade's *Drink*, a version of *L'Assommoir*.[11] French adaptations were considered more subtle than English ones in their substitution of sensationalism for natural truths, yet they too crudified the broad strokes of the novelist. Frederick Wedmore, for instance, roundly condemned both. Of the French production of *L'Assommoir*, in January 1879, he wrote:

'As the labour of a serious, although often a mistaken artist in literature, it lost greatly in the drama . . . it lost its balance, its reasonableness, its natural sequence, and it became melodrama. . . . So it is that what was in the book a true and elaborate, though often painful and repulsive study—in which the art of fiction preached a lesson with a power denied to the mere wielder of statistics or platform furtherer of philanthropy— so it is that the good study becomes in part a vulgar melodrama, such as might have been written without the aid of M. Zola's penetration and his unfaltering plainness.'[12]

And of *Drink*, first produced at the Princess's in June of the same year:

'The interest of a rude excitement having been substituted for that of a development of character through circumstance, why—except for the chance of retaining the novel stage effects of the *lavoir* and the water pails—invite us to suppose that the scene passes in France instead of East London?'[13]

Some slight interest was shown in Zola's two important theoretical statements, *Le Naturalisme au Théâtre* and *Nos Auteurs Dramatiques*. An article in *Progress* in 1884 noted that:

'The coming dramatist must study not man in general but individuals, each in his *milieu*. That *milieu* must be reproduced with fidelity hitherto unattempted by the scene-painter, the costumier, the property-man.'[14]

And it focused some of its attention upon the relation of décor to play and character to structure.

'His action will be too simple to require any of the *ficelles* of Scribe and Sardou. Acts and scenes will be more or less arbitrary divisions. He will drop his curtain upon a mere conversation whenever his characters have said all they have to say. Each personage will speak a language appropriate to himself, moulded to suit his character and the dialogue will be distinguished by a plentiful lack of wit.'

But prolonged attention to his dramatic theory was rare— obviously discussions of Zola concentrated on the novels, with only occasional allusions to the plays. A famous if eccentric article, W. S. Lilly's pious castigation of the novels entitled 'The New Naturalism', opened with a justifiably scathing account of the Paris production of *Nana* (1881). He described the nine tableaux: the first was an outdoor scene with a real waterfall, after which

'. . . came a drawing room furnished *à la Japonaise*, a species of upholstery just then in the height of fashion; after that a racecourse with real horses, and then a boudoir hung with real blue satin. In the eighth *tableau* a noble town house was burnt to the ground before our eyes. The ninth and last was a perfect copy of a room in the *Grand Hotel* in which Nana lay dying of confluent smallpox.'[15]

But by associating the over-ambitious realistic settings in *Nana* with quotations from Zola himself he was able to misrepresent the whole theory and reduce it to absurdity.

'. . . the experimental drama must be a material evocation of life on the stage; and who can now doubt the possibility of effecting this by the art of the scene-painter and the upholsterer? No: "après les décors si puissants de relief, si surprenants de vérité" (possibly M. Zola was thinking of the nine *tableaux* in *Nana* which I have described) "on ne peut nier la possibilité d'évoquer à la scène la réalité des milieux." So too the language must be real—the language of the street—*un morceau de rue*. The old notion of a style differing from that of common life, more sonorous, more nervous, more highly pitched, more finely cut, is an abomination to M. Zola, and it must be allowed that he scrupulously avoids it.'[16]

This was the prelude to a concentrated indictment of the morality and subject-matter of the novels, and the naturalistic theatre was an obvious and easy butt.

Conversely, a sympathetic involvement in the trammels of French realism endowed the better-informed with a receptiveness to the new possibilities within Zola's dramatic theory. French critics had been perturbed by his automatic transference to the drama of a technique that they thought to have originated in theories of the novel. In 1887 Theodore Childs, an American journalist and friend of Henry James, reported their objections from Paris for the benefit of an English readership: whereas the novel was an analytic form composed of an accumulation of contrasts, the drama was synthetic, its characters created through concentration and simplification. Childs countered with Zola's own continual comparison of the art of Corneille and Molière with that of Scribe and Sardou.

'In the dramatic formula of the seventeenth century we find long descriptions, minute narratives, interminable analysis. In the formula of Scribe and Sardou we find no description, no analysis, nothing but action and incident, the desire to amuse continually and rapidly. The spectators of Corneille, Molière, and Regnard, were content to listen; the spectators of today demand the action itself and not the description of it; they want to see the characters going and coming and living in their natural *milieu*. In the satisfaction of this demand dramatic art has gained in scenic reality, but it has lost in superior truth, because the facts have been allowed to predominate at the expense of the personages who have become conventional puppets; in other words, in the piece with a plot there remains nothing but action, while the study of character has disappeared. The whole ideal of Zola is to keep and improve the framework of reality, and to restore, in the composition of the piece, the simplicity of the classical writers, their psychological and physiological analysis, and their secret of allowing the idea to develop by itself from the very logic of the sentiments of the characters. In short Zola regards the stage as a living picture where man is the most important element, where facts are determined only by acts, and where the eternal subject remains the creation of original figures animated by human passions.'[17]

Childs' enthusiasm was such that he even justified the realistic paraphernalia of the French production of *L'Assommoir*: 'the old melodrama can be transformed by exactness in scenery and characters, and by the presentation of a simple and popular story in a framework of reality.'

Although information about attempts to establish a naturalist theatre in Paris had filtered through, the English theatre, coyly apprehensive of French profanity (even when, like *Drink*, translated into melodrama), was still unprepared for exposure to its triumphant realisation in the productions of Antoine; and when his company visited London for a season in 1889, advance notices concentrated upon the reputedly scandalous repertoire,

'the Théâtre Libre being the happy hunting ground of the ultra-realistic or fin-de-siècle dramatist who specially affects the horrible and the revolting.'[18]

The company had been invited to London by Mayer, impresario and owner of the Royalty Theatre who, although more accustomed to presenting French classics, had been struck by Antoine's production of Hennique's *La Mort du Duc d'Enghien*. Mayer paid well, and Antoine was pleased to go, for his visit enabled him to study the London theatre at first hand (surprisingly, he was especially impressed by Irving's *Macbeth*). But the English did not respond to his techniques with the reverence traditionally accorded the French classical companies. Mayer was interviewed in the *Pall Mall Gazette*:

'*Interviewer*: And what about mise-en-scène?—For that is the point in which M. Antoine's originality chiefly manifests itself.
'*Mr Mayer*: The *Duc d'Enghien* will be mounted exactly as in Paris, Antoine's genius as a stage manager does not run in the direction of costly display. As for dresses, they will be of course brought over from Paris; and mark this, they are not mere fancy-ball dresses, but actual costumes of the period, made and worn in the year 1804 or thereabouts.
'*Interviewer*: "The force of realism can no further go!" '[19]

When interviewed by George Moore who, for once, allowed his own personality to be subjugated, Antoine offered himself as manager rather than as naturalist reformer, placing the emphasis upon texts rather than upon means of production.

'The aim of the Théâtre Libre is to encourage every writer to write for the stage, and, above all, to write what he feels inclined to write and not what he thinks a manager will produce. I produce anything in which there is a grain of merit, quite irrespective of any opinion I may form of what the public will think of it, and anything a known writer brings me, and exactly as he hands it to me. If he writes a monologue of half-a-dozen pages, the actor must speak those half-dozen pages word for word. His business is to write the play: mine to have it acted.'[20]

Most of this interview was taken up with details of his own life and the history of his theatre, with only a single excited exclamation from Antoine:

'. . . tomorrow night you will see how they act—no screaming, no taking the stage, no playing to the gallery—real life is the art of the Théâtre Libre.'

Certainly it was not until the art of the Théâtre Libre had actually been experienced that the papers began to make the right connections:

'What naturalism on the stage means, in theory, is the throwing overboard of the conventions—no "points", no "curtains", no "crisis", very often no "dénouement", simply a page cut, without erasure or addition from the book of life.'[21]

'They belong however to the realistic school, and represent the latest tendencies and developments of theatrical art. Whether that art will commend itself to the English public, or indeed to the French public, before which it has been set for a couple of years is doubtful. Last night's entertainment, though well received in the main, provoked at least as much astonishment as interest.'[22]

The dual nature of its 'unconventionality' (subject and technique) was now acknowledged:

'Without any deliberate design on the part of the manager, his theatre soon became a sort of refuge for young dramatists of the most advanced school, whose pieces were too unconventional for the ordinary stage. It must be owned that for some of these productions, 'unconventional' is a very mild term, they were denounced by all but the extremist 'naturalists' as scandalous and repulsive. Others again, were unconventional without impropriety, sinning against nothing but the current formulas of dramatic construction. To the latter class belong 'Jacques Damour' and 'La Mort du Duc d'Enghien', which the enterprise of M. Mayer secured us an opportunity of witnessing on Monday evening.'[23]

The first play that Antoine performed in London was a dramatisation by Hennique of Zola's novel *Jacques Damour*. It had an Enoch Arden theme: a communist exile returns from abroad to find that his wife has betrayed him in his absence. The play was received with moderate approval, and Antoine's performance as the guttural eau-de-vie-drinking 'ouvrier' was highly praised.

Antoine's second offering, *La Mort du Duc d'Enghien*, was acknowledged to be the more interesting work. Much championed by Moore in the years to come, the play made use of a novel method of construction; the three divisions of the piece were entitled not 'acts', but 'tableaux', each tableau presenting a separate episode. In the first, General Ordener brings to his fellow generals Napoleon's order to cross the Rhine and seize the Duc d'Enghien in his neutral territory of Baden; in the second, the Duke's breakfast-party is interrupted by French soldiers and he is arrested; in the third, a court-martial is held in the prison at Vincennes. Construction alone bore the stamp of naturalism, as Archer immediately recognised:

'. . . I am much mistaken if *La Mort du Duc d'Enghien* be not a new departure of great moment. It is an attempt to put an historic episode on the stage in its unvarnished simplicity, without any involution of plot or analysis of motive.'[24]

Unconventional structure drew attention to unusual mise-en-scène. The third act was lit by candlelight alone; with the house-lights turned right out, the actors became barely more than silhouettes. The tribunal sits waiting to cross-examine its prisoner. He enters, but no limelight picks out his face, and he remains in almost total darkness. The cross-examination is heard, the members of the court-martial retire, and the prisoner falls asleep, slumped over the table. A few moments later, a soldier enters and taps him on the shoulder. He is led outside, and a volley of shots is heard.

The grim reality of this scene astonished English audiences:

'The horror of the whole scene and its pathos are indescribable. Had I not seen it, I would not have believed that so great a tragic effect could be produced with such matter-of-fact material—such rigid economy of means.'[25]

Archer commented:

'In the last scene, nothing is left to the imagination but what it claims as its right—for it must be remembered that the most thrilling spectacle in real life will not move us save through sympathetic imagination. The picture presented to the eyes is perfect in its sombre reality. . . . We see the actors' faces only fitfully, as the candle-light happens to fall upon them quite enough . . . if M. Antoine had chosen to posture in a halo of limelight the scene would not have gripped us half so favourably.'*

But one account stands out above all others as a truly searching and inclusive investigation of the dramatic issues raised by the production. This is Henry James' 'After the Play', a fictional dialogue between four members of the audience. Florentia has been bored by the play and Dorriforth attempts to persuade her of its validity.

'*Dorriforth*: Wasn't it a curious, interesting specimen of some of the things that are worth trying: an attempt to sail closer to the real? . . .
'*Florentia*: It was just like any other play—I saw no difference. It had neither a plot, nor a subject, nor dialogue, nor situations, nor scenery, nor costumes, nor acting. . . .
'*Amicia:* It's a *morceau de vie*, as the French say. . . . Though Florentia saw nothing I saw many things in this poor little shabby *Duc d'Enghien*, coming over to our roaring London, where the dots have to be so big on the 'i's', with its barely audible note of originality. It appealed to me, touched me, offered me a poignant suggestion of the way things happen in life.
'*Auberon*: In life they happen clumsily, stupidly, meanly. One goes to the theatre just for the refreshment of seeing them happen in another way—in symmetrical, satisfactory form, with unmistakable effect and just at the right moment.
'*Dorriforth*: It shows how the same cause may produce the most diverse consequences. In this truth lies the only hope of art.'[26]

Dorriforth argues that this 'shabbiness' places extreme responsibility upon the actors, a responsibility that they must be competent to bear. Auberon suggests that it might be possible for a performance to make full use of both acting skills and décor. But the mean ideal remains elusive; as Dorriforth explains, the English situation is such that the clever machinery of stage presentation has assumed the major role and will not be usurped; and pictorial have replaced dramatic values. A comparison builds up between Tree's extravagant production of *The Merry Wives of Windsor* and the austere *La Mort du Duc d'Enghien*.

James' probing discussion accepted Antoine's production on its own terms, passing over the obviously limited resources at his disposal to concentrate upon essentials; something that Archer, despite his interest in Hennique's play, was incapable of doing. When

* Archer's remark that 'the result entirely bears out Professor Herkomer's theory as to the essential identity of pictorial and dramatic truth' shows a confusion about *kinds* of realism. Antoine's interiors approximated to the real with a very different accuracy from that obtained by Herkomer's landscapes and vistas.

he replied to James' piece, prefatory apologia had first to be made—which suggests that a vital part of Antoine's achievement had been overlooked.

'It needed exquisite mounting and consummate acting; it was put on the stage in the most rough and ready fashion, and played by a company of well-meaning amateurs. . . . For all that . . . it interested and moved one. It showed a character in the grip of destiny, and showed it without any (actual or figurative) limelight effect. Now, is not this what we want in the drama of the future—a simplification of mechanism, a diminution of artifice?'*[27]

Still, prompted by the episodic structure of the play, Archer could now begin to identify, however tentatively, the beginnings of a new kind of theatre, comparable with recent experiments in fiction.

'The rhythm seems to have gone out of our lives. Similarly, a drama of scenes instead of acts, a drama without intrigue, without coincidences, without picture poster situations, with no catastrophe, with no solution, with no villain, and perhaps a poor apology for a hero and heroine—such a drama will at first seem formless, purposeless, flaccid. We shall miss the outward, world-struck design, and shall have no eyes at first for inward coherence and unity of idea. A new generation of actors too, will be needed to seize and interpret the new subtleties of character study.'

One of the great frustrations in following Archer's trains of thought is that his considerable ability in observing patterns of aesthetic change are so often mitigated by a too rigid adherence to professional standards, a short memory and a failure to follow through the implications of new phenomena. Here is but one typical example—he was to neglect his own prophecy, and on this occasion

---

* The percipience shown by James' characters in relating staging to play was on the whole rare. Even those who did acknowledge the connection rarely confronted recent developments—compare for instance the out-dated references made by W. J. Lawrence in September 1890. Although he displays a great knowledge of the history of practical theatre, Lawrence stops short at the 'realistic' drawing-rooms of T. W. Robertson's 'cup-and-saucer' comedy, which '. . . marks the limit of artistic progression towards the actual, because the drama, robbed of idealism, has no right of existence. A play, to be an art product, must partake more or less of the beautiful; and beauty cannot exist without an ideal. Left to its own devices, Realism only obtrudes upon us a depressing sense of the ugly and vulgar' ('Realism on the Stage: How Far Permissible?', *Westminster Review*, February 1891, 279), and ends with an excellent example of the stand taken up by idealist reaction.

'Realism is a grateful auxiliary so long as it leaves the imagination unshackled, and remains subservient to the play of action. We must draw the line sharply where it ceases to assimilate with its surroundings, where it inclines to become of itself quite uncontrollable. Illusion is the aim of Art, and Realism is permissible so far as it aids that aim. When Illusion is thrust on one side, Realism, even when reigning in its stead, has not the slightest right of existence.' (Ibid, 288.)

his limited vision was symptomatic of a national tendency. Antoine's specific achievement—the materialisation of the naturalist aesthetic in the actual *staging* of a play, of great importance to the French, was to be only slightly apprehended or absorbed by the English, where even the most interested parties made comparatively little of this aspect of his work. The history of the influence of the naturalist theatre in England indicates the complexity of the routes by which aesthetic theory and example move, and the highly selective ways in which they mature; for closely related to Antoine's work was not only the naturalist doctrine of Zola, whose *novels* were keenly debated in England, but the example of the Meiningen Company, an influence conceded even by Henry Irving, and the very powerful notions of the 'realistic' play, a term that was, unhappily, deployed without reference to the changes that it might offer to the whole theatrical convention.

When the demands for an English Théâtre Libre, resulting in the foundation of the Independent Theatre, again gave the French model a topical interest, its *techniques* had almost become a dead subject. 'Naturalism' had in part become confused with 'Ibsenism', a much more complex and inconsistent body of ideas and associations; Antoine's image was fixed as first and foremost the pioneer of the non-commercial theatre, and it was to remain so.[28]

Although it had provided George Moore with an education in theatrical technique, and although 'naturalism', its origins usually unacknowledged, is found at the root of many of his later pronouncements, its full context was often obscured by the polemical demands of the moment. For the time being Antoine, by describing his achievements and aims, had only seemed to have suggested to Moore a convenient way of uniting his loathing of actors, his disgust with the hierarchy of managers and his admiration for the French drama into a coherent programme. Moore had ended his interview with Antoine with demands strikingly similar to those that were to be put forward by Archer two months later, on his own rather different hobby-horse, in 'A Plea for an Endowed Theatre';[29] still Moore did have the advantage of Antoine as a prototype, an immediate practical example which Archer was too grandiose to discern.

'Then I thought of my country, where actors aspire only to be gentlemen, and where plays are written by those who can write nothing else. We are charitable barbarians, nothing more; thousands are subscribed yearly for the maintenance of indigent nondescripts who call themselves actors; but a pound could not be collected were the object an artistic one—for instance, to found a free theatre in England.'[30]

As early as the 1870s, in an exchange of letters with Bernard Lopez, a retired French playwright, prefacing their jointly written play *Martin Luther*, Moore had expressed his appreciation both of the French romantic dramatists and of exponents of 'le théâtre bien fait' at the expense of all those English poets, from Wordsworth onwards, who had unsuccessfully attempted to revive the poetic drama. Moore writes a dream fantasy in which the astonished ghost of Sheridan speculates on the changed state of the London theatre:

'The novel has improved
The poem too; forward all things have moved,
Except the play. Nay, tell me, how is this?
There must be something serious amiss. . . .
Is vice stamped out, and do you go to church,
And flog your sinning bodies with the birch?
Are drunkenness and prostitution dead,
And human nature now quite perfected?
If such be not the case, why, why then not
Write comedies as I did? Where are thought
And wit?'[31]

At the end of his vision, he is confronted by two naked men, each carrying a large French dictionary. They proffer 'the list of their achievements': a programme of the London theatre, dated 1878, listing eleven theatres and thirteen plays, all of which are French in origin.

The chief interest of these letters, with the young Moore adopting as always a pose of jaundiced sophistication and intent on conveying an impression of considerable knowledge, lies in their unmasking of what was as yet basically a highly conventional taste: it was probably not until 1879 that he became personally acquainted with Zola and, through him, with writers such as Daudet and the Goncourts.

In 1881 Moore collaborated in London with his brother Augustus on a libretto for *Les Cloches de Corneville*; in 1885 a satirical attack on the acting profession was published, *A Mummer's Wife*, and in 1888 there appeared *Confessions of a Young Man*, in which he referred to Théâtre Libre playwrights Catulle Mendès and Théodore de Banville. In the *Confessions*, while continuing to insult the London theatrical establishment, he poured lavish praise on the music-hall:

'. . . better than a *fricassée* of Faust garnished with hags, imps and blue flame; better far better than a drawing room set at the St James', with an exhibition of passion by Mr and Mrs Kendal; better, a million times better than the cheap popularity of Wilson Barrett—an elderly man posturing in a low-necked dress to some poor trull in the gallery.'[32]

The music-hall could be extolled because it was a genuinely *popular* art, and as such very different from the legitimate theatre, where a play's impact was artificially stimulated by the lavish trappings which the public had now come to expect as their right. Because it was on these that hung any kind of commercial success, the stage—Moore wrote anonymously in 1885—could never be regenerated by the establishment of a National Theatre which would have to economise with cut-price settings. The music-hall, where are 'incarnate the life and joys of the living world', was a forcing-ground for a new drama that would grow out of traditional sketches and comic business:

'They would be written simply, without regard to M. Sardou's method of bringing down a curtain; they would be produced with little scenery and few dresses, and their success would therefore be determined by the amount of life they contained.'[33]

And here it seems very likely that he was making an implicit connection with the stand adopted by naturalist theory against the artificial convolutions of formal plot. In the *Confessions* he also returned to a theme touched on in *A Mummer's Wife*, and at that time a subject of general discussion, the newly elevated status of actors, making Mrs Kendal a particular object of attack.

Moore renewed his practical activities in the theatre during the same year, and on 12 April 1888 a group of amateur actors appeared in his one-act play *The Honeymoon in Eclipse* at St George's Hall, a means of production which bore a striking resemblance to that of the Théâtre Libre, also of course an amateur organisation. A reviewer in *The Evening News* recognised the parallel and criticised the actors for not doing justice to the play. Moore came back with a spirited defence.

'In my opinion the view that your critic takes of amateurs in general is a mistaken one; and, bearing in mind the depth of degradation in which our stage is sunk, and the real use that amateurs have been put to in France, and the literature they have brought to light I venture to suggest that this subject is not one that should be at once dismissed as unworthy of consideration and experiment, even if the performance of my play had been less satisfactory.
'Personally I believe that amateurs will prove of real service to those who would break with the soul-wearying conventionalities of the modern stage.'[34]

The spring and summer of 1888 was for Moore a period of rapidly increasing involvement; he reviewed from Paris performances that included de Banville's *Le Baiser*—'the triumph of the Théâtre

Libre'[35]—and reprinted a short article on Dumas fils' play *Francillon*: 'if it be not the best, it is at least the best our age has to give.'[36] Both appeared in *The Hawk*, a scurrilous journal with a surprisingly eminent list of contributors (Clement Scott, Bernard Shaw, A. B. Walkley, Justin McCarthy, James Runciman, Robert Hichens and Frank Harris).

Later in 1888 came the sensational 'Mummer-Worship', an inventive article, packed with scandalous examples, in which an ebullient Moore amplified his hatred of actors. The profession had become pompous; its hypocrisy had grown with respectability; it had assumed a social position which was the prerogative of artists; it was exploiting its new status to insinuate itself into the world of the bourgeois villa. Respectability was but one manifestation of vanity, and vanity was behind an actor's every move, even to the writing of his autobiography. He noted the recent publication of memoirs by the Bancrofts, Toole and others; and compared the cultured salons of the eighteenth century with those of the present day, dominated by vulgar theatricals. With its insidious hints, its false prudery, 'Mummer-Worship' was not to be forgotten by the theatrical profession.

'Our contention is a threefold one: first, that acting is the lowest of the arts, if it be an art at all; secondly that the public has almost ceased to discriminate between good and bad acting, and will readily grant its suffrage and applause to anyone who has been abundantly advertised, and can enforce his or her claim either by beauty or rank; thirdly, that the actor is applauded not for what he does, but for what he is—that of late years the actor has been lifted out of his place, and, in common with all things when out of their places, he is ridiculous and blocks the way.'[37]

In nearly all Moore's later skirmishes in the theatre a violent distrust of actors is somewhere evident; 'Mummer-Worship' went far beyond the staid and philosophical debates sparked off by the publication of Diderot's *Paradoxe sur le Comédien* four years earlier. Frustration in getting his own work performed no doubt played its part, but a conviction that the growing cult of star personalities and their increasing influence, not only within the theatre itself but in all other areas of society, connect with a naturalist belief in the primary importance of the play, undistracted by unbalancing individual performances and intrusive settings, as well as with a strong suspicion of a social conspiracy, financially motivated, to suppress reform.

Robert Buchanan, author of the famous 'Fleshly School' attack on the Pre-Raphaelites, was among the many who resented Moore's insinuations. In his article 'The Modern Young Man as Critic',[38] he divided his subject into three categories: the 'Superfine Young Man'

(Henry James), the 'Detrimental Young Man' (Paul Bourget), the 'Olfactory Young Man' (Guy de Maupassant). For his fourth type, the 'Young Man in the Cheap Literary Suit', he chose William Archer. Archer, he protested, was not only ignorant; he was opposed to true imaginative art. He had chosen in Ibsen, 'the progeny of Schopenhauer', an idol whose morbidity lacked even Zola's redeeming 'balm of a subtle interpretation', and who might reasonably be associated with 'Jack the Ripper'.

From Archer he switched to Moore, who typified 'the Bank Holiday Young Man, the new upstart, the new prophet of straightforward animalism'. Moore summarised for Buchanan all the deficiencies of the younger critics: their cynicism, their 'realism', above all their 'impertinence'.

In November 1889 Moore returned to the fray with 'Our Dramatists and their Literature',[39] a major diatribe against English dramatists. As the range became wider, so the judgements became more harsh; the article was clearly intended as a manifesto. Moore disposed of all the supposedly major dramatists of the time—Gilbert, Burnand, Wills, Jones, Pinero, Grundy, Hamilton and Augustus Harris—none had produced a single play of literary merit. He lambasted the current London season, criticising Pinero's recent success, *Sweet Lavender*, for being illogical, and inaccurate in its presentation of social classes, and damning Pinero's other play, the much-acclaimed *The Profligate*, as inconsistent: its hero had reformed by the end of the first act. Jones' *Wealth* and *The Middleman* were both dismissed, and Irving's production of *Faust* he found close to pantomime, refusing to respect a cast that included Squire Bancroft, Ellen Terry and Irving himself.

The failure to find literary value in any of these plays inevitably involves a comparison with the state of the novel: they lack its 'logic and elemental philosophy'; and furthermore raises the question of the demands of the age. In a reply to critics of 'Our Dramatists' he drew on Swinburne's theories of the Elizabethan drama:

'Mr Swinburne says that as the intelligence of Elizabethan England was poured into the drama, so the intelligence of today is poured into the novel and the poem. This is my article in essence.'[40]

The slogan 'drama as literature' on which Moore's article was founded was enough to rouse Buchanan to another onslaught against 'impertinence'. This time the objects of attack were the advocates of immoral realism (such as Moore) who also questioned the present organisation of the theatre. In attacking those who wished, in their own terms, to reinstate the drama as a literary form, he asserted that in creating a theatrical experience words are but a contribution and a means to an end, their importance transcended 'in defiance of literary analysis'. The kind of literary realism that *he* admired was that practised by the modern descendants of T. W. Robertson, who included Gilbert, Jones and Burnand:

'I contend that the art of the modern, with all its small talk, with all its superficiality, with all its familiar characterization and apparent absence of ethical purposes, does include Literature, and *is* literary, in the sense that it employs language for the purpose of securing an artistic and perfect dramatic atmosphere. The art may be coarse and common, but it is there; the speech may be the cackle of the modern, but it is the speech of Nature; and over and above it all is the skill, the sentiment, which touches the sympathy of human beings.'[41]

What Buchanan abhorred about the decadent realism of Ibsen and Zola, where 'moral, or rather immoral, problems [were] argued out behind the footlights', was that its much-vaunted claim to be literary was, in his view, a blind allowing the inclusion of distasteful and unnatural subject-matter in the guise of ethical problems; in the complete theatrical experience ('dramatic atmosphere') the ugly reality of life becomes transformed into art.

A match for Moore in the dubious skills of polemical journalism, Buchanan is an extreme example of idealism on the defensive, but he is still representative of the old guard, the Clement Scott generation, who, morally outraged by the new plays, hold it against them that they lack some essential theatrical quality only to be achieved in the old forms and through established means of presentation.

In fact, throughout these quarrels two issues, obviously interrelated, were played off against each other: one was to do with the authority and traditions of the established commercial theatre, the other with the function held by the play in a theatrical performance. Moore's 'Our Dramatists' was only a prologue to a whole nexus of articles in 1890 in which these two issues were again confronted.[42] It was inaugurated by an article in the April *Fortnightly Review*, in which Oswald Crawfurd, an undistinguished journalist, surveyed the past season, noticing in particular a vogue for melodrama (a category in which he placed Pinero and Jones), the survival of farce, and the demise of the classical genres. Crawfurd objected to the existence of the gallery, with the obligation that it placed upon playwrights and actors to gratify 'the uneducated provincials'. He also blamed the actor-managers, whose egocentricity determined the choice of play and who underpaid their supporting casts in order to finance the special effects and scenery needed to bolster their own performances. He concluded that there were four reasons for the present state of degradation:

'First, the mixed audience; then, the apathetic behaviour of the educated portion of audiences; thirdly, long runs; and perhaps strongest cause of all, the actor-manager system; and the final product of these causes is melodrama of a very false and foolish kind, and almost nothing but melodrama.'[43]

The diagnosis was familiar enough by this time; Archer had made the same points continually. Crawfurd proposed a scheme for an initially endowed organisation made up of several theatres working under a joint stock company and offering a wide range of dramatic material to a larger public. By stressing the need for a 'well-judging and self-asserting public' Crawfurd contrasted his plan with 'the reform movement now on foot in favour of a so-called "Théâtre Libre" in London', which he saw as a movement towards minority art. What Crawfurd was really aiming at was a kind of improved popular theatre; although he admired Ibsen for having dispensed with empty heroics and false sentiment, he rejected what he considered to be his intent to edify. He decided that the real battle was between the artists—actors and playwrights—and the impresarios and agents who controlled them.

The article was widely read. In June there came a reply from Beerbohm Tree, who took as premise 'that art is best which is broadest': the finest drama appealed as much to the gallery as to the stalls; the gallery must be preserved. Tree, quoting Moore in his support ('to agree with whom is a sensation as pleasant as it is novel'), was optimistic to the point of complacency, eager to please all sides; he offered some support to the Ibsenites, but at the same time defended the long-run system on the grounds that without it rehearsal time would have to be cut, both author and manager would suffer financially, and the public would never adjust to a repertory system. He provided historical evidence to support the value of the actor-manager, using this to counteract demands for an endowed theatre.

Other actor-managers—Irving and Wyndham amongst them—rose to the bait, claiming in their defence the demands of the market and the protection of invested *capital*: a theatre, its properties, a company, and finally their own talent. With all this at stake, how could they afford to take risks, and why should popularity, worked for and deserved, be considered heinous and disreputable? And they could cite history—from Shakespeare to Garrick through to the managers of the nineteenth century the theatre had always been controlled, maintained and developed through the initiative and courage of the acting profession. Or if these arguments for responsible autocracy were unacceptable then they could refer to their companies as corporate, even benevolent, societies, set up for the mutual good of all participants, which included everyone from the stars to the minor players, from the designers to the carpenters, even the humble playwright himself, who benefited from the guaranteed draw of a popular star, attractive settings and the hope of a long run. By discounting, with shocked self-righteousness, the accusations of monopoly and self-seeking, Tree, Irving and Wyndham set out to defend themselves as the unjustly maligned and hard-done-by guardians of art, of public taste and of a national heritage.

But behind their statistics, their opposition of laissez-faire capitalism to rule by some kind of élitist, coercive and possibly immoral minority lay a more subtle debate. Crawfurd had been much perturbed by signs that nineteenth-century popular taste led only to Farce and Melodrama, and that the higher genres of Comedy and Tragedy had all but disappeared. The gallery audience he happily relegated to the music-hall, where they might find their own level, leaving the more discriminating audience free to revive a taste for the ancient arts and, the phrase recurs, to re-establish 'the drama as literature'. Ways would have to be found to make the process economically and artistically viable, and one tactic might be to substitute for extravagant stage carpentry methods that were both cheaper and more conducive to an imaginative response. Like Moore he involved the Elizabethan stage and referred to a recent article by John Addington Symonds, who 'shrewdly suggests that the wealth of lyrical and exalted descriptive poetry in the Elizabethan drama was intended as an appeal to the imagination of audiences in the then complete absence of scenery and stage decoration.'

'Drama as literature' meant to Crawfurd plays that could never achieve full popularity with the theatre in its present situation. For Tree, the very idea that the theatre was ailing was quite incredible. It was a special activity in its own right, and reformers should avoid the error of equating advance in the theatre with advance in other art forms. Of course the public might lag behind progressive tastes, but they had the right to expect certain standards in production, for these were part of the *theatrical experience*.

Henry Arthur Jones, as wary of really new ideas as he was of subvention, made his distinction between the theatrical and the literary in terms of the 'decorative' and the 'intellectual':

'When the history of the Lyceum comes to be reviewed in the memory of those who are now young, the leading impression will be one of lurid sunsets, gorgeous processions, torchlights, banners, armour, music, incense, and moving across this background, the two figures of the great magician and his radiant enchantress.

'What will be the leading impression remaining of the French stage when it comes to be similarly reviewed in memory? Probably some intense scene from a drama of modern life by a modern author, played in front of the most meagre and conventional drawing room scenery. The one impression will be mainly intellectual, the other mainly decorative.'[44]

Jones here exemplified the English compromise: his respect for the intellectual style still acknowledges the other two criteria of an inspirational ideal and popular success. He complained of the difficulties confronting the playwright, who had to produce a work both elevating and popular out of contemporary situations and modern colloquial speech, and ended by according total responsibility for the present state of affairs to the playwrights themselves; the business of the manager was no more creative than that of a publisher. By minimising the importance of conditions, Jones tactfully succeeded in offering no solutions and causing no offence:

'But in our present situation I am for trying all experiments, for throwing out a restless energy of adventure and enterprise in every possible direction. Actor-managers? Yes. Independent managers? Yes. National Theatres? Yes, if a workable scheme can be found. Municipal theatres? Yes. Théâtres Libres? Yes. Boards of management? Yes. Let us make a trial of them all, and see which works best for the general good.'

Tree's practical solution to the problems raised in this exchange was to organise the series of experimental productions—they began with Henley and Stevenson's *Beau Austin*—that were known as his 'Monday-Nights'. Moore, discussing them in an unsigned article in October,[45] raised a point that had so far been overlooked: Antoine, the most significant figure in the European theatre at the time, was himself an actor-manager.

At last all the issues were joined. Moore praised Archer for having campaigned single-handed for reform over the years, commended the boldness of Tree's venture, but drew attention to Tree's possession of the Théâtre Libre classic *La Mort du Duc d'Enghien*, and urged that it be produced.

By the autumn of 1890 it had become almost impossible to consider reform without reference to the Théâtre Libre, and it was as a result of these discussions that the Independent Theatre was formed. It resulted from the organisational labours of one man, J. T. Grein. Yet its precise origins are difficult to pin down, not least because of

George Moore's indefatigable attempts to claim the achievement as his own without actually denying the role played by Grein.

Although Archer took no part in the foundation of the Society—he was fully engaged at the time with the series of Ibsen productions—his contribution was to have created a more sympathetic climate of opinion over the previous decade, and he was now prepared to cast a benevolent but critical eye over the whole proceedings. He had observed the increase of Little Theatres and special performances in England, the revival of interest in the classical theatre at Oxford, the Shelley Society's performance of *The Cenci*, and the vogue for pastoral performances. John Todhunter's play *Helena in Troas*, performed at Godwin's Greek theatre, had, in particular, set him thinking of what he called 'the Impossible Theatre'[46]—an organisation subsidised by men of wealth and taste which was to produce rare plays, old and new, for a small audience of connoisseurs. But he more consistently advocated an 'endowed theatre', which would produce a variety of plays that, but for the cramping organisation of the commerical theatre, would reach a normal public. This preference was to be behind his qualifications of the Independent Theatre venture.

In 1889 Archer was confronted with something that approximated to his Impossible Theatre when the Théâtre Libre visited London. But as he confessed, he knew little more about the Théâtre Libre than he had read in the gossip columns. His first reaction was to say that such an organisation could only exist in Paris; because only there were there playwrights of unconventional talent. There were no such new playwrights in England, and here he stood by the abused managers. Not only were there no playwrights, there was no public and no critics: 'compared with us, Sarcey is a Radical and Vitu an anarchist.'[47] Archer was always a discriminating observer rather than an active participant—and one of his duties was to indicate difficulties.

It was not until some months after Antoine's visit that Moore began seriously publishing propaganda for an English equivalent, by which time J. T. Grein had started making similar demands.

Grein was born in Amsterdam in 1862, and his youth was spent both there and in Antwerp. His first writings on the theatre, published in Amsterdam, included articles on *Nana* and *An Enemy of the People*, and a book, *Dramatic Essays and Sketches*, appeared in 1884. At this time his ideas were neither new or unusual, and he admired both Scribe and Sardou. He must have been aware of Dutch theatres organised in ways that were unknown in England, of the Netherlands Stage Society, for instance, founded in 1876, which presented Molière and Shakespeare as well as the work of native playwrights.

In 1885 Grein left Amsterdam for London. His first article on the English stage appeared on 8 November and was a general and condemnatory survey. In the summer of 1887 he visited Paris, and *The Dramatic Review* carried his reports of this visit, which made no reference to Antoine or the Théâtre Libre.*

On 20 March 1889 he started his own periodical, *The Comedy, A Fortnightly Review of Art*, which ran for five months and included much gossip, a series on contemporary dramatists, an article on Archer by C. W. Jarvis, the usual reviews, and one article on the Théâtre Libre. Grein's contributions to these little magazines are distinguished by their mild tone and tolerance, although a defence of *A Doll's House* and references to *Ghosts* are indicative of future concerns.

The Comedy was replaced by *The Weekly Comedy, A Review of the Drama, Music and Literature*, and it was here that his campaign got properly underway. The eighth issue, of 30 November 1889, included a formal demand for the foundation of a British Théâtre Libre, published with approving comments from Archer, James and Hardy. An offprint was circulated, immediately followed by four more articles on the same subject. In November Grein read a paper on subsidised theatre to the Playgoers' Club.

The response to this activity was considerable. Archer drew attention to the scheme and discussed it at length, but still doubted whether there was suitable talent in England to sustain it.[48] In June George Moore, in company with Arthur Symons, visited Paris to see *Ghosts* at the Théâtre Libre. On their return both men wrote articles about the performance, and both ended with a *cri de coeur* for the play to be produced in England. Symons put it like this:

'We have not yet a Théâtre Libre and it is possible that the Lord Chamberlain might have but little desire to license a play which is not even an adaptation from the French. But a Théâtre Libre could be improvised for the occasion, and *Ghosts* in this way at least, performed—privately, if the guardians of our morality forbid the production of a play which contains so much that is "properer for a sermon".'[49]

The Paris visit gave Moore another opportunity to meet Antoine, and also to test his conviction that plays that read well also acted well. Although he praised Antoine's performance as Oswald, the

---

* Schoonderwoerd (59) suggests that Orme (52-3) is wrong in saying that he saw the Théâtre Libre at this time.

real subject of this article (the first of a series of four in *The Hawk*)[50] was the play itself, and, as might be expected, he was carried away with enthusiasm. He concluded:

'Why have we not a Théâtre Libre? Surely there should be no difficulty in finding a thousand persons interested in art and letters willing to subscribe five pounds a year for twelve representations of twelve interesting plays. I think such a number of enthusiasts exist in London. The innumerable articles which appear in the daily, the weekly and monthly press on the London Stage prove the existence of much vague discontent, and that this discontent will take definite shape sooner or later seems more than possible.'

Moore's articles start with a plea for 'three or four thousand' people to found an English equivalent to the Théâtre Libre, and they attempt to provide the basic principles on which plays for its repertoire should be selected.

'Plays which a manager of a regular theatre will not produce, not because they are bad, but because he thinks there is no money in them. What kind of plays are these? Plays in which the characters, although true to nature, are not what are known as "sympathetic characters", plays in which there are no comic love-scenes—plays that contain no comic relief—plays that deal with religious and moral problems in such ways as would not command the instantaneous and unanimous approval of a large audience drawn from all classes of society—plays in which there is no love-interest, plays composed entirely of male or entirely of female characters, etc.'[51]

He called for a variety that could, on occasion, embrace the bizarre, that could include unconventional, and not necessarily distinguished, material. 'That the play should be "rare" is the first and almost the only qualification necessary to secure for it the right of representation.'

Moore was much more concerned about choice of play than organisation and referred to Archer's opinion that plays of literary merit were not submitted even to the commercial managements; Antoine himself had had to find half his repertoire outside France. Moore's tentative list therefore included foreign plays: Tolstoy's *The Dominion of Darkness*, *Ghosts*, *La Mort du Duc d'Enghien*, *Jacques Damour* and Metenier's *En Famille*, and he also suggested that approaches be made to 'all the novelists', as well as to Henley, Grundy, Jones and Pinero.

Meanwhile Augustus Moore, still editor of *The Hawk*, had started to campaign against the enterprise and against Grein in particular. The reasons for this curious move are difficult to determine, but perhaps it was his behaviour that brought Grein and George Moore together; from this point on they were, nominally at least, colleagues. Moore publicly dissociated himself from his brother's attacks:

'. . . If anything I have written on the subject has suggested to Mr Grein the way out of the present dramatic deadlock, it would indeed be ungracious for me to disclaim sympathy with him. I have talked the matter over with Mr Grein, and have advised him to appeal to the most prominent men of letters—Mr George Meredith, Mr Thomas Hardy, Mr Robert Louis Stevenson, etc. In truth, it rests with them. If they have any dramatic actions which they wish to see represented, there is no reason why Mr Grein should not succeed. If on the contrary, they decide to hold aloof, the movement, which is purely a literary one, must fall to the ground.'[52]

As a declaration of intent this clearly did not satisfy Grein, for soon afterwards he himself wrote setting out further details of his scheme. He ended with a defiant joke:

'When the hostile criticism comes, as of necessity it must come, I shall be prepared to meet it. Only let no man tell me of the Théâtre Libre that the public don't want it. Sir, the general public won't get it.'[53]

Although one important reason for founding an Independent Theatre was to bypass the rulings of the dramatic censor, Moore had already, when it came to it, been prepared to defend that institution on the grounds that the decisions of a single intelligent man were likely to be preferable to those of a democratic jury which 'represented the public' (an alternative suggestion put forward by Archer) or, worse, the whims of public opinion itself.[54] The prosecution of Vizetelly, publisher of Zola's novels, in 1888 had recently shown how public outrage could affect a private activity such as novel-reading; the lesson to be drawn from that painful episode was that a dramatic censor was actually *needed* to protect the vulnerable literary playwright and his special audience from decisions about the moral rectitude of their minority interest being thrown into the hands of a philistine majority. By the discriminating use of the closed performance and the limited edition individual judgements on artistic merit could be kept separate from the demands of public success.

Even in the autumn of 1890, before the opening of the Independent Theatre the following year, disinterested observers (had there been any) could have perceived areas of contradiction. Grein is wildly energetic, his commitment untouched by theory or doubts about the kind of audience he needs; an excess of enthusiasm and tolerance which might allow guiltless revision later on. Moore rests for the time being with the idea of the 'literary', sometimes equated with realism, always carrying with it an implied comparison with the novel: 'literary' means an accurate description of life without the constricting obligation to please an audience. Watching them both is the temperate Archer, uncomfortably trying to bridge the gaps between his appreciation of new tendencies in the drama, his criticisms of commercial rule, and a basic belief that, as he put it later when Moore tried to exclude critics from Independent Theatre performances, 'the drama is essentially a social art. . . . Moreover, even in matters of art, man is a proselytising animal.'[55]

The Independent Theatre opened on 13 March 1891 at the Royalty Theatre with the legendary first English production of *Ghosts*; a programmatic choice, as Grein acknowledged.

'The selection of *Ghosts* is in itself a manifesto—a demonstration of my plan of campaign. The question whether *Ghosts* is a moral play or not has nothing to do with the case. The point is, does this drama embody, in every sense, the purpose of the Independent Theatre? Is it, to express my policy in a few telling words, "a play that has a literary and artistic, rather than a commercial value"?
'And to this question there can be but one, an affirmative reply. There is another reason why I have chosen *Ghosts*. In nearly every centre of civilisation—in Berlin, in Paris, in Christiania, in Copenhagen, in Amsterdam, in Brussels—the earnest students of the advancing drama have had an opportunity to see this work, read and discussed as it is by everyone, and have applauded it. The London stage alone, ruled by an iron rod of medieval narrowness and dictatorship, ruled by the fear of Mrs Grundy and Sweet Fifteen, dared not produce the most modern, the most classical drama of the age. Thus the Independent Theatre Society, where art, not money or long runs, is the cry, has stepped in to free the London stage from the taunt of artistic orthodoxy.'[56]

The inevitable vilification that resulted from this production was, as they must have suspected when choosing the play, to oblige the founders to restate their purposes in defiance of widespread public disapproval.[57] But there had always been another ambition besides the presentation of neglected and scandalous works. Grein's announcement had continued:

'. . . above all I wish to stimulate the production of a native unconventional school, and to give a hearing to those who strive to foster the undeniable *renaissance* of the drama. At present unconventional dramas are scarce, not to say absolutely non-existent, here, for want of an outlet; but the impetus being once given, the endeavours will follow; and, as a first result of the movement, I am happy to state that plays have been promised by many writers of distinction, from all of whom one may expect that they have something new to say, and will say it well.'

The Independent Theatre was intended to have stimulated those younger writers whose notion of playwriting was, as Grein put it elsewhere, 'that real human emotion should be aroused by the presentment of real human life.'[58]

But by the end of the first year there came something of a modification of policy. Now it seemed that the Independent Theatre had been founded 'not to oppose, nor to compete with, the existing theatres, but, in a certain measure, to co-operate with them.'[59] It was to 'test' new plays that were 'original, unconventional, and literary', and, if they were found to be successful, 'every effort [would be] made to transfer the rights of that play to any management who may wish to produce it at his theatre'—which suggests that the interest in popular success that Moore had renounced altogether was still to some extent being applied. There were to be other compromises. The truth is that the Independent Theatre never did succeed in attracting the promised new English playwrights, and this weakness was soon seized upon by its critics.

The second choice was *Thérèse Raquin*, performed on 9 August 1891 before an audience which included Shaw, Wilde and James. The production of Zola's play, with its macabre treatment of adultery, murder and double suicide, received a good deal of praise, but between Archer and Moore (who had revised De Mattos' translation) there can be seen an important divergence of opinion. Archer pointed up the differences between Zola and Ibsen:

'It is thirteen years since I first read it, ten since I saw it acted in Rome; and I have never ceased to regard it as the strongest, simplest, sternest real-life tragedy as yet extant. Ibsen's dramas have not displaced it from that position in my esteem, for Ibsen is not really a realist. He is a poet, a symbolist; life, in his hands, becomes supersaturated with spiritual import. *Ghosts*, *The Wild Duck*, and *Rosmersholm* are far greater, subtler, more potent and pregnant pieces of literature than Zola's play. One would infinitely rather have written *Hedda Gabler* than *Thérèse Raquin*.'[60]

Moore, in a passionate defence of the Independent Theatre,[61] opposed suggestions that *Thérèse Raquin* be given the chance of a commercial run, asserting the need to protect serious plays from wide exposure: he was concerned not for the poetic drama ('as dead as the civilisation that produced it') but for the 'realistic drama'—and under that heading he put both *Thérèse Raquin* and *Hedda Gabler*. *Hedda* he had already praised in naturalistic terms for its 'purely human and scientific shape'.[62]

Here are signs of a crucial split in terminology. Objection to the naturalistic principles laid down by Zola in the preface to *Thérèse Raquin*, 'which in 1873 was a futility', Archer considered to have 'become an anachronism in 1891. It belongs to the Stone Age of aesthetics'.[63] The battle had long been won, now the orientation had changed, and with it a whole set of terms. W. S. Lilly, in his attack on realism, had made reference to an ancient Platonic conception of the function of art, the 'union of spiritual substance and material symbol';[64] now it was as 'symbolism'—by which he may not have meant the same as Lilly—that Archer, groping towards a new conception of his drama, wished to place Ibsen; and for Moore to speak in general terms of the 'realistic drama' and still to apply that phrase to Ibsen and Zola together suggests that in 1891 he too might have been on the way to becoming an anachronism. His own attempt at writing for the Independent Theatre shows that this may well have been the case, and that he returned to the task of playwriting with a new and considerable disadvantage (although he would hardly have seen it as such)—long experience in the composition of novels.[65]

Towards the end of 1892 *The Pall Mall Gazette* invited novelists to contribute personal statements to a series called 'Why I Don't Write Plays'. Their replies are remarkable both for their apparent ignorance of recent events in the theatre and for their instinctive hostility to the dramatic form. Thomas Hardy admitted the divorce between stage and literature, but found it only 'inimicable to the best interests of the stage'. The blame was placed squarely upon the *conditions* imposed by the theatre.

'. . . In general, the novel affords scope for getting nearer the heart and meaning of things than does the play: in particular, the play as nowadays conditioned, when parts have to be moulded to actors, not actors to parts; when managers will not risk a truly original play; when scenes have to be arranged in a constrained and arbitrary fashion to suit the exigencies of scene-building although spectators are absolutely indifferent to order and succession, provided they can set before them a developing thread of interest. The reason for the arbitrary arrangement would seem to be that the presentation of human passions is subordinated to the presentation of mountains, cities, clothes, furniture, plate, jewels, and the other real and sham real appurtenances, to the neglect of the principle that the material stage should be a conventional or figurative area, where accessories are kept down to the plane of mere suggestions of place and time, so as not to interfere with the required high relief of the action and emotions.'[66]

George Gissing confessed that invariably his first impression of an Ibsen play was that it would be improved if written as a novel.

Although he went on to concede the plays' effectiveness once seen upon the stage, his initial reservation was symptomatic of a deep mistrust of the form as a whole.

'In dealing with the complex life of today I am not content to offer only dialogue. The artist, I agree, must not come forward among his characters, but, on the other hand, it appears to me that his novel will be artistically valuable in proportion to his success in making it an expression of his own individuality. To talk about being "objective" is all very well for those who swear by words. No novelist was ever objective, or ever will be. His work is a bit of life as seen by *him*. It is his business to make us feel a distinct pleasure in seeing the world with *his* eyes. Now, to be sure, a skilful dramatist does this, up to a point. For my own part, I wish to go beyond that point, to have scope for painting, to take in the external world and (by convention, which no novelist has set aside) his unuttered life of soul. Stage directions and soliloquy will not answer my purpose.'[67]

Only George Moore made reference to specific plays—*Beau Austin* and *Thérèse Raquin*—noting that discord between writer and audience preceded disjunction between writer and form.

'I find, therefore, that the general taste corresponds encouragingly with my taste regarding novels, but is in hopeless opposition to my taste regarding plays. And this difference of taste means something more than the mere taking or losing of a little money on my part. Some collaboration on the part of the multitudes is necessary to enable the artist to produce art that is vital, and so it seems to me that those who would interpret the life of their time do well to choose the novel, rather than the play, as a means of expression. The success of *Anna Karenina* proves that the narrative form permits the novelist to put his best thoughts and his most accomplished art into his work and still be read, whereas the failure of the plays I have named and the success of plays which I shall not name prove that the dramatic form of today is disregard for every kind of moral sequence and the violent dislocation of the inevitable course of human action.'[68]

Moore announced that he intended to write a play for the Independent Theatre in answer to a challenge issued by G. R. Sims after the Society had invited William Poel to stage *The Duchess of Malfi* in August: as the Independent Theatre seemed to have failed in its declared intent of presenting new English plays, he would offer a hundred pounds for something suitably 'unconventional'. Archer, for one, pointed out, in his reasonable way, in a review of a one-act play by Grein and Jarvis, *Reparation*,[69] that the directors of an unconventional theatre were under no obligation to write unconventional plays themselves; Moore's success or failure would prove nothing for or against the Independent Theatre.

Meanwhile Moore set about abridging *The Strike at Arlingford*, a five-act social drama that he had written in collaboration with Arthur Kennedy some time earlier. It was performed at the Opera Comique on 21 February 1893. The hero is John Reid, a Socialist leader who had in his youth an understanding with a certain Lady Anne, the daughter of his nobleman employer. After Lady Anne had realised the impossibility of furthering their relationship, Reid had left his position and became a poet, Socialist and professional agitator. Now sent to Arlingford to lead a colliery strike, he discovers that the collieries are the property of Lady Anne, who runs them with the advice of her friend, a millionaire businessman, Baron Steinbach. Reid is now engaged to a fellow Socialist, Ellen Sands; but on seeing his former flame his old love revives, partly under the advances she makes towards him. There follows a struggle between duty and inclination, although the two are not entirely opposed, for an examination of the account books plainly reveals the truth of what he has been told by Lady Anne—that to yield the increase demanded by the men would lead to a catastrophic loss for the colliery. Reid therefore resolves to persuade the strikers, who are already starving, to resume work; but at this juncture an anonymous cheque for two thousand pounds reaches him, to be distributed among the men with a view to prolonging the strike. He withholds it. Challenged with the offence by his uncompromising fiancée, he vows that he was acting in the long-term interests of the men. He puts this point of view to the strikers; they attempt to murder him; he escapes, but sees Lady Anne being taken away to safety by Baron Steinbach; in a fit of conscience, and anticipating a further attack by the men, he takes poison.

The political content of the play was not Moore's main concern, and his own account of his intentions was probably, despite its portentousness, accurate enough.

'What I have tried to do is to depict a weak man in a position too strong for him—a kind of modern Hamlet, so to speak, whose mind and resolution were overborne by his circumstances.'[70]

'In my own conception of my play the labour dispute is an externality to which I attach little importance. What I applied myself to in the composition of *The Strike at Arlingford* was the development of a moral idea. I leave the play itself to explain this idea.'[71]

The intent was to make an audience accept 'ideas' in a play as they would in a novel; but Moore's 'moral idea' was overshadowed by the long discussions of political 'ideas', or so at least it was generally thought.

'. . . long dreary dialogue upon questions of capital and labour which are not necessary to the play, and as they were utterly trivial and commonplace proved exceedingly tedious.'[72]

'. . . interpolation of undramatic arguments on social questions. . . .'[73]

'He has over-burdened the story with dialogue, and we have half the time a play and the other half polemical discussions upon capital and labour.'[74]

And most damning of all,

'. . . would probably be found to read far better than it plays.'[75]

Actually Moore had made some genuine if heavy-handed efforts to relate ideas and action. That Steinbach, the intelligent, articulate businessman, is representative of Capital is obvious, but his position as adviser and onlooker rather than protagonist places him outside the central debates between Reid and Lady Anne: he's 'context' rather than 'subject'. And the use of a peripatetic journalist called Hamer, who is present for much of the play searching for a story, and who subjects Steinbach first to rigorous questioning and then to a formal interview on political issues, is another enlarging device.

The real weakness of *The Strike at Arlingford* is here within the dialogue, in the substitution of interview or statement for exchange, in Moore's failure to find suitably dramatic modes of expression. Reid's declarations of love (he is, we know, a poet of the Pre-Raphaelite School), if unlikely in themselves, appear even more absurdly incongruous when punctuated by Lady Anne's own prosaic comments.

'*Reid*: I could not remember where I had met that perfume. It seemed to recall a far-off time, a dead past; but when I tried to define what it did recall, the illusion vanished. Ellen's description of you did not help me. It was when my thoughts were occupied with other things that the haunting odour seemed on the point of whispering its secret. I put the flowers away, but the soft, insinuating odour pursued me, held me sleepless. . . . Suddenly I cried out—"It is she!"
'*Lady Anne*: I remember the day you left Torrington Park. I saw you walk across the park in the rain; you had told me that I had broken your heart.
'*Reid*: I did not speak false. You were a cruel, heartless girl, as you are now a cruel, heartless woman.
'*Lady Anne*: (dashes the tears aside) I am sorry you think so badly of me, but it can't be helped . . . I did treat you cruelly, I know.'[76]

So, as the play proceeds, the personality of Lady Anne becomes more of a caricature and less deserving, it might seem, of Reid's attention:

'The worst of servants is that one can't speak before them, unless one speaks in French. You don't, do you? . . . I cannot imagine how you could have ever thought of marrying a woman who wasn't a lady.'[77]

The development of character is restricted by the paucity of diction and implication. There is no sense of memories of the past being, consciously or unconsciously, distorted; no ambiguity in the present inheritance of earlier behaviour; unlike Ibsen, recollection has to be taken at face value.

Undisputably 'serious' in subject, but by no means as 'unconventional' as Moore claimed,* *The Strike at Arlingford* is not even convincing in its realism. For the most part, development is conveyed through discussion. Characters being established mainly *outside* the events of the play, they cannot profoundly change within it. Emotional crises are indulged, political declarations devitalised. It's not so much that Moore tries to transfer the habits of novel-writing to the drama as that he is unaware of the resources of the dramatic form. He is unable to write dialogue that is self-sufficient, that is resonant of relationship and suggestive of more than is articulated; and tied to the limited expression of his characters, without the novelist's freedom to intervene or explain, he flounders between the immediacy of his subject and the actuality of his chosen form—the realistic drama. Sims, in answer to whose challenge the play had been written, was to express satisfaction with what he called Moore's 'psychological' drama.[78] The word that he chose could hardly have been less appropriate; as a piece of critical description it is as unhelpful as 'serious' or even 'literary'.

There is a lack of density in the images and metaphors of *The Strike at Arlingford* (it is also noticeable in Pinero and other 'literary dramas'), that connects with an incapacity to deal with inductive thought and expression. The literary drama is essentially linear; in these plays characters are obliged to explain themselves even *to* themselves through monologue (not soliloquy) and formal debate; and their explanations are often singular, either in terms of the kind of emotional expression they use or in that they can offer themselves only one set of reasons for their behaviour. This failure serves as a reminder of the complex achievement of the true playwright, who successfully inter-relates action with articulation on several levels, a playwright such as Ibsen at his greatest.

The audience for *The Strike at Arlingford* had included at least one less satisfied member—G. B. Shaw, who wrote a disgruntled letter

* Recent plays on labour themes had included *The People's Idol* by W. Barrett and V. Widnell (Olympic Theatre, 4 December 1890); *Work and Wages* by W. Bourne (Pavilion, 23 June 1890); *Capital and Labour* by W. J. Patmore (Lyric, 28 November 1892).

to Moore warning him that his 'strikology' was inaccurate ('he has confused the master collier class . . . with the financial class'), and another, in protest, to Archer.

'In fact, from the realistic point of view, the whole play is utter nonsense: it was so unreal to me that it bored me to distraction. The first act only needed some practical knowledge to be made very amusing, especially the deputation. Moore's counterpoint is weak; he runs too much into duets. A master of polyphony like myself would have made a fine concerted piece out of that quartet and chorus.'[79]

Comparisons between Moore's play and Shaw's *Widowers' Houses* (produced by the Independent Theatre a year earlier, and admired by Moore as 'a really brilliant social satire')[80] were inevitable. Archer in effect replied to Shaw's letter in a later article:

'It would be better of course, that the sociology should be correct as well; but if the human nature is correct, that is the main point. There is, at a low estimate, ten times more flesh and blood in Mr Moore's play than in a certain entertaining production of unimpeachable Fabianism but doubtful humanity.'[81]

'Flesh and blood' versus 'sociology': the choice seems particularly narrow when recent critics have shown how ingeniously Shaw appropriated and parodied established dramatic forms in the composition of his own highly self-aware plays.[82] Characteristically, it was Shaw himself who provoked the complaints by advertising *Widowers' Houses* as 'An Original Didactic Realistic Play', and by following its performance with a Fabian address to the audience. Archer, who had collaborated on the first draft, certainly missed the ironic juxtapositions in the sub-title.

Widowers' Houses is the first example of Shaw's anti-climactic technique. No character undergoes a surprising reformation— Sartorius ends as he begins, a slum landlord, Trench enters into an overt financial relationship with him *not* by compromising his moral principles but by acknowledging a previous covert complicity. The play's moral impact depends on the author's conviction that the opportunities offered by a corrupt society will always prove more attractive than an individual's desire for change. Archer saw this as good propaganda but bad art: a dramatisation of the parliamentary 'blue book' prevented a convincing portrayal of human relationships and must therefore be 'unrealistic'. '. . . It is the business of the realistic drama (and Mr Shaw vaunts his realism) to lead us through appearances to realities,' but Shaw 'skips appearances to go direct to realities.'[83] Archer seems to invest appearances with an almost Hegelian significance: unlike Oscar Wilde, who appreciated Shaw's 'superb confidence in the dramatic value of the mere facts of life' and 'the horrible flesh and blood' of his characters,[84] he protested against his cynical 'inhumanity', and the absence of those qualities he had particularly admired in Moore.

'Truly, for a set of blood-suckers, Mr Shaw's middle classes are strangely bloodless. And he fails withal—partly by reason of his summary and paradoxic psychology, partly from other and subtler causes; no breadth of humanity, and least of all from any *odor de femina*, gets over the foot-lights.'[85]

A comparison of this kind does not go to the heart of the matter. Moore's play, with its violent climax of a suicide that has as its cause a romantic love-affair as well as a social crisis, obviously expects a response to its 'humanity'; Shaw's more bathetic mode requires a very different kind of identification, invited by an idiosyncratic re-working of old dramatic forms.

When Grein defended the part he had himself played in the presentation of *Widowers' Houses* it was with an abnegation of certain responsibilities. A play, he wrote, was accepted by the Independent Theatre if it was 'artistic' and 'interesting' and 'literary'; its 'tendency', its 'form', its 'practicability' were of no concern to the management, who only provided certain facilities through which the literary could 'examine' their work:

'For through the performance, and the performance *only*, they will see their work under a microscope, as it were; they will see its strong points; they will be forced to admit its weak ones; they will be able to judge whether they possess the gifts that make playwrights.'[86]

Grein allowed performance to be a means as much as an end; the value ('literary', 'artistic') of a play exists prior to its staging, which is a test of its form.

Indeed the 'form' of *Widowers' Houses* provoked very little comment elsewhere, and was not a topic towards which even Shaw, in his elaborate and cunning self-analyses, drew attention. But then his writings about his early plays are part of a personal campaign; even more than his criticism of other writers they are deliberately and wilfully misleading. Issues are only raised if they can be resolved, and claims are sometimes based upon inappropriate comparisons. Thus he could write, aligning himself with 'all great masters of fiction' and dissociating himself from mere manipulations of plot:

'As a fictionist, my natural way is to imagine characters and spin out a story about them, whether I am writing a novel or a play. . . . At the same time I am quite aware that a writer with the necessary constructive ingenuity, and the itch for exercising it for its own sake, can entertain audiences or readers very agreeably by carefully constructing and un-ravelling mysteries and misunderstandings; and that this ingenuity may be associated with sufficient creative imagination to give a considerable show of humanity and some interest of character to the puppets contrived for the purpose of furthering the plot.'[87]

But Shaw, as he sometimes admitted, reconciled the freedom of character and the restriction of plot through use of stereotype (Sartorius, for instance, is 'an exceptional and superior specimen of the middle-class man'),[88] and types act according to type. An audience is intended to respond and judge by recognition and, ultimately, by identification. When critics suggested that his portrayals were too harsh, Shaw could reply,

'Let us not try to encourage the hypocrisy of the theatre, already greater than that of the conventicle, by being more austere in our judgement of *dramatis personae* than of real men and women.'[89]

The equating of life on and off the stage can be used to encourage the participation of the audience, who become involved with the characters on stage on the same terms that those characters become involved with each other; which also allows for lively discussion, for if behaviour is predictable there is time to debate its implications. The types are socially determined: Shaw's characters are invariably placed by class, by work, by social position alone. Their consistency is maintained because of Shaw's apparent belief (expressed openly in his more pessimistically Fabian moments) in a basically un-changing society. Fixed within a static environment, and having no life outside it, his characters have a very restricted range of values and concerns (Raymond Williams has pointed out how uncon-vincing the moments of personal passion invariably are).

It is suspicious that Shaw should have backed up his declared hatred of constructed, 'inorganic'[90] art by references to Shakespeare and the novelists. When he claimed that there is no willed 'con-sistency' in his own plays,[91] he chose not to mention the consistency imposed by theories of social determinism. It is part of the deceitful strategy of his declarations that life, inconsistency and realism should be set against the theatrical, the patterned, the imaginary; yet his own plays adhere closely to time-honoured theatrical gambits—misalliance, mis-identity and delayed disclosure—all of which belong within the most rigid dramatic convention of all, the melo-drama. Where no distinction is made between artifice and life, it is life that suffers. It cannot be denied that Shaw's theatricality is often stunningly effective, but in its dramatic disclosures it only reveals those underlying truths that have always existed (which is why the melodramatic form is so appropriate), and, within a corrupt and limited society, presents only those experiences that its members are permitted. This is what Shaw means by realism, which because of society should aspire to nothing more than comedy or farce.[92]

Shaw's early theory does not entirely suit his early plays—but there is perhaps a sign of his own sense of insecurity in *Candida*, where the poet Marchbanks is allowed a secret 'beyond' the action and its issues, a secret that the drama can only allude to and cannot assimilate.

The only considerable new English dramatist that the Independent Theatre had presented was Shaw; and yet, when offered *The Philanderer* and the daring *Mrs Warren's Profession* in later years, Grein baulked at the risk. Shaw's plays depend on the audience's complicity in the events on stage, often via the presence of a surrogate and always by the deceptive manipulation of paradox and irony, and it took time for them to find an audience of willing and amused victims.

A study of *Widowers' Houses* and *The Strike at Arlingford* makes one thing abundantly clear. All that is meant by 'a sense of theatre'—pace, construction, emotions that are convincingly engendered and compellingly shown without the help of authorial explanation and description (what Thomas Hardy had called 'the high relief of the action and emotions')—are skills that even a novelist has to learn from scratch, and have traditions of their own.

Apart from *Widowers' Houses* the new plays staged by the Independent Theatre were not distinguished, failing dismally even to attempt Shaw's level of wit and irony. Michael Field's *A Question of Memory*[93] is set in Hungary. A Hungarian soldier, captured by Austrians, is threatened with the death of his mother and sister unless he discloses vital information. On his refusal the women are shot. Told that the death of his sweetheart will follow he is prepared to talk, only to discover that under the strain of inquisition he has actually forgotten the information.

Mis-identity is the theme of Dorothy Leighton's *Thyrza Fleming*.[94] It concerns an actress who has in the past been rescued from ignominy by the husband of her recently-married daughter who, not knowing of her previous circumstances or even that she's her mother, becomes jealous. Thyrza, rather than reveal the truth, attempts suicide. Fortunately the daughter overhears a conversation in which all is revealed, and is able to forestall her mother's act and to forgive her.

A Man's Love,[95] a Dutch work translated by Grein and Jarvis, is a simply constructed play about the love of Frank Upward, a weak vacillating barrister and poet manqué, for his wife's sister Emily. His love is rejected by her on the grounds that if he is capable of betraying his own wife then he is also capable of betraying her, a moral conclusion that the play seems to endorse, for it ends with Frank returning to his wife and child.

Mrs Oscar Beringer's *Salve*[96] ('A Fragment in One Act'), performed at the Opera Comique on 15 March 1895, might be selected as the end-point of pseudo-realistic drama. A prodigal son returns home incognito to find his parents in desperate financial straits. His mother, thinking him a rich stranger, kills him; on discovering his true identity loses her wits.

For all their 'realism' most of these plays also preserved the well-worn devices of plot manipulation: the overheard conversation, mis-identity and so on. Earlier on A. B. Walkley, prominent critic of *The Speaker*, had pointed out,[97] with particular reference to *The Goldfish*[98] (translated by Texeira de Mattos from the Dutch of Van Nouhuys and first performed by the Society on 8 July 1892), how such plays respected other, if more recent, conventionalities. The first act of *The Goldfish* introduces a dissatisfied middle-class couple, the Koorders: a husband burdened with financial problems, a frustrated childless wife. When a doctor friend mentions in passing that a neighbour's baby is dying of convulsions, Koorders, noticeably shocked, leaves immediately, followed by his suspicious wife. The second act opens with their arrival at the house. The child is dead, its distraught mother beseeching retribution upon herself and the child's father. This turns out to be Koorders who, she claims, left her to marry for money. He abjectly submits to the recriminations of both his mistress and the doctor, and goes to the bedside of his dead child. Fitting punishment comes in the third act in the form of bankruptcy, but his wife offers forgiveness on the condition that he uses her money to pay off the creditors, which he does with due humility.

Walkley's point was that the play made use of recently established moral stereotypes—a pusillanimous husband and a magnanimous wife (both to be found in *A Doll's House* and *The Profligate*), a friend who silently adores the wife (as does Dr Rank in *A Doll's House*) and a child as the focal point of a catastrophe. So although *The Goldfish* is to be associated with the New Drama in its aspirations to 'vigorous analysis and direct observation', it also shares with it a 'morbid, over-strained, almost inhuman morality'; a failing which even the high-minded Archer saw as a lack of 'subtlety, irony and distinction'.

One of Archer's solutions to the problem of combining the virtue of 'seriousness' with the need for sophistication was to award a play tragic stature wherever possible. This he did with *Alan's Wife*, by Elizabeth Robins and Mrs Hugh Bell (first performed by the Independent Theatre at Terry's on 28 April 1893).[99] The play is set in the North of England; a working girl smothers her deformed child, is condemned to death but refuses to repent. In its time the simplicity of treatment and the harrowing nature of the subject provoked vigorous debate: a defence from Grein based, as so often in his case, on the 'slice of life' formula embracing 'psychology' as well as 'simplicity';[100] a protest from Walkley about the play's intellectual vapidity—no 'arrangement', 'development', 'design' or 'ideas';[101] and, from Archer, affirmation of the power of a sober exposition of a tragic idea, 'life at the mercy of brute chance'.[102]

Because of the problems involved in making a descriptive reference to form that also accounted for the gravity of subject-matter, these plays forced critics into a troubled revision of terms. Yet the contradictory basis of their realism went undetected. In each case the inevitable catastrophe—most of the new plays staged by the Independent Theatre end with death, many with suicide—was precipitated in the context of a fixed morality, so that although their methods look like objective social realism, society had actually been cast in the role of fate. The result was a moral impasse, disallowing the multiple access to character and the presentation of social ironies on several levels that were needed if the drama was to operate with its full power to involve.

The Independent Theatre was known as a realists' theatre; it followed a continental model that proclaimed itself to be 'naturalist'. Naturalism was itself a double term, almost equally applicable to treatment and subject—one could not change without the other. But naturalist habits were tenacious; the mode altered from within; which is also to say that plays called naturalist (or of course more often realist) were often little or nothing of the kind. Both the time-lag between the arrival of a new approach and its absorption into manifestoes, and a deliberate muddling of terms to suit personal bias, confuse an understanding of a complex situation, as does, in a different way, the English unwillingness to consider the text and its theory within a whole theatrical context. At the centre lies Ibsen, whose plays became, simultaneously, symptoms, examples and influences upon critical response. An examination of early reviews reveals subtle attempts to incorporate his plays within realist theory; which in turn involved a strong resistance to Ibsen's own apparent efforts to free himself from what had become constricting forms.

When the Independent Theatre came to stage *The Wild Duck* on 4 May 1894, understanding and appreciation of the Norwegian playwright had reached a certain degree of sophistication. Reviewers encountered some difficulty in trying to determine the overall tone of the play, but this was probably caused as much by the particular performance as by the strong element of self-satire which the play contained. Many came to the conclusion that its style was curiously mixed; although Shaw, whose case this play had so admirably suited, had placed an exclusive emphasis upon Ibsen's questioning of his own idealism,[103] it was now widely recognised that that was not all the play contained.

'. . . a curious medley of dramatic styles, ranging from portentous tragedy to puerile farce.'[104]

'[The audience] . . . roared with laughter at the scenes intended to be serious, and they yawned ominously at the master's ponderous and heavy-handed wit.'[105]

'Few appeared to know the real character of the work—perhaps it was played in some ways too gravely for the understanding of its audience. That it is a kind of colossal jest, a burlesque *reductio ad absurdum* of principles dear to the author, never was clear to those who flattered themselves that they were merely laughing with him.'[106]

The idea of mixed style was to affect consideration of the symbolic duck itself, although its 'mode' (that of a variable symbol which reflects and identifies characters through the interpretation they give it) was recognised and discussed at once.

'The question of the wild duck being symbolical to those who in sorrow descend the lowest depths, and are eventually rescued, is left for the audience to solve.'[107]

'As for the "wild duck" of the title, it is like the elephant in the Cambridge problem, its weight may be neglected. It is at once a real bird and a symbol: it symbolises many things, Ekdal's daughter and Ekdal's disreputable old father and sometimes Ekdal himself. Ibsen *must* have his symbol and I should be very sorry not to admit the real poetry of this symbol as Ibsen introduces it. But it does not help our comprehension of the stage; it obscures it rather—all the talk about it, from the rigorously dramatic point of view, only retards the action.'[108]

In the most developed and enthusiastic reviews, mixed style and variable symbol coalesce in an appreciation of ironical technique. Thus Archer wrote of

'. . . that smooth, unhasting, unresting, movement which is Ibsen's greatest invention in the technical sphere—every word at once displaying a soul-facet and developing the dramatic situation. . . . Hardly ever before, as it seemed to me, had I seen so much of the very quintessence of life concentrated in the brief traffic of the stage. Its poetry and its prose, its humour, its irony, and its pathos, its commonplace surface suddenly yawning into unplumbed abysses.'[109]

The Wild Duck is not, it has always been agreed, an especially difficult play in the Ibsen canon, nevertheless Archer's comment, his awareness of a world behind the events and exchanges represented on stage, signals the presence of an important nodal point in the history of nineteenth-century theatre—the rediscovery and rehabilitation of dramatic symbolism within the auditorium itself.

Five years before, in his 'Ibsen and English Criticism', Archer had attempted to defend Ibsen against charges of being 'a dramatic preacher rather than a dramatic poet', of his art having been 'vitiated by didacticism'. He had begun by conceding that there were certain areas in which his message did become obtrusive.

'Not his direct teaching—that, as it seems to me, he always inspires with the breath of life—but his proclivity to what I may perhaps call symbolic side-issues. In the aforesaid dramas in verse this symbolism is eminently in place; not so, it seems to me, in the realistic plays. I once asked him how he justified this tendency in his art; he replied that life is one tissue of symbols. "Certainly," I might have answered, "but when we have its symbolic side too persistently obtruded upon us, we lose the sense of reality, which, according to your own theory, the modern dramatist should above all things aim at." '[110]

Apart from 'symbolism' (examples of which he did not provide), Archer had claimed for Ibsen the ability to 'vitalise' his work, to 'humanise' it, to imbue characters with 'an intense and palpitating life, and so give intense dramatic life to modern ideas'; Ibsen achieves 'typicality' not through dogma or systematic thought but through paradox and 'the "broken-lights" of truth, refracted through character and circumstance.'

'The telling of absolute truths, to put it another way, is scarcely Ibsen's aim. He is more concerned with destroying conventional lies, and exorcising the "ghosts" of dead truths; and most of all concerned to make people think and see for themselves.'

He exonerated Ibsen from accusations of didacticism in *A Doll's House* by citing Nora's final speeches, where there is 'the very mingling of truth and falsehood, of justice and injustice, necessary to humanise the character and the situation.' After the early dismissal of symbolism Archer's argument became a moderate plea for the dramatic significance of 'relative truth' in the creation of 'a sense of reality'. In retrospect, the discarding of Ibsen's symbolism on the grounds of its relations with didacticism is the most intriguing ploy in this early explication.

Socialists and the socially conscious had indeed seized upon Ibsen with a didactic intent; but the channel soon ran dry once its current had been diverted. Ibsen's plays then assumed centrality in other respects, as part of the morphology of the drama, of the evolution of a medium and the changing ways of responding to it. In the annals of dramatic history this is sometimes too neatly recorded as a complete shift from realism to symbolism, from the play as direct representation to the play as poem. Symbolic content had been recognised early on as one aspect of Ibsen's writings, especially by those who knew *Peer Gynt*. Even the later preoccupation with his subject-matter (syphilis, feminism, insanity), although often distorted by howls of outrage and squeals of distaste, could on occasion be more searching, provoking questions about what the 'subject' of a play really is and whether it could be discussed apart from its containing form.

A full appreciation of Ibsen came to demand an acceptance of symbolism as an integral part of a play's subject rather than as substitute for it; a crucial requirement that was made more difficult to fulfil by the justifiable suspicion that as far as symbol as substitute was concerned, Ibsen himself might not be innocent of allegory. No longer was it enough to view the drama as an illusion of reality; what was now necessary was a willing suspension of disbelief, an admitted susceptibility to potent atmosphere but unlikely events, a profound involvement. All of which sometimes seem to have needed a vast transformation of sensibility: an impression which the oddly poignant efforts to understand made by ill-informed writers in popular newspapers go some way towards strengthening.

But at first reviews complained of an absence of moral and stylistic balance in Ibsen, connecting a taste for the well-made play with assumptions about the well-rounded playwright. Ibsen is charged with falling short of professionalism—versatility and a sense of proportion. He is accused of being neurotic and obsessive: obsession with social problems becomes transferred to an 'obsessive' technique. Thus his symbolism is 'heavy', 'profound', or 'weighty', often 'intrusive', nearly always 'unintelligible'. The neuroses of his characters can be easily explained away in terms of 'madness' (and if the character is mad, then so perhaps is its creator?). Labelling Nora, Hedda, Solness as mad clears the critic of the responsibility to understand them, moreover the study of an individual psychology can be discounted as undramatic theorising, with the characters serving as *examples* of ideas about heredity, disease and so on.

The first principle of realism—that dramatic action and behaviour must be probable according to established terms of character and situation—had come to the fore in discussions of *A Doll's House*. It was objected that Nora, first seen as the dominated child-wife, was suddenly transformed in the last act into a violent and articulate adult.[111] This was a fairly simple debating point, although capable of expansion into arguments turning on an opposition of 'theoretical discussion' (which permits such apparently unlikely changes in behaviour) to 'real life' (often disguised as 'realism').[112]

Perhaps *Rosmersholm*, produced in February of 1891, should have produced more insights into matters of form than it did. Archer, sniffing symbolism on the wind, made an obscure reference back to Nora's tarantella in *A Doll's House* as a moment when 'theatrical convention and artifice' asserted itself, and announced a final break with the 'well-made' tradition:

'Of the plays in his latest, or penultimate manner, *Rosmersholm*, I repeat, is the one which most conspicuously, one may almost say wantonly, defies the technical maxims of constructive orthodoxy. If there are two rules of stagecraft on which all authorities are agreed, they are these: first, that you must always get on with your action; second, that you must not mystify your audience.'[113]

The word 'mystify' sprang readily into the minds of other critics:

'The new play, one of the least objectionable, most mystical, and surely the best written in the whole of the Ibsen series. . . . The old theory of playwriting was to make your story or your study as simple and direct as possible. The hitherto accepted plan of a writer for the stage was to leave no possible shadow of doubt concerning his characterisation. But Ibsen loves to mystify. He is as enigmatical as the sphynx.'[114]

Ghosts was said to present the unnatural (that is, the unbalanced or the distorted or the simply obscene), when the true function of the drama, as of all art, was to celebrate the beautiful triumphs of the natural; the word naturalism was commonly applied to the play only in order to exploit the contradiction. *Black and White*, for instance, was typical in protesting that it was Ibsen's 'ignorance of nature that is one of his worst failings'.[115] The anonymous but sympathetic reviewer in *The World* (not on this occasion William Archer), who wrote of 'a play wherein the infinitely tragic possibilities of modern existence, and the nemesis that attends rebellion against the law of nature, form the leading interest',[116] was very unrepresentative in his perceptiveness.

On 20 April 1891 Elizabeth Robins gave her celebrated matinée performance of *Hedda Gabler*. The heroine was taken to be 'modern woman', a tangle of wild and distracted nerves, with all the attributes of the modern temperament. Her states of mind, oscillating violently between withdrawn autonomy and a passionate, always unrealised, desire to merge the self with another, were described as *phases*—a choice of word which, with its connotations of unteleological evolution, seems in itself to imply recognition of an unstructured psychological sequence.

'I know of no play [admitted *The Hawk*] in the whole range of modern comedy, or tragedy, which presents so true and so terrible a picture of certain phases of human life familiar to all who observe.'[117]

And from *The St James' Gazette*:

'If from the dramatist we are to demand nothing more than the portrayal of certain phases of life as they present themselves to his eyes or are conceived by his imagination, no exception need be taken to Henrik Ibsen's latest play *Hedda Gabler*.'[118]

But that Hedda was a product of the modern condition was not necessarily, for the same reviewer, a justification of the play itself:

'It is enough for his purpose that he finds in the character of his heroine a subject to probe and analyse, heedless that nothing can be gained by so futile an operation.'

For the *Times* reviewer, it was 'a study in *nervosité*', and its apparent objectivity was justification enough:

'He allows the case to explain itself . . . that the play should be more acceptable than some of its predecessors is a necessary consequence of the very plainness of its thesis, which precludes all discussion of its heroine's action upon ethical grounds.'[119]

Two critics displayed a special and personal involvement in their response to *Hedda*. They were A. B. Walkley and Henry James, and it seems likely that the first had learnt from the second. In his review of *Rosmersholm* Walkley had referred to Gabriel Nash, Paterian aesthete, a study in composite modernity, in James' *The Tragic Muse* (1890):[120]

'. . . along with his new subject-matter, he has brought a new *technique*. It is because, then, of the novelty of his theatre . . . that so many of us are attracted to Ibsen; not, as a vain people supposeth, because we approve the conduct of his personages, or regard ourselves as the addressees of his ethical "message"—whatever that queer missive may be. We take a purely aesthetic delight in him, because he gives us new impressions. There is an impressionist in one of Mr Henry James' novels, whose *animula vagula blandula* is summed up in this way: "I drift, I float, my feelings direct me—if such a life as mine may be said to have a direction. Where there's anything to feel I try to be there!" Well, dramatic criticism just now is impressionist; it is drifting and floating. There is always something to feel in the playhouse, when Ibsen is being played, and we try to be there.'[121]

The identification is absolute: Walkley, one of the most literate of critics, was to offer himself as being of the 'impressionist school',

'. . . a vagabond, who accepts his impressions as they come, and changes his moods with his horizons. . . . The enunciation of positive judgements, of absolute truths, I hold to be no part of my business: on the contrary, to be negative and relative was a point of honour. To have as many impressions as fortune willed—if irreconcileable, no matter—about the same work.'[122]

Even *The Stage* opened its review of *Hedda* with an allusion to impressionist criticism:

'The new school of critics—for here is a new school of criticism nowadays, as of everything else—tells us that the critic can only judge of a work of art by his own personal impressions, and that all general principles must be thrown over as old-fashioned lumber. So many critics, so many opinions. This is necessarily the axiom of the new school, for as no two nervous systems and temperaments are exactly alike, so no two human beings can feel exactly alike. There must be shades of difference in their opinions as there are in their faces. When the impressionist critic addresses himself to Ibsen he finds either a great deal to praise, or a great deal to blame. On the other hand, the writer who subordinates his personal impressions to what he conceives to be the general principles of art— finds in Ibsen, as a general rule, much to blame and little to praise, the reason being that in the Ibsen drama most of the current conventionalities of characterisation or treatment are set at defiance.*[123]

---

* Compare this with the defence of Irving's *Lear* against the strictures of both Archer and Walkley, published in *The Speaker* on 10 December 1892.

'The impressionist school has done good service in dramatic criticism as well as in painting; but a recent article on *King Lear* written by the very accomplished "A.B.W.", set me wondering whether the purpose and the limits of the new school had, in this country at least, ever been rightly understood. An impressionist should record his impressions—*entendues*: in other words, he should say what he feels—he should do for the shifting imagery of the play what the impressionist artist tries to do for the passing vision of this material world which absorbs his sense of colour and of form. But is not this another way of saying that the new school tries to observe with keener concentration of the intellectual and aesthetic apparatus than the conventionalists whom it is tending to supersede? Assuredly it does not mean that the writer about the drama is to tumble onto paper the mere siftings of his crudest sense-impressions—say, the feeling that his stall was not quite comfortable, or that a fly had settled on the leading tragedian's nose. . . . But then Mr Walkley will have his answer—he has his "impressions"; they are different from mine, and there's an end on't. . . . And now I have a lance to break with Mr Archer, who has of late been catching Mr Walkley's trick of impressionising . . .'.

In the early months of 1891, when *Hedda Gabler* and *Rosmersholm* were performed, 'impressionist' criticism was of topical interest— Oscar Wilde's manifesto, largely plagiarised from Pater, 'The True Function and Value of Criticism', had appeared in *The Nineteenth Century* in July and September of the previous year. Impressionism was particularly appropriate to *Hedda*, as Walkley explained:

'The "hard-shell" Ibsenites, who insist upon regarding Ibsen as a moralist rather than as a dramatist, will be sore put to it to find the moral of *Hedda Gabler*. More wary persons, who recognise that the purpose of art is not to point morals, but to create impressions, will be content to accept the play as a picture of a peculiar type of *révoltée*, a dramatic study in mental pathology, a nineteenth-century tragedy. . . . The play is a bit of sheer "impressionism". '[124]

James concentrated on the formal implications.

'It is doubtless not the most complete of Ibsen's plays, for it owes less to its subject than to its form. . . .'

'The demonstration is complete and triumphant, but it does not conceal from us—on the contrary—that his drama is essentially that supposedly undramatic thing, the picture not of an action but of a condition. It is the portrait of a nature, the story of what Paul Bourget would call an "état d'âme", and of a state of nerves as well as of soul, a state of temper, of health, of chagrin, of despair.'[125]

The moment of these plays, of *Hedda Gabler* in particular, was felt to mark the theatre's belated participation in a new wave of ideas already manifesting itself in literature and literary criticism, and, retrospectively this was to be its main importance, it acted as a kind of catalyst in the transition from realistic to symbolic drama, a preparation for symbolism. What Walkley predicates, and what James' alert cultural antennae sense in the offing, is a changed relationship between audience and play, where the play requires a particular kind of audience or mood, the crucial relationship upon which an understanding of Ibsen's subsequent work was to depend.

But impressionism never interfered with Walkley's respect for immediate credibility, in fact it reinforced it. He disliked intensely what was generally considered to be a bad production of *The Lady from the Sea*, because it 'embodied dreams; and dreams . . . fade in the garish light of the stage.'[126] Qualifying a lecture by H. A. Jones, in which he advocated a first attention to character rather than to plot, he cited the work of Antoine and the Théâtre Libre ('naturalism' in its pure French form) and again invoked James:

'. . . there are some temerarious spirits who go a step farther than Mr Jones. Nature, say these, shows no plot, design, construction, at all; why then should the drama, whose function it is to hold the mirror up to nature? "The strange irregular rhythm of life" (as Mr Henry James puts it), that is what the uncompromising realists want the drama to imitate. . . . Life is not only the raw material for the stage, it is the model as well. True, you cannot transfer life to the stage in its entirety: limitations of time and space forbid that; there must be selection, arrangement, concentration. But, even with selection, "the strange irregular rhythm of life" might be imitated. The ultra-realists have a better case than Mr Jones suspects.'[127]

Either *Hedda* or, for example, *La Mort du Duc d'Enghien*, which was composed of three scenes unconnected by convolutions of plot, could have served as examples in his allusions to plays that imitate not only the material but also the form and patterns of life: Walkley had found his own way of absorbing Ibsen into a broad naturalistic category.

But there are pitfalls ahead for the investigator who amasses his evidence in sequence of date; for ideas travel quickly, travel underground, and they can be accepted, quoted or returned to sender before they're even understood, with their message unread, half-read, unfinished. So it was with these early problems, which—still only half-solved—were largely relegated to history to make way for the questions raised by the arrival of *The Master Builder*. When Archer and Walkley came to confront the new and crucial issues, it had to be in terms that neither was yet quite accustomed to handling.

Their gentlemanly quarrel began when Archer introduced his new translation of the play, in *The Pall Mall Gazette* of 12 December 1892, with a glance backward at *Hedda*.

'. . . the new play is a curious reversion from the type of *Hedda Gabler*. Mr Quiller-Couch described *Hedda* as a piece of "frank impressionism".'*

Himself conceding that *Hedda* was 'extraordinarily objective, and, so to speak, unsymbolic', Archer sets up, with an apparently immediate precision, the comparison with *The Master Builder*.

'Impressionism has given way to a symbolism more complex than that of *The Wild Duck*. The dramatic action, as in *Rosmersholm*, is almost entirely outside the frame of the picture.'

Thence (the progression could not have been otherwise) to symbolism's natural partner:

'. . And so far from passing on the solid earth, it takes us into a region of *mysticism* [author's italics] more uncanny than that of *The Lady from the*

* Probably a reference to a remark passed by A. T. Quiller-Couch in his review of *Peer Gynt*, *The Speaker*, 7 August 1892. (Repr. *Adventures in Criticism*, 1896, 297.)

Miss JANET ACHURCH
as NORA HELMER
IN ACT II

23   Pen and ink drawing of Janet Achurch dancing the tarantella in Act II of the 1892 revival of *A Doll's House* at the Avenue Theatre, with Charles Charrington as Helmer and Charles Fulton as Dr Rank.

24   Elizabeth Robins as Hedda Gabler, 1891.

25 Artist's impression of the fall from the tower in *The Master Builder* at the Trafalgar Square Theatre, 1893 (*Pall Mall Budget,* 23 February 1893).

26 Elizabeth Robins as Hilda Wangel in the same production of *The Master Builder*.

27   Poster by Edouard Vuillard for
Lugné–Poe's production of *Solness
Le Constructeur*, first performed in Paris
in 1894.

3   Design by Maurice–Denis for the programme
Pelléas et Mélisande, produced by the Théâtre de
Oeuvre in Paris in 1893.

29 'Scène de théâtre', oil painting by Vuillard,
possibly of *Pelléas et Mélisande*, c. 1890

Sea. To be strictly accurate, I should say rather that there is no corporeal, tangible action at all, whether within or without the frame of the picture. There is one event, at the very end; but even it can scarcely be said to happen on the open stage at all.'

Archer finds that mysticism quickly overtakes the conventionality of the opening scenes: the major part of the play is a duologue about the meaning of past events which, though apparently not remembered in full by Solness, have somehow been transferred to Hilda by what Archer describes as 'occult sympathy'. When these memories are expressed in terms of 'castles in the air' and 'kingdoms', the conversation loses its 'objective reality'. But this observation does not prevent Archer from resuming with an orthodox moral reading of the story as the trials and penance of an ambitious will.

'Solness has advanced in worldly prosperity, and has been enabled to achieve his ambitions, at the cost of other people's happiness.'

And in case this distillation of the play's essence fails to account for all its elements he then issues a brisk warning against any further inferences.

'And what does it all mean, you ask? Frankly, I don't know, and I don't very much care. Those who go to Ibsen for doctrine, reproof and correction may, at their leisure, unravel the skein of ethical purpose, and weave it into the fabric of "Ibsenism". What I look for in Ibsen is primarily emotion, and I find it in plenty in this strange, ironic, bitter-sweet fantasy.'

Falling back on the metaphor he used of *A Doll's House* he concludes,

'So far as its symbolism is concerned, the play, to my thinking, resembles one of those stained-glass windows which are composed, almost at haphazard, of the fragments of the original design. I catch only "broken lights" of ethical purpose; but the whole effect is nonetheless rich and impressive.'

Symbolism has, as before, been associated with a meaning that it would be futile to pursue, and the drama is offered, despite all that Archer himself has managed to find within it, as 'a castle in the air of pure imagination'.

The Master Builder opened on 20 February. A day or so earlier, Archer had some more observations to make on the play, which appeared in print two days after the opening night.[128] He spoke of it as 'a drama which, while realistic in form, is in essence as poetic, as mystic, as fantastic, as *Faust*, or *Peer Gynt*, or *Prometheus Unbound*.' The notion, first applied to *A Doll's House*, that a play allows of as many different interpretations as the various truths that it contains, is repeated with a slight change in terms—'we shall each of us trace different dream-forms, and read a different prognostic for the coming day.' Dream-forms perhaps, but the most important subject located by Archer holds a conveniently ambiguous position between dream and reality. The strange relationship between Hilda and Solness has, for Archer, its foundation in 'hypnotism', Ibsen's use of which 'goes straight to the limit of the conceivable, and relies upon our very scepticism as to what may or may not be physically possible to make us accept the situation which is poetically necessary.'

In thus bringing *The Master Builder* within the realms of credibility, Archer had found a way of shifting his emphasis nearer to the representation of reality. A piece written after the performance and published five days later furthers the retreat from his earlier views, at the same time as attaching new prominence to an alternative formula.

'. . . disregarding the element of hypnotism, is there anything inconceivable, anything insane in it? The whole conception of the character is poetical—granted; but to what a pass has criticism come if all that transcends the most ordinary everyday probability is to be denounced as insane! I shall be told, no doubt, that there is no more magic virtue in the word "poetic" than in the words "symbolic" or "allegoric", and that a dramatist cannot escape from the laws of his craft by calling his extravagances "poetic". But that is precisely where I venture to join issue with the great body of the critics. I say that a dramatist has a perfect right to produce a great poem under the guise of a great play.'[129]

It is perhaps surprising that the alternative, poem rather than play, which begs so many questions (and is incidentally proleptic of certain twentieth-century approaches to the drama), should not have become a topic for discussion at the time. That formula was only another aspect of Archer's attempt to defuse symbolism by protecting the central action of *The Master Builder* from its dangerous fall-out.

Archer's prolonged analysis, if conscientious on the surface only, makes an undeniable contrast with the sardonic and impatient dismissal that the Robins performance drew from Walkley.

'The accident, in Hilda's cant phrase, would be "frightfully thrilling", if we could only see it, but we cannot. So that on the stage itself nothing of a material external nature can be said to happen. The whole drama consists in the development of—or rather in the exposition of already-developed — character. Solness and Hilda are both remarkable people. I am bound to say I never met anybody in the least like either of them. . . .

'Why is the hypnotism dragged in? What are the "castles in the air"? Why all the prolonged metaphor about "churches", and "homes for human beings", and "towers pointing up, up, up?" Many commentators have come forward to explain the whole thing is all allegory. Solness is Dr Ibsen, the buildings are his plays, Hilda is the New Spirit and so forth. But this is only to make the darkness visible. Allegory, mysticism, and symbolism are all very well in their place, but I submit that they are not in their right place on the stage. On the stage I want lucidity, and if I don't get it I am angry.'[130]

But this was too assumptive even for the hard-pressed journalist, and in April Walkley delivered an extended and again decisive verdict, with 'lucidity' now promoted to a position as the *sine qua non* of dramatic art. The influential history of symbolism, however, had to be acknowledged first.

'The symbolic drama is practically unknown in the English, and, indeed, in the whole of the modern theatre. On the Greek stage it was familiar enough—the *Prometheus* of Aeschylus, to name the classic instance, is a piece of Titanic symbolism. . . . And now, after many centuries, art seems to be returning to symbolism, partly by way of reaction against a crude and excessive naturalism, partly in the attempt to annex new tracts of thought, as yet imperfectly surveyed. . . . Ages ago, Socrates, who asked so many questions, raised this important one, "Whether the invisible can be imitated?" Symbolism is the outcome of the effort to demonstrate that it can. And now we see this effort at length reaching to the drama—the keep, the inmost stronghold of the Castle of Art, which has always been the last to yield to the beleaguering forces of change.'[131]

A symbolist tradition allowed, its present manifestations respected, Walkley went on to define the nature of drama:

'In the playhouse it is essential to my enjoyment that I understand, then and there; I must know what's going on. For, on the spot—whatever suggestions it may offer for subsequent reflection—the drama deals with the surface of things. . . . It may have all sorts of other meanings later on, but, above all, it must have a meaning at the moment.'[132]

Next he provided a theory of symbolism:

'. . . Now obviously, it is in the very nature of symbolism to elude this demand. There are three elements in your perfect symbol, are there not? It must have profundity, it must have complexity, it must have obscurity. A symbol is a veiled truth? Then it must be all veil. . . . Meaning, it must have, then—and its meaning must not be insignificant. . . . Again, your symbol must show various facets of the truth in varied lights—or, if you like, there must be veil within veil. . . . Again, the bird which gives its name to Ibsen's *Wild Duck* is a complex symbol—now it is Old Ekdal, now Hialmar, and now a real bird, something to be served with cayenne-pepper and a slice of lemon. Finally, a symbol must be obscure. Why be at pains to invent a riddle which anyone can guess at first shot? It is the vagueness, the mystery of the symbol which contributes so greatly to its power over the imagination.'[133]

By bringing the two together, he could show their incompatibility.

'But, in determining the three elements of the symbol, have I not named the very qualities in which the stage is most deficient? The symbol is profound, the stage is superficial; the symbol is complex, the stage is simple; the symbol is obscure, the stage lives by clearness. . . . A sharp line of demarcation will have to be drawn between the outer story and the inner significance, between the veil and the thing veiled, the concrete image and the abstract idea—in other words, between the form of the symbol and its content. No matter how abysmally profound, how subtly complex, how mystically obscure the content may be, it will be all labour wasted unless the form comply with the fundamental and immutable laws of dramatic art.'[134]

This brought him at last to *The Master Builder*, which failed on both counts: it was unclear both in content (inner symbolic meaning) and in form (outer subjective meaning).

'Nor has the "form" an existence independent of the "content" . . . in *The Master Builder* we are constantly baulked by passages which, until we introduce the symbolism to give them some meaning, are sheer nonsense; as, for instance, the professional evolution of the architect from "church" building to the erection of "homes for human beings", and thence to "castles in the air". That is to say, the symbolism has to be dragged in, the "form" to be pieced out, by the "content", not so much to explain as to explain away the play.'[135]

He concluded that the illusion of reality which is essential to drama was here irrevocably destroyed by symbolic fantasy, and Archer's view of the play as 'realistic in form' but 'fantastic in essence' met with a firm rejection.

Walkley's attacks prompted Archer to append a reply, 'The Melody of *The Master Builder*', to the cheap edition of the play when it appeared later in the year. Pursuing his earlier inclination, he substituted the words 'melody' and 'harmony' for 'story' and 'symbol', and set out to account for the whole play in terms that recognisably belong to orthodox theory. Thus

'It is no doubt with a symbolic sub-intention that Ibsen has made Solness an architect; but since, on the realistic plane, he might just as well be an architect as anything else, it cannot be said that even ordinary probability has been sacrificed to symbolism.'[136]

The 'kingdoms', the 'castles in the air', Archer described as mere 'metaphors'. The reasons for this lie within territory that he himself admitted to be obscure; in fact it was more treacherous than perhaps he realised. He now had to envisage a situation in the theatre where an audience's understanding of a character's behaviour and speech needed to be greater than the character's own self-awareness, but at the same time he was hesitant in allowing his imaginary audience the knowledge of what they themselves had to infer or contribute. This is at the very heart of a crisis in realism, for once openly admit the need for active imaginative participation in an illusion (however much that participation has been silently assumed before), and the drama's capacity to represent can be challenged at a most vulnerable point. Archer put it like this:

'Simply because the deliberate and conscious use of metaphors by the characters in a play is not at all what is meant by symbolism. There is doubtless symbolism in these "castles in the air" *in so far as they represent to Ibsen's mind* (and are intended to convey to us) *something different from what they represent to Hilda's.*'[137]

The metaphors are 'meaningless . . . as between herself and Solness, and significant only as between poet and audience.' The implications of these remarks, and their tacit acceptance of the 'play as poem' were, for the time being, left unexplored, and Archer's account ends—and it's not insignificant—with 'the dramatic style of the play—so tense, so surcharged'.

The force of symbolism dissipates as soon as it can be taken as allegory, which is just what many critics, understandably enough, presumed *The Master Builder* to be. Unable to find a simple inner meaning they floundered, at a loss for any meaning anywhere in the play.

'But—urge the hard-pressed Ibsenites—the play is symbolical. A symbol, the dictionaries tell us, is the sign or representation of any moral thing by the images or properties of natural things. Well, here are the images and the properties—presumably in the *personae* on the one hand, and, on the other, in the churches and towers, the "home for human beings", and the castle in the air for Halvard Solness and Hilda Wangel. What are they symbolical of? There can be no symbolism without consent of parts—and this farrago of unreason can be united with nothing in reason. The whole business is a crazy one—whether from design or unconsciously we do not pretend to say.'[138]

If they despaired of ever disentangling the strands of its symbolism, the peculiar power of the theatrical experience nevertheless remained to be puzzled over, and by more critics than one might have expected.

'A piece of fantasy, an allegory, a fable, the play unquestionably is; inconclusive, vague, obscure; outraging at every turn the laws that rightly and necessarily govern dramatic construction; yet, consciously enough, offering ample matter for thought and reflection and stimulating the imagination to a high degree.'[139]

Like Archer but without his persistence and experience, these day-to-day critics fell back on 'strange dramatic force', 'weird intensity' and 'poetic imagination'—phrases that carry a weight greater than their ostensible meaning—testifying not only to the need for a new set of terms but to a genuine dislocation of sensibility, and the startled apprehension of a large intent. 'The whole play seems to us to be nothing but one desperate, raging, cry of revolt against human destiny,' confessed *The Spectator*.[140]

By staging *The Wild Duck* in 1894 (which had after all been written some ten years earlier) the Independent Theatre had chosen a play that could, up to a point, be assimilated within now established frames of reference. Like the last Ibsen productions of the nineties—*Little Eyolf* in 1896 and *John Gabriel Borkman* in 1897—it inspired the familiar phrases. *Borkman*, although again raising the possibility, in its most acute form, of 'modern tragedy', was still either written off as 'an ugly dream'[141] or praised for its 'poetic atmosphere'.[142] Discussions of *Little Eyolf* concentrated on the Rat-wife. The viability of a symbolic *character* was quite willingly conceded, with the rider that it be *placed* within a credible reality:

'We do not object to symbolism "by itself", of course. But there are conditions to be observed if it is to be artistic. Either your symbolism must be clear and determined, or, if it is to be vague, it must leave room for explanation on common grounds. This is not the case in *Little Eyolf*. The "Rat-wife" incident contains features inexplicable on common grounds. She stands for death: well and good, but either the incident should have been determinately symbolical, or she should have been a possible "rat-wife" as well, and she was not.'[143]

'It is dramatic; the characters—the abnormal characters, as I contend—are clearly drawn. There is a possible doubt about the artistic value of the symbolism because, while it is shadowy in itself, actuality is sacrificed to it.'[144]

Archer's inquiry into Ibsen's symbolic art in *Little Eyolf* makes use, as it had done with *The Master Builder*, of suggestions that the mysteries are conveyed through reminders of a possible supernatural agency:

'The story he tells is not really, or rather not inevitably supernatural. Everything is explicable within the limits of nature; but supernatural agency is also vaguely suggested, and the reader's imagination is stimulated without any absolute violence to his sense of reality.'[145]

Ibsen's ability to evoke in his plays intimations of a hidden process, so often recognised if not always fully admitted even by hostile critics, still remained for Archer explicable only within the terms of realistic representation—the immediately referential nature of the theatrical experience remained inviolate.

In such faltering ways new ideas adumbrate new forms; both were available from several sources for the few, the very few, who could recognise them. In the course of a chaotic honeymoon in London in 1893, spent partly with the Greins, August Strindberg stirred up enough interest for plans to be mooted for a production of *The Father*, but these were never implemented. Strindberg's powerful ideas and personality had already been introduced to England with an abbreviated version of the preface to *Miss Julie*[146] and by a rather unperceptive article in *The Fortnightly Review*[147] from his most fervent champion Justin Huntly McCarthy, who described him as 'a realist among the realists'. Strindberg wanted to see the end of a middle-class drama dependent upon popular ideas; 'closed' for the very reason that it was 'open' to whatever single interpretation its audience wished to impose upon it, its limitations derived from characters that were identifiable solely by phrase and mannerism. He claimed to have created characters who could be recognised by the universality of their experience and understood only by the natural ambiguities of life: mixture of experience would replace fixity of character. Hence Strindberg's modern personages are

'... more vacillating, more worn out, more composed of a mixture of old and new ... conglomeration of past degrees of culture and fragments of the present time, fragments borrowed from books and newspapers, bits of men, tattered pieces from gala-robes turned into rags; just as the soul is patched together.'[148]

Where naturalism, confident that what can be shown can be explained, 'demands happiness', so the spectator trained to this presumption provides his own remedy for whatever crisis he is shown upon the stage. It is to frustrate and challenge these 'progressionists' and 'men of the programme-party', in defiance of their ameliorating response, that Strindberg announces in the *Miss Julie* preface his intention to write tragedies about 'hysterical modern personages in a desperate fight against nature'. So too in this assault does Strindberg appeal to a common sub-strata of deep experience; but despite the curiosity displayed by Grein and McCarthy, there is little evidence in England, at that moment, of any full understanding of what he might do for the drama.

A growing involvement in the possibilities of dramatic form can be observed in John Todhunter's otherwise unremarkable plays of the early 1890s—*The Black Cat*, put on by the Independent Theatre at the Opera Comique on 8 December 1893, and *The Comedy of Sighs*, presented during Florence Farr's brief management at the Avenue Theatre in March 1894, together with W. B. Yeats' *The Land of Heart's Desire*. In his preface to the Independent Theatre edition of *The Black Cat*, Todhunter, the patriarch of Bedford Park and once the harbinger of a new poetic drama, attempted to bring himself up to date by clumsily embracing a version of naturalistic theory (though he himself did not apply this term). He emphasised both character and dialogue ('action itself is language'), whose importance was currently being reinstated in 'problem plays', and contrasted them with the superfluous plot and sensational activity of the previous well-made play. The new ideal, 'vital not academic, organic not mechanical', includes 'our so-called realism', which is

'. . . but the first wave of a new romantic movement, on the stage as elsewhere. For when the old ideals are decrepit, we must go back to nature to get the stuff wherewith to make new ones.'[149]

In the true representation of nature, playwrights unearth more profound levels of action: 'not merely the external incidents, but shifting phases of thought, emotion, character in the *dramatis personae*.'

Todhunter's all-inclusive formula confuses distinctions as it makes them. Still the main preoccupations do come through, and his eccentric preface suggests the ways in which the concept of naturalism applied less to a rigid technique and more to an approach that included, implicitly, some reference to the emotional, the internal and the unstated processes of the drama. Dramatic action becomes then more than what is seen to occur, more even than what is known to occur.

At the same time as English critics were preoccupied with the task of assimilating the symbolic tendencies of Ibsen's middle period, the avant-garde of the *Quartier Latin* were coping with the explosive birth of a drama that was unashamedly symbolic in its every respect. The directors of the Independent Theatre acknowledged its arrival first by making plans, in 1893, for a performance of Maeterlinck's *La Princesse Maleine* by marionettes (this came to nothing), and then, two years later, by inviting Lugné-Poe's Théâtre de l'Oeuvre to London for a short season.[150]

The Théâtre de l'Oeuvre, like its predecessor, the Théâtre d'Art, was part of a conscious reaction to Antoine's Théâtre Libre and naturalist theory.[151] Although documentary evidence for the Théâtre d'Art is scanty, and there are no photographs or illustrations, a number of contemporary statements do make its intentions reasonably clear. They start with a paradox: while, as Pierre Quillard put it, 'la parole crée le décor comme le reste',[152] no physical décor can match the vision aroused in the imaginations of an audience by the poetry alone. The Théâtre d'Art aimed to create settings which accompanied the drama only by suggesting atmosphere, that is, by 'symbolising' the indefinable. Scenic values became abstracted; whereas the naturalism of the Théâtre Libre stood or fell by its fidelity to a specific historical location, the primary standards for the décor of the symbolist theatre were the efficacy of its colours, its textures, its mood, placing it in direct opposition to any 'illusionist' theory which strives, hopelessly, to find ways of reproducing an immediate reality. It was to the painters that Paul Fort, founder of the Théâtre d'Art, turned for his décors; and, fittingly, to the poets that he turned for his material.

For Pierre Quillard's medieval poem *La Fille aux Mains Coupées*[153] Paul Sérusier provided a golden backcloth decorated with angles, which was seen through gauze and a tulle curtain. Many of the Théâtre d'Art's productions originated as poems: they reached an apotheosis with *The Song of Songs*,[154] which drew upon all the classic texts of synaesthesia: from Baudelaire, from René Ghil, from Chardin-Hadancourt. Wagner had long been a source of inspiration to French poets; now one outcome of their enthusiasm was to be seen on stage—a musical analogy runs obsessively through all discussions of the symbolist theatre. *The Song of Songs* aspired to total art: music, words, colour, even perfume, were to be harmonised; all the senses were to be involved, simultaneously, in the one overwhelming experience.[155]

But Fort's work already contained two alternative possibilities for décor, either of which were relevant whenever the symbolist aesthetic was manifest in the theatre: whether it was to be the major visual component in a total theatrical experience or whether it was to be a subsidiary towards evoking a mood and elucidating a text. It was this second function which Fort's successor, Lugné-Poe, who founded the Théâtre de l'Oeuvre in 1893, explored. He was able to make use of his experience of acting with the Théâtre Libre, and his personal involvement with three painters who, early heirs of both Pont-Aven and Bayreuth, were themselves deeply concerned with establishing a closer relationship between the fine and applied arts. For these men, Maurice Denis, Edouard Vuillard, Pierre Bonnard, theatrical décor and, more famously, the theatrical poster, offered ideal media. Painters were welcomed by Lugné-Poe in their professional capacity, working to enhance the imaginative mood of the plays and to provide harmonious accompaniment to words and actions. They were not required as 'archaeologists', neither were their designs in any way confined by natural dimensions or conventional rules of perspective.

In 1895 Lugné-Poe opened his London season with *Rosmersholm* and *The Master Builder*. Both plays invoked comparison with their English productions, but it was *The Master Builder*—though Lugné-Poe's intentions were barely understood—that was seen as the most striking example of the variety of ways in which Ibsen's plays could be presented. How far the French company were able to recreate their original production on an English stage is impossible to determine: it is known that they had problems in transporting the properties. In Paris, Vuillard's set had featured scenic innovations of some significance, for instance—a simple form of symbolic décor—a sloping stage that displayed every movement; but it is certain at least that the collapse of the church tower in the final moments of the play did, as in Paris, actually take place on stage.

The acting too was of a radically new kind to which English audiences were quite unaccustomed. Lugné-Poe's Solness was 'violent and almost brutal in manner, jerky and hard in delivery, and curiously abrupt in demeanour',[156] and his performance emphasised 'the imperious will, the compulsive magnetism of the man'.[157] He wore a startlingly bright red face make-up and an unusual goatee beard. Suzanne Després played Hilda as a 'loud-voiced, brazen girl, utterly unmysterious';[158] 'Hilda translated into everyday prose'.[159] When critics complained that she missed 'the poetry' found in the part by Elizabeth Robins, the failure was, in a sense, theirs for not responding to a new, less lyrical style. These were not, as some took them to be, clumsy amateur portrayals aimed at crude realism: in both cases, it seems reasonable to assume, a bold emphatic characterisation had been adopted deliberately. They approached a 'caricature' style—exaggeratedly typical, an over-emphasised normality that seemed to stress the *ab*normality of what was being said, a tendency in symbolist acting that was to reach a climax in the work of Jarry and the art of the grotesque.

Lugné-Poe's success in using painters in the theatre was exemplified in his production of Maeterlinck's *Pelléas et Mélisande*,[160] which managed to contain the play's nineteen scenes within two basic settings: a forest and a castle, which like the traditional castles of fairly-tale, had no specific historical or architectural character. The backcloths were of dark and indefinite patterns which gave them the look of old tapestry. As there were few properties, colour effects assumed paramount importance—shades of mauve, purple, orange, dark blue and green imparted a mysterious gloom, a rich and romantic melancholy. Maeterlinck himself had suggested the medieval costume designs, modelling them on pictures by Hans Memling and Walter Crane. Apart from Mélisande, who wore pure white, the colours blended with the setting. Finally the whole effect was subdued even further by a minimal use of lighting and the presence of a gauze curtain, which divided the audience from the stage, distancing and blurring the picture. The motives and effects were pictorial, the methods impressionistic; Lugné-Poe had created an animated stage-painting, and actors were to the setting as figures are to the background of a picture, sharing in a reciprocal imaginative relationship.

London's bewildered response to this production must in part be blamed upon the company. The sets were badly constructed, even on occasion disintegrating during performance, intervals were inexcusably long, and the cast had embarrassingly frequent recourse to the prompter.[161] The novelty of the forest backcloth attracted a remarkable range of allusion from an audience that was genuinely at a loss.

'An "impressionist" daub representing a forest.'[162]
'A Pre-Raphaelite forest.'[163]
'A wood with trees of the Aubrey Beardsley growth.'[164]
'. . . what seemed to be a large diagram representing a coal or other mine, the seams of "metal" being depicted in dull buff on a dark ground. A reference to the book informed us that this was meant to indicate a forest.'[165]

The gauze at least was unanimously recognised as a device to create an atmosphere of mystery, if with some cynicism.

' "Why the gauze curtain?" was a question heard in the stalls of the Opera Comique during the performance . . . but most players knew that a "gauze" is the favourite aid of the writer of melodrama who desires to convey the idea that his story is of the nature of a poetical dream.'[166]

In fact that gauze, one of the most commented upon of all the Théâtre de l'Oeuvre's innovations, might have been seen as visible evidence of a symbolist quandary; for while it placed the dramatic action in a removed world in which the audience was invited to participate imaginatively, at the same time it manifestly *separated* them from that action. It may be in the nature of a 'pictorial' scene as opposed to a 'realistic' illusion for an ambiguity to be inevitable: so the gauze, which suggests an infinite multiplicity of time and space, may also remind spectators that they are present to witness a spectacle, in a particular place, at a particular time.

This is only a reminder of the paradoxical nature of any symbolic art. In the symbolist theatre the whole presentation, together with its occasion, form a composite: colour and shape, gesture and movement, together with drama, together with event, co-operate in the evocation or creation of multiple symbol. The décor, whether it 'accompanies' or 'contributes', is thus inevitably elevated far above its position as stage carpentry; symbolist theatre requires a deep trust in the affective power of stage components, and its anti-materialist philosophies paradoxically rely upon the beauty of its material conventions.

But *Pelléas et Mélisande* in itself did not generally produce this kind of theoretical speculation. Simplicity, shades of the Elizabethan theatre, were noted, as were the strange rhythmic chanting and the ethereal gestures of the performers, but understanding was limited to admissions of susceptibility to a mood.

'. . . that weird fascination, which, whether it be merely a pictorial and rhythmic appeal to emotional imagination, or whether it be the compact of symbolism and allegory, is not to be realised by those who have not seen, or, rather, felt it.'[167]

L'Intruse, the other Maeterlinck play, a drama of inaction set in a deserted Flemish farmhouse where an old man awaits death to the accompaniment of a ticking clock, was greeted with more enthusiasm, and the semi-darkness of the stage, the hushed voices of the performers and their silent movements made their impression. But then *L'Intruse* possessed the theatrical appeal of any play that is based on suspense.

If the visit of the Théâtre de l'Oeuvre drew fresh attention to the many issues raised by symbolism, it was as much Maeterlinck's own presence in London at the same time as the performances of his plays that precipitated a reinvigorated inquiry into the theory. In his interviews with reporters from the daily papers, Maeterlinck seemed to suggest that his real interest was not in the theatre at all, but in a mystical vision too delicate and intangible ever to be materially realised. Naturally when face to face with the man himself his interviewers politely bypassed the peculiar dichotomy of a playwright openly professing a hostility to his own medium (a rather different line from that taken by tough professional journals such as

The Era,[168] whose leader-writer gave full vent to his patronising contempt). To *The Daily Chronicle* he remarked:

'With the greatest admiration for the talents of my interpreters, I cannot say that any theatrical representation, whether of my own plays or of others, gives me real pleasure. On the contrary, it is apt to worry (*agacer*) me. I think that almost all plays that are not mere stage-carpentry can be better appreciated in reading than on the stage.'[169]

And to *The Sketch*:

'. . . I myself take little or no interest in the practical side of dramatic life. I always enjoy reading a play far more than I do seeing it acted, for on the stage the delicate symbolic essence of what every thoughtful writer wishes to convey cannot but escape.'[170]

The renunciation included almost the whole body of dramatic literature, with only one or two partial exceptions—one of them, significantly, *The Master Builder*.

Close questioning about his notion of a puppet theatre only received the evasive answer that, preferable though they might be to clumsy human beings, marionettes would have to be neither 'primitive and limited in their motions', nor 'too exact and detailed'.[171]

'Are you a musician, M. Maeterlinck? [enquired *The Daily Chronicle*, looking for another clue.] It has always seemed to me that in the echo-like repetitions which characterise your dialogue you were aiming at a musical, what I may almost call a fugal, effect?'

Maeterlinck's reply at least hinted at the considerable importance he placed upon the power of dialogue to convey more than direct information.

'The repetitions to which you allude are a fault of my early manner which I am striving to correct. . . . There are times, no doubt, when repetition is a legitimate dramatic effect. Take, for instance, the scene in the fourth act of *Macbeth*, where Rosse tells Macduff of the murder of his wife and children. Here Macduff's mechanically-repeated questions are of the essence of drama.'

It was towards just this problem of dramatic language and its wider meanings that Archer (he had first shown an interest in Maeterlinck in 1891) turned—talking now quite openly in terms of a symbolist approach.

'M. Maeterlinck has invented, or at any rate perfected . . . a new and very beautiful method of dramatic expression. Perhaps "expression" is scarcely the word, for the peculiarity of the method is that nothing is fairly and squarely expressed. Language is in M. Maeterlinck's hands quite literally the veil of thought and emotion, revealing through concealment; so that the film of gauze interposed, at the Opera Comique, between the audience and the stage, had a symbolic as well as a picturesque value. Very seldom, except in passages in impersonal moralising, do his characters give direct utterance to what they are thinking and feeling. Often, indeed, they could not if they would, for they do not themselves realise what is passing in their hearts. The poet's art lies in so working on our imagination that, through their seemingly irrelevant and sometimes even trivial babble, we divine more than they could possibly tell us if they could "unpack their hearts with words".'[172]

Even Walkley could accept *L'Intruse*. Although it contained 'no rhetoric, only little driblets of commonplace talk, no dramatic action, only dramatic inaction,' it was still 'the one impression which the playwright has sought', and he enthused over *Pelléas et Mélisande* for 'the sheer beauty, the tender pathos, the romantic enchantment', its 'artistic success'.[173]

The display of sympathy, in both cases, is intriguing but explicable. Both Archer and Walkley had found extreme difficulty in assimilating the puzzling equivocation and irony of *The Master Builder*. Walkley had been unable to cope with elements which had seemed at the time incompatible with his own dramatic theory, and Archer had felt the need to provide credible explanations to bring the play in line with realistic principles. Maeterlinck's plays, where there was no immediacy, no recognisable reality at all, involved no such heart-searching; indeed, they even served to gratify a lingering nostalgia for idealism.

Lugné-Poe's season was not the first opportunity that Londoners had had to see Maeterlinck on stage. *L'Intruse* had been put on by Beerbohm Tree as an experimental performance at the Haymarket on 27 January 1892, less than a year after its première (and the first performance of any Maeterlinck play) at the Théâtre de l'Art in Paris. While in France the publication of his first play, *La Princesse Maleine*, in 1890, and the production of *L'Intruse* had met with immediate acclaim and endorsement of Octave Mirbeau's phrase 'the Belgian Shakespeare', reactions in England tended to be more cautious.[174] Tree himself preceded his production with some dismissive remarks to the Playgoers' Club, and Hall Caine, in an introduction to the English translation, wrote of its lack of 'dramatic structure', of 'dramatic form', even of 'dramatic idea'—'it has no tug of emotion, no clash of incident.'[175] Archer, more receptive, wrote an article about this 'Pessimist Playwright'[176] in which he commented on his 'musical rather than literary effect' and his old-fashioned reliance on 'morbid fantasy'. He conceded that Maeterlinck's use of 'mechanism' sufficiently stimulated the imagination to 'make it meet him halfway'. Yet a conscious artifice permeated the whole ('all nature and the world he treats as his machinery'), so that dramatic action was merely the workings of fate: 'Fate—a blind, non-moral fate—the beginning and end of M. Maeterlinck's philosophy.'

Maeterlinck's major theoretical statements were not written until after the early plays, but were quickly translated. *The Treasure of the Humble* appeared in English in 1897, and it contained the influential essay 'The Tragical in Daily Life', in which he put the case for a drama of silence and gesture rather than one of violence and action: the most profound experiences occur at times of normality and solitude. For Maeterlinck, Hamlet's inactivity made him a more significant tragic hero than Othello.

The drama of silence and of stasis is best relayed through impersonal devices, through masks and marionettes, or actors pretending to be marionettes, non-human figures that evoke an awareness of the non-material world. The sense of the noumenon can also be found in certain dramas of quotidian life, where characters and audience both became aware of a sub-stratum of meaning beneath their conversation, a sense of 'otherness', of their own remoteness from each other and from their true selves. *The Master Builder* assumes a particular importance for Maeterlinck for this reason.

'Hilda and Solness are, I believe, the first characters in drama who feel, for an instant, that they are living in the atmosphere of the soul; and the discovery of this essential life that exists in them, beyond the life of everyday, comes fraught with terror. Hilda and Solness are two souls to whom a flash has revealed their situation in the true life.'[177]

They speak, that is, a language in which are blended together a simultaneous awareness of both inner and outer experience. In a later essay, 'The Modern Drama', Maeterlinck was to assert that

'It is in a small room, round a table, close to the fire, that the joys and sorrows of mankind are decided. We suffer, or make others suffer, we love, we die, there in our corner.'[178]

Modern dramatists had turned to the problems of contemporary dramatic morality and made their drama out of conflicts of passion and duty, of duty and desire. But although they had touched 'the highest point of human consciousness' yet for Maeterlinck, the mystic, the ultimate revelations eluded them.

'Here we touch the limit of the resources of modern dramaturgy. For, in truth, the further we penetrate into the consciousness of man, the less struggle do we discover. It is impossible to penetrate far into any consciousness unless that consciousness be very enlightened. . . . But a consciousness that is truly enlightened will possess passions and desires infinitely less exacting, infinitely more peaceful and patient, more salutary, abstract and general, than are those that reside in the ordinary consciousness.'[179]

Maeterlinck was still striving after something above and beyond the claims of duty, and he considered Ibsen, for all his profound understanding of human consciousness, to be hampered by external obligations; hence the 'unjust pride', 'a kind of soured and morbid madness', of his tragic heroes.

'For, if it be true that Ibsen has contributed few salutary elements to the morality of our time, he is perhaps the only writer for the stage who has caught sight of and set in motion a new though still disagreeable poetry, which he has succeeded in investing with a kind of savage, gloomy beauty and grandeur (surely two savage and gloomy for it to become general or definitive); as he is the only one who owes nothing to the poetry of the violently illumined dramas of antiquity or the Renaissance.'[180]

Thus Ibsen's plays were only part of a necessary and difficult process of emancipation from worldly gloom and division.

This is obviously nebulous stuff; but for those who already inclined towards mysticism Maeterlinck's thoughts about the theatre had their attractions, especially after the publication of *The Treasure of the Humble*:

'Plot and action are to be relegated to an entirely secondary position, the stage is to be swept clear of cheap trickery and superficial effects, and the eternal mystery life is to rise up in an almost palpable sense before the spectator.'[181]

Arguments about the 'literary drama' deployed Maeterlinck in support of various issues. The symbolist drama could be seen as a highly 'literary' way of avoiding the problem of contemporary degraded subject matter, at the same time as the lessened involvement in character and plot gave free rein to the personality of a playwright to express itself through mood and atmosphere alone. In 1891 Tree had rejected *Les Aveugles* because it was not 'acting drama —we may respectfully relegate it to the bookshelves of literary curios.'[182] The quasi-Shakespearean *La Princesse Maleine* was granted 'picturesqueness', but 'our author forgets that the picturesque is not the end and aim of dramatic art, but rather the vehicle to be employed toward that end.'[183]

The relevance of a 'picturesque' mode to an immediate dramatic situation was a crux in investigations of this kind; but, given a willing commentator, the use of symbolism offered a viable solution. Arthur Symons, the most verbal of these, was to say of Villiers de l'Isle Adam's *Axel* that it was 'the drama of the soul, and at the same time . . . the most pictorial of dramas.'[184] Deeply involved in marshalling a full symbolist canon, he perceived in the plays of Maeterlinck and de l'Isle Adam a powerful antidote to realism.

'The modern drama, under the democratic influence of Ibsen, the positive influence of Dumas fils, has limited itself to the expression of temperaments in the one case, of theoretic intelligences in the other, in as nearly as possible the words which the average man would use for the statement of his motions and ideas. The form, that is, is degraded below the level of the characters whom it attempts to express; for it is evident that the average man can articulate only a small enough part of what he obscurely feels or thinks; and the theory of Realism is that his emotions and ideas are to be given only insofar as the words of his own command can give them.'[185]

Besides the freedom to express *himself*—'to Maeterlinck the theatre has been, for the most part, no more than one of his disguises'[186]—the symbolist playwright has access to deeper levels of consciousness. The means available to him are artificial yet precise. The strutting motions of a marionette, by parodying phenomenal life, demonstrate the ways in which that life appears to the mystic intelligence, a vehicle only for 'some elaborate invention, planned for larger ends than our personal display or convenience'. Symons' enthusiasm for masks and marionettes relates also to a general concept that would have won recognition from Wilde and Godwin. (And so the idea of the drama as invoked or recreated *mood* and aesthetic whole returns to the English theatre, its potency reinforced by French symbolism. Although, significantly, Forbes-Robertson's immensely popular revival of *Pelléas and Mélisande* in 1898, with Mrs Patrick Campbell, had a far more representational setting than that used by the Théâtre de l'Oeuvre.) 'Atmosphere,' Symons wrote of Maeterlinck's early plays, 'the suggestion of what was not said, was everything . . .'.[187]

Maeterlinck's symbolism also acted as a focus for more conventional theorists. His drama omits the 'will' that they connected with action and realistic speech. The dream plays, in which character has a reciprocal relationship with setting and a passive relationship with the overall action, are fundamentally different from those realist plays where situation conditions event and dilemma, and resolution is manifested through crisis. Symbolism was, though, accorded a cautious respect—mainly because of its capacity to transmit the promptings of the unconscious in images of mystery and fate. Archer got that far:

'The tendency of all his thought is to minimise the operation of the will—that is why some people, vaguely realising that morality rests on the hypothesis of free-will, call his work morbid and immoral. . . . His characters very seldom give direct utterance to what is passing in their minds. They talk of everything else in the world, and, by the aid of an indefinable, elusive symbolism which is the poet's peculiar secret, we are enabled to divine more than they know themselves of their innermost emotions. . . . And just in this (I intend no paradox) our symbolist is often more real than the realists. . . . This is, on the whole, an inarticulate world. Comparatively few real-life dramas work themselves out in analytic scenes, like those of *Rosmersholm*, or *The Notorious Mrs Ebbsmith*.'[188]

Already there had been plays that contained strands of both articulate will and unknown motive: *Hedda Gabler*, which starts with the will's collapse, and *The Master Builder*, where the will is initially dominant but collapses later, had been the critical instances, explicable at first only in terms of disinterested, unstructured observation in the one case, and intimations of the supernatural (or the *barely* credible) in the other. Dramatic convention inevitably makes this part of the problem of a character's own self-cognisance, the degree of confidence and understanding with which he views his own identity and voices his own feelings. Solness, for example, is obviously puzzled by his own state, and by what Hilda tells him about himself; he can only be said partially to understand his past and present behaviour; the audience either shares his bewilderment or notices certain ironical discrepancies in his conduct.

Maeterlinck's drama of inuendo and suggestion, artificially manipulated in a deliberate attempt to involve the audience into making its own imaginative contribution, also invites participation. But in Maeterlinck, the directing power of an external fate (most often death) must be recognised by the audience, and probably by the character as well; a diminishing of the opportunities for irony that the complicity between figure and romantic setting, and the dateless time, corroborate.

The single level of the mystic drama runs the suicidal risk of ignoring the multiplicity of human intercourse, and without such ironies (which are after all only a special if absolutely vital level of conflict) there can be no drama at all; hence, at base, the instinctive reluctance shown by both Archer and Walkley to swallow *The Treasure of the Humble* quite whole: Archer by pointing out that even Maeterlinck's own plays, which isolate and externalise events that occur within the soul, preserve, as they must, elements of dynamic conflict as much as they try to evoke a static mood;[189] Walkley, in a very non-committal preface to the English translation, concentrating upon sources for the mystic doctrine rather than upon a dramatic theory which he hinted might be 'an unrealisable dream'.[190]

But already symbolism was drawing on other, older resources for its present realisation. Lugné-Poe was much taken with the revival of interest in England in the Elizabethan theatre, which had been nurtured by the productions of William Poel, and in 1896 he came to London again, this time to assist Poel with his *Two Gentlemen of Verona*. In the Elizabethan conventions he observed just that same combination of simplicity and artifice whose subversive possibilities were being exploited by a rebellious protégé—Alfred Jarry: 're-monter à l'antique, à cette naïveté savante me semble bien le secret du nouvel art pour lequel M. Jarry écrit.'[191]

Jarry's theories of décor were extreme: in some statements he rejected it completely, in others he compromised with a demand for a return to the bare Elizabethan stage. The single setting for *Ubu Roi* is obviously, on one level, the logical end point of earlier symbolist work which had aimed at reducing décor to a minimum number of atemporal settings. But Jarry also demanded the transference of the action to an unspecifiable location, the use of masks, reliance on universal gestures, depersonalisation of the actors. Once released from the constraints of place and personality, his characters were quite free to perpetrate their outrage.

Like the Elizabethan theatre, the theatre of Jarry has no pretensions to illusion. By openly acknowledging the need for explanatory intervention, it re-opens the hidden gulf between the reality of what is enacted and the artificiality of its surroundings. An inescapable and useful irony—Maeterlinck's attempt to overcome it had produced only a bland monotony.

The continuing power of the naturalist ideal depends in part on such antithetical upheavals from inside. Explosions occur when the tension between conflicting pressures becomes intolerable—on the one hand a passionate desire for a full description of life in its entirety and on the other frustration at the impossibility of achieving an irresistible illusion with the techniques of realistic stage art. So with Jarry the theatre burst out in anarchy, and naturalism deliberately set out to destroy itself by menacing the audience with the threat of its own breakdown and by indulging the absurdity of its theatrical pretensions. Jarry insults his audience by implicating it within the incohate ugliness and imprecision of his fictive world.

W. B. Yeats and Arthur Symons saw *Ubu* together in Paris, and the horrified comment of the poet, appalled by what he termed the 'objectivity' of the play, which seemed to announce a hideous new phase—'After us, the Savage God'—has entered legend. Symons, eager to account for the amazing experience in terms of his all-embracing symbolist programme, ventured that the means developed by Maeterlinck for the evocation of sublime states had, in Jarry's mischievous hands, become inverted so that it was a way of releasing terror, bestiality and (the word seems proleptic) cruelty.

'Just as the seeker after pleasure whom pleasure has exhausted, so the seeker after the material illusions of literary artifice turns finally to that first subjugated, never quite exterminated element of cruelty which is one of the links which bind us to the earth. *Ubu Roi* is the brutality out of which we have achieved civilisation, and those painted, massacring puppets the destroying elements which are as old as the world, and which we never chase out of the system of natural things.'[192]

Recent dramatists have (perhaps unconsciously) taken up an interrupted cue not from their immediate predecessors but from the dramatists of the turn of the century—from the silence of Maeterlinck and the anarchy of Jarry. Inaction ends in existential nothingness, the symbolist farce foreshadows the absurd, the dream turns to nightmare.

When in 1898 the Independent Theatre staged its last production, it had to a large extent fulfilled the purposes for which it was founded, if only by offering an example of a viable means of sustaining minority theatre. Evidence of the power of that example lies in the foundation of descendant organisations, even within its own lifetime. In 1897 the New Century Theatre opened, with a revival of *John Gabriel Borkman*; in 1899 the Stage Society was founded and first moves were made to found a theatre in Ireland that would be a vehicle for both revolutionary art and nationalist politics; and 1904 was to see the first of the Vedrenne-Barker seasons at the Court. Shaw and Yeats and Synge, all raised in this new climate, are the three English-language dramatists of the beginning of the century who are most remembered and, in two cases, still regularly performed (the exception, significantly, being the one who was most involved in exploring new modes of theatrical experience). Developments on the continent were, in contrast, dominated by the rapid and portentous ascendancy of the great creative director—Stanislavsky and Meyerhold in Moscow, Reinhardt in Berlin, Copeau in Paris. By largely ignoring form and staging, at least in its own productions, the Independent Theatre certainly had not made any real preparation for the advent of such figures in the English theatre, which, although a generous and welcoming host, was for a long time to offer little in return to its visitors either in the way of imitation or of progression; Walkley and Archer may, however little they realised it themselves, even by 1900 have witnessed its most receptive years.

The reasons for a period of cultural lethargy are often difficult to locate. One line of diagnosis should begin with a consideration of what *might* have happened, of those newly taken directions that should have been still potent. But these were ambivalent, and they were only partially followed through. By the end of the century the non-commercial theatre was established as, at worst, a stop-gap: as either a dry place safe from the commercial flood or, better but more rarely, as an occasional breach in the solid walls of money and popular taste. (All metaphors are inexact when it comes to describing only a mutating existence.) At the same time the theatre was on the way to becoming a disastrously, if necessarily, self-conscious art; and that is where the struggle for organisation and the efforts to understand new forms really touch.

Symbolism's great and most sophisticated claim was that it had the power to disturb composure by indicating the hidden meaning behind a surface of normality (as, more recently, the flamboyant, violent attacks on bourgeois sensibility that derive from Jarry), and in its purest form it required an audience desirous of and prepared for a deep involvement. Yet there was a serious contradiction in the wish of reformers to 'involve' or 'disturb' because—it's more than preaching to the converted—minority theatre inevitably ends up aiming its power to disrupt only at those who are already engaged. And that *is* contradictory because the theatre's recurrent claim for recognition depends upon a sense of its own social centrality—yet it must continually find new ways of achieving it, which means joining in an advance guard, participating in a cultural guerrilla warfare. Protests against the Independent Theatre and the kinds of play it supported stemmed from feelings of mystification and shock; there was rage at the image in the mirror, not only at what it showed but also at those who held it up to a resentful face.

Respect for what was thought to be accurate and comprehensive observation permitted a limited acceptance of naturalism. In the case of Maeterlinck and the symbolist drama the clash came less with their transcendent ideas (which automatically carried a moral cachet) than their opaque form. How could an audience know what it hadn't been shown, how could it understand what wasn't explained, how could a playwright depict when he seemed to deny most of the conventions of dramatic representation?

Drama is a matter of action and gesture as of verbal language, although when these become too closely associated with a static tableau or a dominating setting, then the prime verbal statements have a diminished impact and, maybe, the progress and impetus of the drama become stultified. A novelist such as George Moore or a novice such as the young Shaw was confronted with the task of learning the rules of a unique mode, in which verbal sequence is only a part (made more difficult by the demand of the realistic drama for speech to be composed of an actual, colloquial and debased language). Description, analysis, commentary, data of all kinds, are either impossible to present or become clumsy and intrusive; there were alternatives, but they were not always obvious, and they lay in the resuscitation of ancient verbal devices—chorus, soliloquy and imagery; when used skilfully, all these too require or invite the response of a specially alert audience.

It has been argued that the main tendency of nineteenth-century art is towards an historical and intellectual stasis, and that the fixed quantities and inevitable resolution of melodrama are the model for its characteristic expression.[193] Certainly the closed domestic interior and the fixed pictorial setting have it in common, particularly in a proscenium theatre, that they set a single, confined vista before the eyes of the audience. This is a kind of physical and social stasis; and there is a stasis of moral frustration too in the final gestures of the naturalist drama, in the murders and suicides that dominate last acts from *Thérèse Raquin* onward.

If this general pattern is correct then what gives modernity to the semi-symbolic dramas of Ibsen's late period is their final escape from the innate acknowledgement of the rigid moral laws that operate in melodrama and pseudo-realism, or, as in the case of the wholly symbolic drama, from reference to an other than human control. They evoke in their closing moments that mood most associated with tragedy, immediate but insoluble: that living stasis born of a dilemma endured by a hero and shared in part with his audience.

The Independent Theatre, uncertain of its social role (which means essentially its relation to its audience), founded as a protest but eclectic in its repertoire, reflected and even contributed to a confusion in the theatre of its time. Changes in form and changes in organisation are interdependent, which is not to say that they are synchronised. Theatre as ritual, theatre as therapy, theatre as protest, theatre as politics, even theatre as entertainment: much as their advocates may deny it, all are subject to the benefits and ironies of a single law—popular or not, a public medium it is.

Notes

I INTRODUCTION: DOCTRINE AND REPERTORY (pp. 1–29)

1. *The Nineteenth Century*, August 1879, 242–3.
2. Ibid, 238.
3. Ibid, 242.
4. *The Scenic Art*, 1949, 44.
5. Ibid, 119.
6. 'The English Stage', *The Quarterly Review*, February 1883, 388.
7. *The Fashionable Tragedian*, 23–4.
8. *Henry Irving. Actor and Manager. A Critical Study*, 1883.
9. *The Saturday Review*, 30 May 1896, repr. *Our Theatres in the Nineties*, II, 1948, 139.
10. *English Dramatists of Today*, 17.
11. 'What does the public want?', *The Theatre*, June 1885, 272–3.
12. *About the Theatre*, 247–8.
13. See Allardyce Nicoll, *History of English Drama*, V, 1962, 20–2.
14. *The World*, 7 May 1886.
15. 'A Plea for an Endowed Theatre', *The Fortnightly Review*, May 1889, 615–16.
16. Ibid, 616.
17. *The Fortnightly Review*, January 1873, repr. Edmund Gosse, *Northern Studies*, 1890.
18. 'Breaking a Butterfly', *The Theatre*, April 1884, 214.
19. *The Dramatic Review*, 4 April 1885.
20. Laurence Irving, *Henry Irving*, 1951, 535.
21. 363.
22. *Dramatic Opinions*, 9 December 1891.
23. *The Dramatic Review*, 24 December 1892.
24. *The Dramatic Review*, 27 January 1894.
25. Henrik Ibsen, *The Pillars of Society and other plays*, 1888, xxiii–xxix.
26. *Progress*, January 1884, 24–9 and February 1884, 91–7.
27. *Shelley's Socialism*, 1888, 18.
28. *Theatre and Friendship*, 1932, 29.
29. *The Saturday Review*, 8 May 1897, repr. *Our Theatres in the Nineties*, III, 127.
30. *The Quintessence of Ibsenism*, 1891, 6.
31. *Bernard Shaw and the Nineteenth Century Tradition*, 1958, 154.
32. 10 December 1887, 162.
33. *William Morris. Artist, Writer, Socialist*, ed. May Morris, I, 1936, 390.
34. *The Pall Mall Gazette*, 17 October 1887.
35. J. W. Mackail, *The Life of William Morris*, II, 1899, 343.
36. 'The Socialist Ideal of Art', *The New Review*, January 1891, 1.
37. *The Saturday Review*, 10 October 1896, repr. *Our Theatres in the Nineties*, II, 213–14.
38. *The Saturday Review*, 14 March 1896, repr. *Our Theatres in the Nineties*, II, 70.
39. *The Saturday Review*, 21 March 1896, repr. *Our Theatres in the Nineties*, II, 79.
40. For a just appraisal of Jones see John Russell Taylor, *The Rise and Fall of the Well-Made Play*, 1967.
41. *The Renascence of the English Drama*, 1895, preface, vii–ix.
42. A. B. Walkley, *Playhouse Impressions*, 1892, 114.
43. See Jones' preface to *Saints and Sinners*, 1891.
44. 'The Dramatic Outlook', 1884, lecture first delivered at the opening of the Playgoers' Club, 7 August 1884, repr. *The Renascence of the English Drama*, 163.

45. *The World*, 20 March 1895 and 27 March 1895.
46. *The Saturday Review*, 16 March 1895, repr. *Our Theatres in the Nineties*, I, 60.
47. Mrs Patrick Campbell, *My Life and Some Letters*, 1922, 98–9.
48. *The Benefit of the Doubt*, 1896, 12.
49. *The World*, 23 October 1895.
50. *The Saturday Review*, 19 October 1895, repr. *Our Theatres in the Nineties*, I, 218.
51. *The Saturday Review*, 7 December 1895, repr. *Our Theatres in the Nineties*, I, 268.
52. Ibid.
53. See for example Kenneth Graham, *English Criticism of the Novel, 1865–1900*, 1965.
54. 'The Realist's Dilemma', *About the Theatre*, 1886, 329–41.
55. *Dramatic Criticisms*, 1899, 260.
56. Ibid, 38.
57. See J. C. Trewin, *Benson and the Bensonians*, 1960.
58. Robert Speaight, *William Poel and the Elizabethan Revival*, 1954, 60.

II AN AESTHETIC THEATRE: THE CAREER OF EDWARD WILLIAM GODWIN (pp. 31–68)

1. E. Watson, *Sheridan to Robertson*, 1926, 196.
2. *The Architect*, 31 October 1874—26 June 1875. Repr. Edward Gordon Craig's journal *The Mask*, May/June 1908—April 1914.
3. *The Western Daily Press*, 11 October 1864; see Kathleen M. D. Barker, 'The Terrys and Godwin in Bristol', *Theatre Notebook*, Autumn 1967, 27–43.
4. *The Architect*, 8 May 1875, 271.
5. *The Architect*, 12 June 1875, 344–5.
6. Letter to *The Times*, 23 April 1875.
7. *The Story of My Life*, 1908, 106.
8. *Mrs J. Comyns-Carr's Reminiscences*, ed. Eve Adam, 1926, 31.
9. *The Morning Post*, 19 April 1875.
10. *Thoughts and Afterthoughts*, 1913, 44. See also W. Moelwyn Merchant, 'On Looking at *The Merchant of Venice*', *Nineteenth-Century British Theatre*, ed. K. Richards and P. Thomson, 1971, 171–8.
11. Queen's Theatre, 16 September 1876.
12. 'Henry V. A Theatrical Experience', *The Architect*, 9 September 1876, 142–3.
13. *The Architect*, 23 September 1876, 188.
14. 'Henry V. A Theatrical Experience', *The Architect*, 30 September 1876, 192–4.
15. Godwin to John Coleman, 2 September 1886, Enthoven Collection.
16. Sadler's Wells Theatre, 20 September 1880.
17. From a detailed review in *The Portfolio*, November 1880, 184.
18. Lyceum Theatre, 3 January 1881. There were many discussions of this production in contemporary periodicals, and during the following years, e.g. P. Fitzgerald, 'The Scenic World', *Cornhill Magazine*, January–June 1886, 281–6; Juliet Pollock, '*The Cup* at the Lyceum', *Macmillan's Magazine*, February 1881, 316–20.
19. *The Story of My Life*, 196–7.
20. Court Theatre, 7 May 1881.
21. Letter to *The World*, 11 May 1881.
22. Wilson Barrett to Godwin, 31 March 1881, Enthoven Collection.
23. Haymarket Theatre, 26 October 1881.
24. Royal Globe Theatre, 14 January 1882.

25. See C. Halford Hawkins, 'Dramatic Art: The Meiningen Theatre', *Macmillan's Magazine*, April 1877.
26. *The British Architect*, 17 June 1881, 303.
27. A copy remains in the Enthoven Collection together with a great deal of correspondence about the foundation of the society and its first, and probably only, publication, dated 1883, which contained sketches of medieval costumes.
28. See Beerbohm Tree, 'The New Costume Society and the Stage', *The Theatre*, February 1883, 96–8.
29. Hesketh Pearson, *Beerbohm Tree*, 1956, 37–8. See also Max Beerbohm, *Herbert Beerbohm Tree*, 1920, 19.
30. Royal Adelphi Theatre, 14 March 1883.
31. Gaiety Theatre, 30 November 1883.
32. Princess's Theatre, 6 December 1883.
33. See Freeman Wills, *W. G. Wills. Dramatist and Painter*, 1898, 228.
34. *A Few Notes on the Architecture and Costume of the Period of the Play of Claudian, A.D. 360–460*, 1883. See also *The British Architect*, 7 December 1884, for illustrations.
35. *The British Architect*, 14 December 1883, 277.
36. *Index to the Story of My Days*, 1957, 58.
37. *Modern Society*, 15 December 1883, 47.
38. *The Daily News*, 7 December 1883.
39. Ibid.
40. Princess's Theatre, 26 February 1885.
41. *Life*, 16 August 1884, 312.
42. Princess's Theatre, 16 October 1884. See *The British Architect*, 15 April 1881, 192–3, for costume designs.
43. *Life*, 16 August 1884, 312.
44. Ibid.
45. The Enthoven Collection contains minutes for ten meetings between 28 July 1881 and 26 September 1881, several copies of the 'Foundation Rules', and several salary lists.
46. *The British Architect*, 29 July 1881, 379.
47. *The British Architect*, 15 October 1886, 348.
48. *The Theatre*, September 1884, 158–9. See also *The New York Mirror*, 28 July 1884. An example of an open-air production, seized on by journalists, but not acknowledged either by Godwin or Lady Archibald, was the Oberammergau Passion Play.
49. The description of stage and costume is compiled from contemporary reviews of both the 1884 and the 1885 performances. See especially Alfred Austin, 'In the Forest of Arden', *National Review*, September 1884, 126–36; T. F. Thiselton Dyer, 'Tongues in Trees', *Belgravia*, July 1885, 45–51, and 'Foresters at Home', *The Art Journal*, October 1885, 301–4; Janey S. Campbell, 'The Woodland Gods', *Woman's World*, November 1888, 1–7.
50. *The Dramatic Review*, 6 June 1885, 296.
51. 27 July 1884.
52. 6 June 1885.
53. *The Dramatic Review*, 6 June 1885, 297.
54. *Truth*, 31 July 1884.
55. *The Dramatic Review*, 6 June 1885, 297.
56. '*The Faithful Shepherdesse*', June 1885, 1031–42.
57. Todhunter to Godwin, 6 July 1885, Enthoven Collection. The 'pastoral drama' that Todhunter mentioned may in fact be the later *A Sicilian Idyll*,

produced after Godwin's death, which comes more accurately under this heading than *Helena in Troas*.

58. 6 December 1885, Todhunter Collection, University of Reading.
59. See George Nash, *Edward Gordon Craig 1872–1966*, 1967, and *The British Architect*, 4 June 1886, for further illustrative material.
60. *The Nineteenth Century*, June 1886, 914–22.
61. *The Morning Post*, 14 May 1886.
62. *The Sunday Times*, 23 May 1886.
63. *The Dramatic Review*, 22 May 1886, 162.
64. *The Playgoer's Pocketbook for 1886*, 1887, 105.
65. *The Dramatic Review*, 7 August 1886, 12.
66. May 1889, 260–1.
67. *The World*, 30 July 1884.
68. J. S. Campbell, 'The Woodland Gods', *Woman's World*, November 1888. *Woman's World* was edited by Wilde.
69. Letter from Lady Archibald to the authors, E. R. and J. Pennell, *The Life of James McNeill Whistler*, 1908, 222.
70. *Rainbow-Musick*, 4.
71. 8 February 1885, 19–20.
72. 24 August 1885, 113.
73. *The Nineteenth Century*, May 1885, 800–18.
74. 'Miss Anderson's Juliet', *The Nineteenth Century*, December 1884, 886.
75. *The Nineteenth Century*, May 1885, 807.
76. 'Is Shakespeare also among the Archaeologists?', *The Dramatic Review*, 23 May 1885, 260.
77. 'Archaeology in the Theatre', *Macmillan's Magazine*, June 1886, 126.
78. Lys, 'Archaeology or Art?', *The Dramatic Review*, 7 August 1886, 13–14.
79. *The Dramatic Review*, 22 May 1886, 161–2.
80. P. B. Shelley, *The Cenci*, ed. Alfred Forman and H. Buxton Forman, 1886.
81. Bedford Park Clubhouse, 5 June 1890; Aubrey House, Kensington (open-air performance), 24 June 1890; St George's Hall, 1 July 1890; Vaudeville Theatre (together with Todhunter's *The Poison Flower*), 15 June 1891.
82. See I. Fletcher, 'Bedford Park: Aesthete's Elysium?', *Romantic Mythologies*, 1967, 194. Performances also continued into the following decade. An entertainment was given at the Clubhouse on 14 July 1892, which included several scenes from *The Cenci*. Florence Farr played Beatrice.
83. *The Stage*, 9 May 1890.
84. *The Referee*, 11 May 1890.
85. *The Stage*, 9 May 1890.
86. *The Daily Telegraph*, 16 June 1891.
87. *The Illustrated London News*, 20 June 1891.
88. Preface to *The Black Cat*, 1895, x-xi.
89. *Letters to the New Island*, 1934, 175.

III A WAGNER THEATRE: PROFESSOR HERKOMER'S PICTORIAL-MUSICAL PLAYS (pp. 69–110)

1. *The Illustrated Sporting and Dramatic News*, 11 May 1882.
2. 'Herr Wagner's New Theatre at Bayreuth', *The Practical Magazine*, July 1874, 8.

3. Joseph Bennett, *Letters from Bayreuth*, 1877, 30.
4. Franz Hueffer, 'The Wagner Festival of 1876', *Fraser's Magazine*, December 1875, 708.
5. *Letters from Bayreuth*, 78.
6. Halford Hawkins, 'The Wagner Festival at Bayreuth', *Macmillan's Magazine*, November 1876, 57.
7. Geoffrey Skelton, *Wagner at Bayreuth*, 1965, 45.
8. F. Corder, 'Richard Wagner as a Stage Manager', *The Theatre*, February 1883, 74.
9. 'Liszt, Wagner and Weimar', *Fraser's Magazine*, July 1855. Repr. *Essays of George Eliot*, ed. Thomas Pinney, 1963, 100.
10. H. A. Haweis, 'Wagner', *The Contemporary Review*, May 1877, 984.
11. 'Wagner and Wagnerism', *The Nineteenth Century*, March 1883, 442–3.
12. *The New Review*, June 1889, 34. Repr. Henry James, *The Scenic Art*, ed. Wade, 1949, 230.
13. 'Wagner in Bayreuth', *The English Illustrated Magazine*, October 1889, 52.
14. W. B. Yeats, *Letters to the New Island*, 1934, 104.
15. *The London Figaro*, 12 July 1890.
16. 'The Dying Drama', *The New Review*, September 1888, 388–9.
17. *The Herkomers*, I, 1910, 58.
18. Louis Engel, *From Handel to Hallé*, 1890, 171.
19. See references to Herkomer throughout *The Complete Letters of Vincent Van Gogh*, 1958, and V . W. Van Gogh, *Vincent Van Gogh in England*, 1968.
20. *From Handel to Hallé*, 183.
21. Ibid, 183–4.
22. J. Saxon Mills, *Life and Letters of Sir Hubert Herkomer*, 1923, 97.
23. Alice Meynell, 'Artists' Homes: Mr Hubert Herkomer's at Bushey', *Magazine of Art*, January 1883, 96–101.
24. Ibid, 101.
25. 'Portrait Painting', *Magazine of Art*, December 1904, 139.
26. 'The New Gallery', *The Speaker*, 7 May 1892, 556.
27. J. Saxon Mills, *Life and Letters of J. Saxon Mills*, 1923, 165.
28. M. P. Bromet, *Response*, 1935, 162.
29. Ibid, 163.
30. H. von Herkomer, *My School and My Gospel*, 1908, 14.
31. W. F. Wayte, 'Round About Bushey', *The Ludgate*, December 1899, 185.
32. *The Herkomers*, II, 32.
33. See W. L. Courtney, 'Professor Herkomer, Royal Academician, his Life and Work', *The Art Annual for 1892;* H. Herkomer, 'How we teach at Bushey', *The Universal Review*, September 1889.
34. See *The Watford Observer*, 23 June 1888, and *The West Herts Post*, 17 June 1892.
35. *The Watford Observer*, 28 April 1888.
36. *The World*, 2 May 1888.
37. *The Herkomers*, II, 43. For further descriptions of *Am Idyl* see Alice Corkran, 'Professor Herkomer's Pictorial Music Play', *The Scottish Art Review*, July 1889; H. Herkomer, 'Art in the Theatre: The Pictorial Music-Play: "An Idyl" ', *Magazine of Art*, July 1889; *My School and My Gospel*, chs. 12–15.
38. *Truth*, 13 June 1889.
39. *The World*, 12 June 1889.
40. *The Watford Observer*, 22 June 1889.
41. *The Herkomers*, II, 42.
42. *My School and My Gospel*, 139.

43. 'Art in the Theatre: The Pictorial Music-Plays: "An Idyl" ', *Magazine of Art*, July 1889, 322 and 323.
44. Ibid, 324.
45. *The Herkomers*, II, 43.
46. Ibid, 316.
47. *My School and My Gospel*, 140.
48. Ibid, 164.
49. Ibid.
50. H. von Herkomer, 'Scenic Art', *Magazine of Art*, 1892, 259–64 and 316–20, 261. The quotations following are also from 'Scenic Art'.
51. *The World*, 2 May 1889.
52. *The World*, 12 June 1889.
53. *My School and My Gospel*, 199.
54. Interview with Archer, *The World*, 30 January 1889.
55. *The World*, 2 May 1888.
56. *The World*, 30 January 1889.
57. *The World*, 12 June 1889. See also W. Archer, 'The Limitations of Scenery', *Magazine of Art*, September 1896.
58. *Index to the Story of My Days*, 1957, 122. See also 107 and 131. For a more detailed estimation of Herkomer's influence on Gordon Craig see Edward Craig, 'Gordon Craig and Hubert Von Herkomer', *Theatre Research/Recherches Théâtrales*, x, I, 1969, 7–16.
59. *The Dialogues of Plato*, trans. B. Jowett, I, 1871, 708.
60. 'Concerning Sense and Sensibles', *The Works of Aristotle*, trans. Taylor, 1812, VIII, 141.
61. *Goethe's Theory of Colours*, trans., with notes by C. L. Eastlake, 1840, 379.
62. Ibid, 309.
63. Ibid, 299.
64. A. G. Lehmann, *The Symbolist Aesthetic in France, 1885–1895*, 1950, 220–1.
65. This lecture was published as a pamphlet in 1895.
66. 'Colour-Music. A Suggestion of a New Art', *The Nineteenth Century*, July 1895.
67. D. D. Jameson, *Colour-Music*, preface, 3.
68. 71.
69. 'Light and Sound', *Quarterly Journal of Science*, January 1870, 1–2.
70. *Harmonies of Tones and Colours*, 15.
71. See for instance Finetta Bruce, *The Mysticism of Colour*, 1912.
72. *Music and Morals*, 1871, 7.
73. *The Nineteenth Century*, July 1895, 130–1.
74. 10–11.
75. *Colour-Music. The Art of Mobile Colour*, xiii.
76. Ibid, 3. In 1895 D. S. MacColl, foremost pioneer of Impressionist theory in England, dismissed the whole business. See *The Spectator*, 15 June 1895.
77. *On the Spiritual in Art*, ed. Hilla Rebay, 1946, 87.
78. Ibid, 92.
79. Ibid, 40.
80. E. H. Gombrich, *Art and Illusion*, 1960, 366.
81. Compare Rudolf Arnheim, *Art and Visual Perception*, 1956, 286: 'The traditional theory of colour harmony deals only with obtaining connections and avoiding separations, and is therefore at best incomplete.'
82. *On the Spiritual in Art*, 29.
83. 'The Embodiment of a Myth' (1940), *Film Essays*, 1968, 85. It is also remarkable to find Eisenstein still showing interest in the French Symbolist

theatre, the ideas of Baudelaire and Rimbaud, and the manifestoes of René Ghil.

84. 'Colour and Meaning', *The Film Sense*, 1943, 113.
85. See Gerald McKee, 'Last of the Glasshouse Studios', *Amateur Photographer* September 1969, 46–7.
86. *The Bioscope*, 30 October 1913.
87. Ibid.
88. *Kinematograph and Lantern Weekly*, 17 April 1913.
89. *Kinematograph and Lantern Weekly*, 26 December 1912.
90. Georges Sadoul, *British Creators of Film Technique*, 1948, 3.
91. *The Bioscope*, 30 August 1913.
92. *Kinematograph and Lantern Weekly*, 14 May 1914.
93. 'The Dynamic Square', *Film Essays*, 55.
94. Ibid, 56.
95. *Signs and Meaning in the Cinema*, 1969, 8.

IV A LITERARY THEATRE: THE LESSONS OF THE INDEPENDENT THEATRE (pp. 111–180)

1. *The Playwright as Thinker*, 1946, 29. Also published in England as *The Modern Theatre*, 1948, 7.
2. *Drama from Ibsen to Brecht*, 1968, 332.
3. Ibid, 337–8.
4. Michael Orme, *J. T. Grein, The Story of a Pioneer 1862–1935*, 1936.
5. J. T. Grein, *Ambassador of the Theatre*, 1963. For a complete list of Independent Theatre productions, see 114–16. I am indebted to this book for a good deal of the biographical information in this chapter.
6. Emile Zola, *Oeuvres Complètes XI*, 1968, 337.
7. Ibid, 339.
8. *Mes Souvenirs sur le Théâtre Libre*, 1921, 89.
9. Ibid, 199–200.
10. See M. Carlson, 'Meiningen Crowd Scenes and the Théâtre Libre', *Educational Theatre Journal*, December 1961, 245–9.
11. See E. E. Prynne, 'Zola's Plays in England', *French Studies*, January 1959, 23–38; C. R. Decker, 'The Naturalists in England', *The Victorian Conscience*, 1952, 78–114.
12. 'The Comédie Française and Monsieur Zola', *Gentleman's Magazine*, July 1879, 61–3.
13. Ibid, 65.
14. N. Britton, 'Zola and the French Stage', February 1884, 78.
15. *The Fortnightly Review*, August 1885, 240.
16. Ibid, 242.
17. 'The Playwrights of Paris', *The Contemporary Review*, May 1887, 723.
18. *The Times*, 5 February 1889.
19. 22 December 1888.
20. 'The Patron of the Great Unacted', *The St James' Gazette*, 5 February 1889. The interview took place on 4 February.
21. *The Era*, 9 February 1889.
22. *The Morning Post*, 5 February 1889.
23. *The Pall Mall Gazette*, 6 February 1889.
24. *The World*, 13 February 1889.

25. *The Star*, 5 February 1889.
26. *The New Review*, June 1889, 30–46, repr. *The Scenic Art*, 1949, 226–42, 227–8.
27. 'The Dying Drama', *The New Review*, September 1889, 371.
28. See for example M. A. Belloc, 'The Théâtre Libre of Paris', *The New Review*, February 1894, which contains very few references to *mise-en-scène*.
29. *The Fortnightly Review*, May 1889.
30. 'The Patron of the Great Unacted', *The St James' Gazette*, 5 February 1889.
31. *Martin Luther*, 1879, 35.
32. 241–2.
33. 'Can the Nineteenth Century produce a Dramatic Literature?', *The Bat*, 28 April 1885.
34. 14 April 1888.
35. 'Two French Plays', *The Hawk*, 5 June 1888, 345.
36. *'Francillon'*, *The Hawk*, unsigned, 7 August 1888, 124. Repr. from *The Hour-Glass*, March 1887.
37. *The Universal Review*, September 1888, 111.
38. *The Universal Review*, March 1889.
39. *The Fortnightly Review*, November 1889.
40. 'My Article and my Critics', *The Hawk*, 12 November 1889, 519–20. Among the newspapers that had attacked him were *The Pall Mall Gazette*, *The St James' Gazette*, *The Sunday Times* and *The Echo*. Archer devoted his column in *The World*, 13 November, to a vigorous defence of Moore. Swinburne had contributed an article to the same issue of *The Fortnightly Review*.
41. 'The Modern Drama and its Critics', *The Contemporary Review*, December 1889, 910.
42. The discussions took place mainly in *The Fortnightly Review* and *The Nineteenth Century*.
    The Fortnightly Review: Oswald Crawfurd, 'The London Stage', April 1890, 499–516; H. Beerbohm Tree, 'The London Stage, I. A reply', June 1890; Oswald Crawfurd, 'The London Stage, II. A Rejoinder', June 1890; H. A. Jones, 'The Actor-Manager', July 1890; H. Beerbohm Tree, 'II. A Stage Reply', July 1890; Oswald Crawfurd, 'The London Stage', August 1890.
    The Nineteenth Century: Bram Stoker, 'Actor-Managers I', June 1890; Henry Irving, 'Actor-Managers II', June 1890; Charles Wyndham, 'Actor-Managers III', June 1890. For Archer's contribution, a well-ordered criticism 'drawn entirely on the historical line', see *The World*, 4 June and 9 July 1890.
43. 'The London Stage', April 1890, 506.
44. *The Fortnightly Review*, July 1890, 8.
45. X, 'Mr Tree's Monday-Nights', *The Fortnightly Review*, October 1890.
46. 'The Impossible Theatre', *The Theatre Annual for 1887*, 1887.
47. *The World*, 13 February 1889.
48. *The World*, 8 January 1890. See also *The World*, 6 August 1890.
49. *The Pall Mall Gazette*, 5 June 1890.
50. 'Le Théâtre Libre', 17 June 1890, 696; 'The New Théâtre Libre', 24 June, 1 July and 8 July 1890. The articles were reprinted, in a revised form, in Moore's *Impressions and Opinions*, 1891.
51. 8 July 1890, 43.
52. *The St James' Gazette*, 19 July 1890.
53. *The St James' Gazette*, 21 July 1890.
54. 'The Dramatic Censorship', *The New Review*, October 1890. For further details of the censorship controversy, see Allardyce Nicoll, *History of English Drama*, V, 20–2.

55. 'The Free Stage and the New Drama', *The Fortnightly Review*, November 1891, 668.
56. 'The Independent Theatre', *Black and White*, 14 March 1891, 167.
57. For a sample of the most savage reviews, see W. Archer, 'Ghosts and Gibberings', *The Pall Mall Gazette*, 8 April 1891.
58. 'The British Théâtre Libre. A Suggestion', offprint from *The Weekly Comedy*, probably December 1889, housed in the British Drama League Library.
59. First Annual Statement, British Drama League.
60. *The World*, 14 October 1891.
61. *The Times*, 15 October 1891.
62. 'Another View of Hedda Gabler', *The St James' Gazette*, 22 April 1891.
63. *The World*, 14 October 1891.
64. *The Fortnightly Review*, August 1885, 244.
65. Comparisons between the novel and the play were *de rigueur* in discussions of the state of the contemporary theatre. See for instance David Christie Murray, 'The Renaissance of the Stage', *The Contemporary Review*, November 1891, 690; W. J. Laurence, 'Realism on the Stage: How Far Permissible?', *The Westminster Review*, February 1891.
66. *The Pall Mall Gazette*, 31 August 1892.
67. *The Pall Mall Gazette*, 10 September 1892.
68. *The Pall Mall Gazette*, 7 September 1892.
69. *The World*, 18 May 1892.
70. *The Pall Mall Gazette*, 21 February 1893.
71. Note to *The Strike at Arlingford*, 1893.
72. *The Westminster Gazette*, 22 February 1893.
73. *The Era*, 25 February 1893.
74. *The Dramatic Review*, 25 February 1893.
75. Ibid.
76. 82–3.
77. 120.
78. *The Westminster Gazette*, 23 February 1893.
79. Bernard Shaw, *Collected Letters 1874–1897*, ed. Dan H. Laurence, 1965, 383.
80. *The Pall Mall Gazette*, 21 February 1893. Date of first performance 9 December 1892.
81. *The World*, 1 March 1893.
82. See Martin Meisel, *Shaw and the Nineteenth-Century Theatre*, 1963.
83. *The World*, 14 December 1892.
84. *The Letters of Oscar Wilde*, ed. Rupert Hart-Davis, 1962, 339.
85. *The World*, 14 December 1892.
86. *Widowers' Houses*, Independent Theatre edition, 1893, editor's preface, vii.
87. Ibid, author's preface, xiii.
88. Ibid, app. I, 'The Author to the Dramatic Critics', 110.
89. Ibid, 107.
90. Ibid, author's preface, xiii.
91. Ibid, xvii. See also 'A Dramatic Realist to his Critics', *The New Review*, July 1894, 56–73.
92. Ibid, xix.
93. 27 October 1893. A copy of the play is housed in the Lord Chamberlain's Collection, British Museum Manuscripts Room (MSS 53, 707).
94. 4 January 1895.
95. 15 March 1895. Printed for private circulation, 1890.

96. 15 March 1895. Lord Chamberlain's Collection.
97. *The Speaker*, 16 July 1892.
98. Lord Chamberlain's Collection.
99. Independent Theatre edition, 1893.
100. Ibid, editor's preface, v-vii.
101. Ibid, Archer's introduction, ix-lii.
102. Ibid, xxx.
103. *The Quintessence of Ibsenism*, 1891, 96–100.
104. *The Star*, 5 April 1894.
105. *The Daily Telegraph*, 5 April 1894.
106. *The Westminster Gazette*, 5 April 1894.
107. *The Stage*, 10 April 1894.
108. *The Star*, 5 April 1894.
109. *The Sketch*, 13 June 1894.
110. *The Fortnightly Review*, July 1889, 31–2.
111. See for example R. Buchanan, *The Pall Mall Gazette*, 11 June 1889.
112. See for example *The Era*, 15 June 1889.
113. *Black and White*, 21 February 1891.
114. *The Daily Telegraph*, 24 February 1891.
115. 21 March 1891.
116. 18 March 1891.
117. *The Hawk*, 28 April 1891.
118. *The St James' Gazette*, 21 April 1891.
119. *The Times*, 21 April 1891.
120. See D. J. Gordon and J. Stokes, 'The Reference of *The Tragic Muse*', *The Air of Reality: Essays on Henry James*, ed. J. Goode, 1972.
121. *Playhouse Impressions*, 1892, 53–4.
122. Ibid, prefatory note, v-vi.
123. 23 April 1891.
124. *Playhouse Impressions*, 62–3.
125. 'On the Occasion of *Hedda Gabler*', *The New Review*, June 1891. *Scenic Art*, 246 and 250.
126. *Playhouse Impressions*, 67.
127. Ibid, 113–14.
128. *The World*, 22 February 1893.
129. *The Illustrated London News*, 25 February 1893.
130. *Black and White*, 25 February 1893.
131. 'Some Plays of the Day', *The Fortnightly Review*, April 1893, 468–9.
132. Ibid, 469.
133. Ibid, 469–70.
134. Ibid, 470.
135. Ibid, 471–2.
136. *The Master Builder*, 1893, 247.
137. Ibid, 249.
138. *The Stage*, 23 February 1893.
139. *The St James' Gazette*, 21 February 1893.
140. 4 March 1893.
141. *The Standard*, 4 May 1897.
142. *The Daily Chronicle*, 4 May 1897.
143. *The Pall Mall Gazette*, 24 November 1896.
144. *The Academy*, 28 November 1896.
145. *The Daily Chronicle*, 23 November 1896.

146. It appeared in Justin Huntly McCarthy's 'Pages on Plays', *Gentleman's Magazine*, August 1892. Significantly, it was printed without his references to reform in staging—the lessons to be learnt from Impressionist painting in increasing illusion by stimulating the imagination. (*Miss Julie* was first performed at the Théâtre Libre 16 January 1893.)

147. 'August Strindberg', September 1892.

148. *Gentleman's Magazine*, August 1892, 209.

149. *The Black Cat*, Independent Theatre edition, 1895, preface, xii.

150. *Rosmersholm* and *L'Intruse*, 25, 28, 29 March 1895; *Pelléas et Mélisande*, 26, 27 March; *Solness le Constructeur*, 27, 30 March.

151. I am indebted to Denis Bablet's *Esthéthique Générale du Décor de Théâtre de 1870 à 1914*, 1965, for much of the information on the French symbolist theatre given in this chapter.

152. 'De l'inutilité absolue de la mise en scène exacte', *La Revue d'Art Dramatique*, 1 May 1891, 181.

153. 19 March 1891.

154. 11 December 1891.

155. The Théâtre d'Art was noted in *The Players*, 23 December 1891, 31, and *Dramatic Opinions*, 13 January 1892, but not generally in England.

156. *The Globe*, 28 March 1895.

157. *The World*, 3 April 1895.

158. *The Westminster Gazette*, 28 March 1895.

159. *The World*, 3 April 1895.

160. Paris première 17 May 1893.

161. See Pierre Caume, 'Le Théâtre de l'Oeuvre à Londres', *La Revue d'Art Dramatique*, 6 May 1895.

162. *The Star*, 27 March 1895.

163. *The Pall Mall Gazette*, 27 March 1895.

164. *The Daily Chronicle*, 27 March 1895.

165. *The Era*, 30 March 1895.

166. *The Daily News*, 23 March 1895.

167. *The Echo*, 26 March 1895.

168. *The Era*, 30 March 1895.

169. 27 March 1895.

170. 3 April 1895.

171. *The Daily Chronicle*, 27 March 1895.

172. *The World*, 3 April 1895.

173. *The Speaker*, 30 March 1895.

174. A useful bibliography of writings in English about Maeterlinck is contained in Arthur Symons, *The Symbolist Movement in Literature*, 1899, 194-7.

175. *The Princesse Maleine and The Intruder*, 1892, xiii.

176. 'The Pessimist Playwright', *The Fortnightly Review*, September 1891.

177. *The Treasure of the Humble*, trans. Alfred Sutro, 1897, 116.

178. *The Double Garden*, trans. de Mattos, 1904, 99.

179. Ibid, 105-6.

180. Ibid, 108-9.

181. Virginia M. Crawford, 'Maurice Maeterlinck', *The Fortnightly Review*, August 1897, 184.

182. 'Some Interesting Fallacies of the Modern Stage', *Thoughts and Afterthoughts*, 1913, 167.

183. Ibid.

184. *The Symbolist Movement*, 48.

185. Ibid, 50.
186. A. Symons, 'Maeterlinck as Mystic', *Contemporary Review*, September 1897, 349.
187. *Plays, Acting and Music*, 1903, 153.
188. *The New Budget*, 4 April 1895.
189. *St Paul's*, 6 April 1897.
190. *The Treasure of the Humble*, 1897, introduction, xiv.
191. *Mercure de France*, October 1896. See also Lugné-Poe, 'Du Spectacle', *To-morrow*, November 1896; *La Nouvelle Revue*, 1 March 1897.
192. 'A Symbolist Farce', *The Saturday Review*, 19 December 1896.
193. See for example Wyle Sypher, 'Aesthetic of Revolution: The Marxist Melodrama', *The Kenyon Review*, summer 1948.

Select Bibliography

SELECT BIBLIOGRAPHY

Antoine, André. *Mes souvenirs sur le théâtre libre*. Arthème Fayard, Paris, 1921.

Archer, William. *About the Theatre*. T. Fisher Unwin, London, 1886.

——. *English Dramatists of Today*. Sampson Low, London, 1882.

——. *The Theatrical World of 1893–7*. Walter Scott, London, 1894–8.

Bablet, Denis. *Esthétique générale du décor de théâtre de 1870 à 1914*. Editions du centre national de la recherche scientifique, Paris, 1965.

Bentley, Eric. *The Playwright as Thinker*. Meridian Books, Cleveland, Ohio, 1955.

Craig, Edward Gordon. *Index to the Story of my Days*. Hulton Press, London, 1957.

Decker, C. R. *The Victorian Conscience*. Twayne Publishers, New York, 1952.

Habron, Dudley. *The Conscious Stone. The Life of Edward William Godwin*. Latimer House, London, 1949.

Herkomer, Hubert von. *My School and my Gospel*. Constable, London, 1908.

——. *The Herkomers*. Macmillan, London, 1910.

Hone, Joseph. *The Life of George Moore*. Gollancz, London, 1936.

Irving, Laurence. *Henry Irving: the Actor and his World*. Faber and Faber, London, 1951.

James, Henry. *The Scenic Art*, ed. Allan Wade. Hart-Davis, London, 1949.

Jones, Henry Arthur. *The Renascence of the English Drama*. Macmillan, London, 1895.

Maeterlinck, Maurice. *The Treasure of the Humble*, trans. Alfred Sutro. George Allen, London, 1897.

McFarlane, James (ed). *Henrik Ibsen*. Penguin, Harmondsworth, 1970.

Meisel, Martin. *Shaw and the Nineteenth-Century Theatre*. Princeton University Press and Oxford University Press, 1963.

Miller, Anna Irene. *The Independent Theatre in Europe. 1887 to the present*. Ray Long and Richard R. Smith, New York, 1931.

Moore, George. *Impressions and Opinions*. David Nutt, London, 1891.

Nicoll, Allardyce. *A History of English Drama 1660–1900. V. Late Nineteenth Century Drama*. Cambridge University Press, 1962 (2nd ed).

Noël, Jean C. *George Moore. L'homme et l'oeuvre. 1852–1933*. Etudes Anglaises, 24, Didier, Paris, 1966.

Orme, Michael. *J. T. Grein. The Story of a Pioneer 1862–1935*. John Murray, London, 1936.

Rimington, Wallace. *Colour Music* (intro. by H. von Herkomer). Hutchinson, London, 1912.

Robichez, Jacques. *Le symbolisme au théâtre*. L'Arche, Paris, 1957.

Rowell, George (ed). *Victorian Dramatic Criticism*. Methuen, London, 1971.

Saxon Mills, J. *Life and Letters of Sir Hubert Herkomer*. Hutchinson, London, 1923.

Schoonderwoerd, N. H. G. *J. T. Grein. Ambassador of the Theatre 1862–1935*. Van Gorcum, Assen, 1963.

Shaw, George Bernard. *The Quintessence of Ibsenism*. Walter Scott, London, 1891.

——. *Our Theatres in the Nineties*. 3 vols. Constable, London, 1948.

Speaight, Robert. *William Poel and the Elizabethan Revival*. Heinemann, London, 1954.

Symons, Arthur. *Plays, Acting and Music*. Duckworth, London, 1903.

——. *The Symbolist Movement in Literature*. Heinemann, London, 1899.

Taylor, John Russell. *The Rise and Fall of the Well-Made Play*. Methuen, London, 1967.

Terry, Ellen. *The Story of my Life*. Hutchinson, London, 1908.

Tree, Herbert Beerbohm. *Thoughts and Afterthoughts*. Cassell, London, 1913.

Walkley, A. B. *Playhouse Impressions*. T. Fisher Unwin, London, 1892.

Williams, Raymond. *Drama from Ibsen to Brecht*. Chatto and Windus, London, 1968.

Index

(Italicised numbers refer to plates)